CW00866704

BEFORE
THE NIGHT
COMES

For Milo.

BRISTOLFISHING13@GMAIL.COM
STAPLETON BAPTIST CHURCH
BRISTOL

BEFORE THE NIGHT COMES

MATT ROPER

mB

MIRROR BOOKS

m
B

MIRROR BOOKS

All of the events in this story are true, but names
and details have been changed to protect the
identities of some individuals where appropriate.

© Matt Roper

The rights of Matt Roper to be identified as the author
of this book have been asserted, in accordance with the
Copyright, Designs and Patents Act 1988.

All rights reserved. No part of this publication may be
reproduced, stored in a retrieval system, or transmitted,
in any form or by any means without the prior written
permission of the publisher, nor be otherwise circulated in
any form of binding or cover other than that in which it is
published and without a similar condition being imposed on
the subsequent purchaser.

1

Published in Great Britain and Ireland in 2024 by
Mirror Books, a Reach PLC business.

www.mirrorbooks.co.uk
@TheMirrorBooks

Print ISBN 9781915306784
eBook ISBN 9781915306791

Cover Design: Chris Collins
Editing: Christine Costello, Simon Monk

Printed and bound in Great Britain by
CPI Group (UK) Ltd, Croydon, CR0 4YY

MIX
Paper | Supporting
responsible forestry
FSC® C171272
FSC
www.fsc.org

CONTENTS

PROLOGUE

Houses Of Parliament,
October 16, 2023

I'm standing at the back, straining on my tiptoes to see over the heads in front of me.

To my left, the murky waters of the Thames hurry by. Tourists continue to stream along Westminster Bridge or turn slowly on the London Eye. Somewhere above us, Big Ben's muffled chimes announce it is half past three. But in this magnificent room, stretching along the side of the House of Commons, time seems to have stood still.

At the far end, under the light of ornate chandeliers, three girls are dancing. They fix their gaze towards me, hiding their nervousness and excitement as they perform their moves to perfection. And as they do, a roomful of distinguished guests – MPs, ministers, civil servants, diplomats – stand watching, transfixed, pressed together to get the best view, some wiping away tears.

Rany is 14, Maluiza, 15 and Moany turned 14 yesterday. They choreographed the dance themselves and meant for it to move people. It's about childhoods violently cut short, adolescence cratered by pain and trauma... and about hope arriving when it seemed impossible, like a flower that blossoms on barren stones. It's poetic but also personal. It is about them and about their friends.

The final scene is a burst of colour and life. The girls smile as they shimmy and twirl, swishing flowery long dresses and the room erupts in applause. It is almost too much to take in. It's hard to believe we are here, that these girls are here, that people are finally seeing them and that something that was unspoken, unreported and deliberately covered up for so long is finally being heard.

My eyes are filling with tears. I'm transported back – as I often am – nearly 13 years to a very different place, to the lonely side of a remote Brazilian highway, to a night so dark it felt like it would swallow us, to the very first girl...

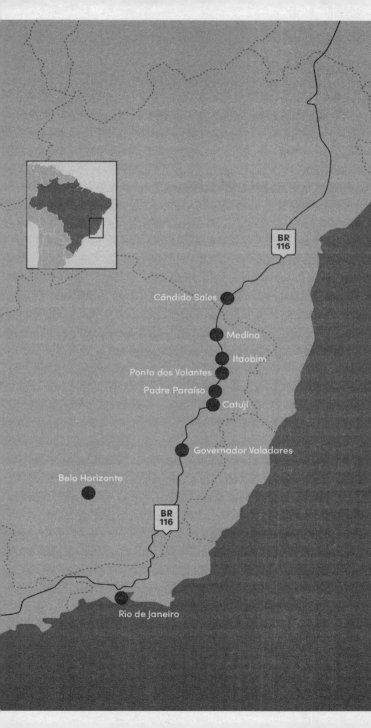

1

LEILAH

I sat forward and gripped the wheel, straining to see past a line of trucks ahead of me.

It looked like there was a young girl standing on the side of the motorway, but we still weren't sure. It was 1.20 in the morning and the whole world was asleep... except for the long-distance drivers, slowing past the murky outskirts of another remote town, and two road-weary travellers trying to find a place to sleep for the night. What would a child be doing out at this time, in that place?

I blinked and rubbed my tired eyes as we edged forward, the trucks now nose-to-tail, hissing and creaking over speed bumps. She was closer now, perched on a concrete verge just inches away from the traffic. As each truck rolled past her she turned her face away, as if ashamed of being momentarily lit up in their headlights. Then, as we passed, she glanced up at us and, in that split second, time seemed to stand still.

She really is just a child, I thought as we passed her. There was no mistaking it now – the girl couldn't have been older than 10 or 11. Her black hair had been brushed back, neatly parted and tied, perhaps by her mum, fussily getting her ready for church or a friend's birthday party... that's how out of place she looked. A lilac dress hung loose on her tiny frame and she wore a purple ribbon in her hair. But it was her eyes that struck me most during that one, fleeting glance. They seemed so full of pain, not frightened or upset, but lost, exhausted, silently pleading for help.

I had been in Brazil for a week now. With two weeks' holiday allowance about to expire, I'd flown out and met a friend, Dean Brody — today one of Canada's most successful country music singers. After a few days we hired a car to explore the vast back-country around Belo Horizonte, a city where I had lived in my twenties. That's how we found ourselves driving towards the town of Governador Valadares, an industrial hub of 280,000 people, in the early hours of January 11, 2011. I remember, just minutes earlier, Dean and I marvelling at a huge full moon, pockmarked with craters, which filled the sky. It seemed like a magical tropical night, one that would stay long in the memory.

It was Dean who first saw the girl ahead of us in the darkness and he who insisted we go back to find out if she needed help.

The next 10 minutes would change my life forever.

We found a broken gap in the central reservation, swung round, then drove back to the place where we had passed her. This time, as I slowed down and pulled off the road, she turned and hurried towards us. Before we could come to a complete stop she was tugging on the rear-door handle, trying to get inside.

"Let me in, before anyone sees." Her voice was high and shrill, her words rushed and stuttered.

"No, no," I said, alarmed. She thought nothing of getting into a car with two strangers in the dead of night. "We just want to talk to you. I'll just pull in over there."

Up close, I could see she was frail, pale and gaunt and even more fragile. Folding her bony arms, she said little at first, clearly wary of being asked questions about her life. But she gradually began to open up and soon the horrific reality of this little girl's life was laid bare before us. Her name was Leilah, she told us. She was 14. We would later discover that neither her name nor her age were correct – she was actually barely 11 years old.

"But what are you doing here so late at night?"

"Helping my mum and dad."

"Oh. Are they nearby too?" I said, looking around.

"They're over there." She pointed into the darkness behind her where shimmering lights revealed a cluster of shanty shacks rising up a hill beyond an overgrown wasteland. "They must be asleep now. Them and my four brothers and sisters. They're all younger than me."

"So, how are you helping them?"

"Doing programmes," she said, matter-of-factly. I knew the term; a way of making prostitution sound like an everyday transaction.

She was more talkative now. "I wait here for the truck drivers. When I get home I leave the money on the table and go to sleep. Sometimes I don't wake up until the afternoon! I do that every night."

"What time do you get home?"

"Dunno. It's always getting light though."

Seeing the anguish on our faces seemed to make Leilah want to tell us more. "You see this," she said, showing us recently healed scars on both her elbows. "When the trucker's finished with me he throws me out of his cabin. Sometimes they let me climb down, or sometimes they just kick me out onto the tarmac. It's a long way down. That's how I got these."

"How many times do you get into a truck every night?" I asked.

"Oh, five or six, sometimes more. They drive off with me, stop somewhere a long way out of town and then leave me right there. Sometimes it's so dark I can't see my hands in front of me. I have to wait for another truck to come along and pick me up and hope they'll bring me back here.

"And how much do they pay you?"

"Sometimes they try to pay me just a few reals, but I don't fall for that one. I never do it for less than 25." That was about £10. She never sold herself short, she thought. As I translated each sentence to Dean, he looked increasingly shattered, as if each word was a hammer blow. Only hours earlier we had stopped on the side of this same motorway to inspect the many roadside stalls that were selling precious stones mined from the surrounding land. Dean had bought a tiny pebble of polished green tourmaline for 50 reals, twice what this beautiful girl thought she was worth.

A huge car-carrier truck thundered past us, blaring its horn and screeching its air brakes. It was the driver's way of catcalling as he passed two men talking with a 'girl of the night'. There was no doubt that this fragile, waif-like young child was seen as a sexual object out here on the motorway. It jolted Leilah out of her train of thought.

"I need to get back. Is there anything else you want?"

I thought for a moment, knowing the words I had to choose were likely the last I'd ever say to this girl. "You're worth much more than you can ever imagine, Leilah. Please, go back home. Don't do this any more. You deserve so much more."

She seemed taken aback, and for the first time managed a

smile. It was probably the moment she realised we were different from the other men who would shudder to a halt beside that crumbling concrete verge. She even offered out her arms and Dean and I gave her a hug. Those last moments were the most painful of them all. We knew we would probably never see her again and, thousands of miles away in England and Canada, it would be impossible to track her down, or lead others to her. Just leaving a vulnerable child, who we now knew was in so much danger and might easily not even make it home at all, out there on a dark highway went against every instinct we had. She turned around and we watched helplessly as she sauntered slowly back into the night, disappearing into a haze of dust, diesel fumes and darkness.

2

THE WRONG WAY

The night we came across Leilah was supposed to have been the end of our road trip through rural Brazil. From there, we'd planned to drive south to Rio de Janeiro, that South American jewel with its golden beaches and breathtaking waterfront promenades. We'd already booked a four-star hotel in the swanky beachside district of Ipanema to enjoy a few days of sea and sand before flying back to our homes and families, mine in Cambridgeshire and Dean's in Nova Scotia. But as we arrived back at the spot where we had stood with her some six hours earlier, golden beaches were the last thing on our minds.

The place was very different in the light of day. Even at 9am a hot sun sapped our energy and the many sounds, sights and smells assailed the senses. Last night's patch of dusty grey earth was copper red, the pitch black behind us, lush green and the hillside shacks where Leilah said she lived were also alive with colour – corrugated iron roofs glinted in the sun, brightly-coloured clothes flapped on washing lines and people hurried up and down the steep hill like lines of worker ants. The traffic was much more intense in the daytime too. All around us trucks manoeuvred, kicking up clouds of dust and spewing out thick black fumes. Just a little further from where she had wandered away from us, the light revealed an electricity substation and a coach station where lines of long-distance buses awaited their passengers.

"Hey Matt, look," Dean shouted over the motorway roar. He was pointing at the ground where the red dust had been disturbed and the imprint of Leilah's sandals were still visible, alongside those of our shoes. We stood and stared in silence for a while, lost in thought, as the harsh sun burned the backs of our necks.

My mind had been racing since we'd arrived at the town centre guesthouse in the early hours. Dean had gone straight to his room without a word, but I'd wandered down to the lobby to get water and try to clear my mind, where an amiable porter seemed to notice my anguish. I told him of the girl we'd just talked to on the side of the road, and he sighed in sympathy. "It's so tragic isn't it? Those girls shouldn't have to do that."

"So there are more of them?"

He quickly hid his surprise at my naivety. "Oh, too many, especially further north with all the misery there. Whenever I see them it breaks my heart."

Back at the place where we had met her, I recognised some of the feelings welling up – that instinct to get to the bottom of the story, or find out how big it might be. How many more children were spending their nights on the side of this motorway? What did the porter mean by 'too many' – tens, hundreds? And what would we really find further north, in what I knew was a vast dustbowl of poverty but imagined was sparsely populated and certainly without many of the social ills that blighted Brazil's big cities? But there was something else, too – those feelings you learn to ignore as a journalist, so you don't lose control of your emotions. What happened to Leilah last night? Did she ever make it home? Why did we just stand by and let her go? Dean and I stood for a while next to her footprints before deciding that we couldn't just carry on with our holiday as planned. We would get in the car and drive, not south according to our itinerary, but north.

* * * *

Our plan was to make it as far as we could before nightfall, the time we imagined we would find some answers. But the fact we were going in the wrong direction, every hour getting further away from where we were supposed to be – from where our flights were due to leave from in a few days – increased our trepidation. Occasionally we'd stop for petrol or a snack at a roadside bar, where we'd leave the comfort of the car's air conditioning and be blasted with the dizzying heat of the sweltering summer air. Urban areas came and went, Teófilo Otoni, Catují, Padre Paraíso, Ponto dos Volantes, Itaobim… and then, some six hours later, a battered green sign announced that a place called Medina was coming up on the left.

The sun was low in the sky, hues of red and orange creeping up from the horizon. We decided to stop here.

Medina was unlike any of the places we had passed through previously, where the road seemed to cut straight through their centres and road humps would slow traffic to a crawl. A small, rural community nestled low between parched hills, it would have been easy to pass by on the motorway higher up on the valley's edge without realising there was a town there. Still, some of its small, terracotta-roofed dwellings spilled up to meet the motorway's edge and barefoot children played chase in the red dirt just metres away from the trucks rolling by. On the other side of the road, a black cloud of vultures circled above an open-air slaughterhouse.

The centre of the town was a different scene again. At the end of a long, potholed road off the motorway, a busy square, dotted with neatly pruned trees, bustled with noise and activity. Outside the municipal market, live chickens stared out of plastic bags with panic in their beady eyes. A straw-hatted man pushed a wheelbarrow laden with greens. I braked suddenly as another man crossed the street in front of us herding three goats with a bamboo pole. We parked up and wandered around for a while, making some discreet enquiries about who might be the best person to speak to about children's issues here.

One name came up multiple times: Rita. She was one of the elected members of the town's 'guardianship council', a body present in every Brazilian municipality responsible for ensuring children's rights. It wasn't long before we were standing outside her door on a dusty cobbled road, just a short walk away, waiting for a metal garage door to roll open.

Rita, a tall, olive-skinned woman with wavy brown hair, smiled kindly as she listened to my introduction, then immediately invited us in for a coffee – one of the traits of Brazilians I've always found endearing. At first she seemed impressed that anyone had thought to stop in her small country town at all, especially two foreigners with no particular business there. I explained that last night we had come across a girl selling her body on the side of the motorway, that we'd been shocked by what she had told us and felt we needed to find out more. We wanted to know if it was something that happened to girls in her town too. The smile suddenly fell from her face.

At first I thought I'd offended her by even suggesting there was a problem with child prostitution in her town. Maybe I'd been way off the mark choosing to stop in a simple community deep in the backcountry that was evidently nothing like the big industrial town we were in last night.. Then tears welled in Rita's eyes. She put her coffee cup down on the table and opened her mouth to speak, but her words were gulped back as tears rolled down her cheeks.

"I… I don't know how you got here, but I think you must be angels," she gasped.

"What do you mean?" I asked, astonished.

"This week it all became too much. The last few days were the worst, I wondered if I could go on and I didn't know what else to do. Then you two turned up."

Her voice trembling, Rita, a social worker, began to describe a tragedy almost too horrific to comprehend. Child sexual exploitation was simply a way of life in Medina, she explained. No-one was shocked to see an 11-year-old girl standing by the side of the motorway, or being offered to clients in the roadside bars or brothels. It was perfectly normal to hear of a parent offering their young daughter around the neighbourhood for a price or just for a food voucher or a packet of cigarettes. Poor families wished for a baby girl not for the reasons most parents would, but because they knew that one day she would be a valuable source of income. The abuse began much earlier, she said, a necessary initiation into the 'work' she would begin aged nine or 10.

"By the time they're 12 it's all they've ever known," she said. "They think that's what happens to every girl."

Dean and I listened in horror. Less than a day after finding Leilah we were hearing that not only were there many more girls like her, even in this small town alone, but that local people were fully aware of what was going on. We hadn't stumbled upon some hidden racket, a shameful trade in children operating under the cover of darkness. Girls, it seemed, were as easy to buy as the products being sold over the road in the bustling open air market.

"But Rita," I said, "This is a scandal. Why isn't anybody trying to stop it?"

Rita leaned forward. "My friend, nobody comes to Medina. There are no tourists, no foreigners, no TV cameras. These girls are worth nothing in Brazil. No-one sees them. Out of sight, out of mind, and people would prefer to keep it that way. Would you like to meet some of them?"

We followed Rita on a surreal tour of her hometown for the next few hours. Without her running commentary, no-one visiting this little country town would have any idea of the horrors that hid behind the quaint colonial walls and brightly-painted cottages. One of those identical terraced houses was actually a brothel specialising in underage girls, she told us. That mud-brick cottage over there? Home to a 12-year-old whose dad built an extra room where he puts her to 'work'. The two girls relaxing on that bench chatting in the warm evening air? That was where they sat to advertise themselves. The whole town knew what they were doing there. Nor were the lines of parked-up lorries along the main street where hard-working local truckers had left their vehicles overnight – hardly any truck drivers lived in the town. No, they belonged to long-distance drivers on their journeys north or south, who knew they only needed to turn in to Medina to find a young girl for sale, theirs for the price of a couple of bottles of beer.

Then there were the names of girls Rita clearly knew well who had walked out of one of those tiny brick dwellings one day and never returned. Jennifer, a 14-year-old, was last seen ambling along the motorway late one night, her school rucksack slung over her shoulder. Sisters Julia and Jessica, aged 12 and 14, who would flag down trucks late at night and would sometimes spend a night or two away from home. The last time they went their family didn't really notice until a week had passed, and now, six months later, they still haven't raised the alarm.

"The girls, they go missing all the time," Rita told us. "For every five who leave, one doesn't come back." She stopped in her tracks and wiped her eyes. "It's like watching sand fall through your fingers. You can't stop it. Every day we're losing them, and as much as I try, I just can't stop it."

Rita brought us to visit the homes of some of the girls she knew in her role as guardianship councillor. The first home was one of those bare-brick constructions we had seen on the motorway's edge, a precarious walk in the pitch dark over uneven, rock-strewn earth. The house, lit by a single bulb hanging from its wire, was home to a man and his four daughters, aged eight to 16, Rita explained.

While the father was away working in a granite mine some 50 miles away, the girls were the breadwinners, offering themselves on the motorway and bringing truck drivers back to their bedrooms. None were home when we arrived, but two of the girls, 12-year-old Viviane and 14-year-old Sâmia, appeared as we were leaving, their arms tightly linked as they wandered back along the motorway's rugged dirt edge. Both giggled shyly as Rita asked them about their schoolwork, the boy band posters we'd seen on their walls and their scraggy pets who had run up to fuss them. What we didn't talk about was what they had been doing out on the motorway. It was a taboo subject in Medina, Rita told us. No-one ever spoke about that.

The second house we visited was lost in a labyrinth of narrow red-earth roads just down the hill from the motorway. It was the home of another father, but this one was beside himself with worry for his daughter. Armando was often at the guardianship council asking for help, Rita explained, when 12-year-old Leticia was missing or spending her nights on the streets. She had been a quiet, well-behaved girl, who even sang in the church choir, until a year ago when she had been raped while visiting her mother in another town, after which her behaviour changed and she began to run away from home. Sometimes she would disappear for days on end. Several times she had been found by police hundreds of miles from Medina, being exploited in brothels or drug dens. "It's killing me, I don't sleep, I don't even go to bed. I just stand on my doorstep waiting for her to come home," he told us, rubbing his face in desperation.

It was past 11pm when we arrived at the last house at the top of a steep, rocky hill on the far edge of town. The cluster of squalid mud-brick houses stood eerily amid huge black boulders. There was no electricity supply up there and it felt like a place for outcasts with dark figures moving around in shadows or hunched near outdoor fires. Approaching the last house, we could make out the scrawny figure of a woman sitting on the dirt track outside, a cigarette glowing between her fingers. She was Maria, the mother of a 13-year-old girl Rita had been trying to help since she was nine.

"Evening, Dona Maria," said Rita. "Is Mariana home?"

I could see her more clearly now. She mumbled something about her being at church – something we knew couldn't be true at that time.

"OK, we'll come back tomorrow then. Tell her to be up early and that I've got some special visitors who want to meet her."

As we headed back into town, Rita filled us in. "Mariana's mum was a prostitute when she was young. So was her grand-mother. So, of course, they expected her to do the same when she was old enough. She's never known anything else. For these people, sending their daughter off for her first 'programme' is as normal as buying her her first Barbie doll."

Rita had found us two rooms in a scruffy pousada above a moneylenders' shop on Medina's main square – the only one she could be sure wasn't involved in the town's lucrative child prostitution business, she said. I lay on an impossibly hard mattress, a rusting air-con rattling loudly above me as frantic thoughts competed with the tiredness in my limbs. Last night I'd struggled to sleep because of one tragic girl; now we had met four, and heard of dozens of others, each just as lost, in just as much peril, and almost entirely alone. In the end, though, it was the subwoofer beats still thumping from across the square at 1.30am that made me give up hope of dozing off so soon. I got up, opened my room door and leaned for a while on the ledge of an open window overlooking the dimly-lit square, and the hills full of twinkling lights beyond it. It would have looked pretty if I didn't know what I knew now.

****

The next day, we returned to Maria's home early – we knew we had a long drive back south if we were going to catch our flight. This time Maria invited us inside, apologising repeatedly for the mess as she shooed away the scrawny dogs and cleared a space on a tattered brown sofa. The room was hazy with lin-gering black smoke from an open wood fire boiling water in the back yard – the house's kitchen – and we stifled coughs as

Maria, who was clearly used to it, chatted as she cut off a slice of tobacco and rolled a cigarette.

Mariana appeared out of breath at the front door a few minutes later. She'd dashed home from a friend's house upon hearing we'd arrived. She was lively and wide-eyed and, of the girls we'd met, she reminded me most of other 13-year-olds I knew back home. Excited to hear that Dean was a famous Canadian singer, she showed us a poster of her heart-throb, Justin Bieber, which she'd kept carefully folded up in a box of her things. Then she dashed off to fetch her notebook, which was filled with girly poems, scribbled flowers and love hearts. I asked Mariana what she wanted to do when she grew up.

"I love dancing, so maybe a professional dancer," she said. "But I'd like to become a judge too, so I can decide what happens to people who do bad things."

She glanced over at her mother, who glared back, puffing on her cigarette. "Ha, you'll never be any of those things," she cackled as Mariana flinched. "She causes me so many problems, Rita. She doesn't respect her own mother. I don't know what to do with her, I really don't."

It was enough to deflate Mariana's initial excitement at having foreign visitors in her home and, over the next few minutes, she grew quiet and subdued, her brown eyes filling with tears. When Maria took Rita into another room, she turned to me and whispered, "I hate it here. It's my mum. She doesn't treat me like a mum should treat her daughter. It makes me want to run away and never come back. But I can't."

We rose to say goodbye and I tried to find some parting words that might give this hurting girl some hope or strength, something that might persuade her to keep herself safe. I'd only spent 10 minutes with her, but my heart was aching for this lost teenager who seemed to be hiding a world of pain. It didn't seem right that all I could offer her were words, however heartfelt. In the end there wasn't even an opportunity to speak to her away from her mother, just a parting hug. As we climbed back down the steep rocky hill back to the road below she stood at the top and watched us, still and silent, until we disappeared out of sight.

We drove away from Medina, taking the motorway back south. Soon the brick buildings and gas stations flashing past us gave way to rolling green hills, dotted with termite mounds and clusters of mango trees but the image of that girl, silently crying out for help as we left her behind, was all I could see. Part of me wished we'd never interrupted our plans to come here, that we'd never stopped to talk to Leilah, never knocked on Rita's door, because then we wouldn't have heard, wouldn't have known. But now we did and not only that, we'd walked down their streets, entered their houses, spoken with them and looked into their eyes.

Half an hour after leaving Medina the motorway cut through another poor town, 20 minutes later another, then another, and another... I began to feel overwhelmed. If what we'd found in Governador Valadares and Medina was happening in all the places in between, then there could be thousands of girls trapped in a similar nightmare. Along the length of this vast motorway, thousands upon thousands. Yet I'd never read a single article or seen a single news report about the sexual exploitation of children in these remote, forgotten places of Brazil.

Six hours later, we passed the place again where we had met Leilah and my mind was made up. It was impossible to just return home, carry on with my life and let what I'd seen and heard fade away. I had to tell people. The least I could do was to tell people.

3

VALLEY OF MISERY

Before that trip to Brazil with Dean, my life seemed to be set-tling into a reassuring pattern. As I reached my mid-30s, I'd been nearly a decade in a relatively secure and rewarding job. I'd been married for about the same time, we'd bought a flat in Greenwich and just had a baby son. For the first time I felt I'd constructed the life I wanted and could clearly see the path it was going to follow.

I'd even managed to escape the stress and unpredictability of a national newspaper newsroom. After eight years as a feature writer on the *Daily Mirror*, I'd taken a new position as the newspaper's correspondent for the East of England. We'd moved out of London to a quiet village outside Cambridge where we planned to buy a bigger house and settle down, away from the city bustle. I remember shaking the hand of the *Mirror* Group's editorial director Eugene as he told me the position was mine, saying "Congratulations Matt, you've got a job for life now. They'll never make you redundant now you're a district man." I got a pay rise and a company car and I'd been in the job for nearly a year.

My first day back at work was the same as ever: stories to follow up, local stringers to call, copy to edit and send over.

But inside me, everything had changed. That remote Brazilian motorway seemed so distant now, almost like a vivid dream, yet I couldn't just forget what we'd seen and heard there and pick up life where I'd left it. I talked it through with my wife Dani, herself Brazilian, and she was just as shocked. Even growing up in Brazil, in the capital city of the same state not 200 miles from where we'd been, she had never heard of such things. But there was another reason why I couldn't just file it away in my mind and move on to the next story, as I did so often in my job, and it had been on my mind since the morning we'd arrived back at the place we had met Leilah.

Four years earlier, the *Daily Mirror* had sent me to Brazil on an assignment. Jean Charles de Menezes, a Brazilian plumber, had been mistakenly shot dead by anti-terror police on the London Underground the previous year, and the long-awaited Independent Police Complaints Commission report into his death was about to be released. The newspaper wanted someone to be at his parents' home to get their reaction when the verdict came through. With knowledge of Brazil and being fluent in Portuguese, I was considered the best reporter for the job.

I'd arrived in Rio and taken an overnight bus north, eventually arriving at a remote coach station in the early hours of the morning, where I hired a taxi to drive me to the family's home, a three-hour journey along dirt roads deep into the Brazilian bush. Late that night, after filing the story, I'd arrived back at the coach station and boarded the long-distance bus which would take me back to Brazil's most famous city. Exhausted after a long working day, and with a long journey ahead of me, I sat back and gazed out of the window as the coach pulled out of the bus station onto the motorway.

As the bus edged slowly out of the station forecourt, a group of girls were milling around on the tarmac down below. My first reaction was alarm — they seemed too young to even be out of their beds at this time, much less be where they were, inches from the slow-moving wheels of buses and HGVs. Ahead of me, one girl who had climbed up a truck's metal steps was peering in through the open cabin window. Just over by the motorway's edge another hung on to another truck's wing mirror as she shouted over to one of her friends. She was at my height and as my coach swung out into the road I passed inches away from her face. It all happened in less than 10 seconds, but felt like slow motion. Then we were off, speeding away down the motorway and, as far as I was concerned, never to return.

I was pretty certain of what I'd seen, but I had pushed it to the back of my mind ever since, never mentioning it to anyone. The memory faded, but not entirely. When I arrived back at the place we'd found Leilah on that scorching summer morning and looked over to the bus station entrance, I had a feeling I'd been there before. Back home, I checked with the *Mirror*'s desk secretary Louise who'd booked my travel and confirmed that it was in fact where I'd hurriedly boarded my coach four years earlier. Not only had I been on that remote patch of Brazilian motorway before, I'd also witnessed the same tragedy. The first time, though, I'd immediately insulated myself from what I'd seen, moving quickly on without much consideration, to continue with my life and career. As I reflected, I began to feel like I'd been placed in the same situation again, and offered another chance to respond.

Confined to my home office and having used up my holiday allowance, I began to dispatch my work as early as possible so

I could spend the rest of my time finding out more about that motorway, the BR-116, from my desk. I spent hours researching online, reading reports, following up on snippets of information and sending messages.

It was easy to find information on the BR-116 itself – it was Brazil's principal haulage route, the longest asphalted motorway in South America which stretched from the border with Uruguay in the south to the city of Fortaleza on the northeast coast. The 2,790-mile-long highway often featured on thrill-seekers' lists of the world's most dangerous roads, nicknamed the Highway of Death because of the high number of fatal accidents along its poorly-maintained, often narrow and twisting route. Long-haul truckers, sometimes travelling for weeks on end, were prone to health problems such as high blood pressure and mental disorders because of their exhausting work schedules and need to constantly concentrate on the perilous road ahead, according to one report. Drivers commonly used alcohol and medication, sometimes even cocaine, to maintain alertness and stay awake for days on end.

It was much harder to find any mention of child prostitution along the highway. That, according to the internet, was only a problem in Brazil's famed coastal cities like Recife and Fortaleza, preferred destinations of foreign sex tourists. But if what we'd encountered during those two days, in the most remote communities of Brazil, was typical of the thousands of other poor towns along the vast BR-116, then this was an even bigger story than I had thought. It was difficult to believe that something so shocking hadn't been widely reported before with little to no discussion about it on social media. My digging eventually paid off when I came across a Federal Highway Police report from the previous year which appeared to have been quietly released with barely any mention in Brazilian media. The study estimated, through interviews with truck drivers, the number of places along the country's federal highways where child sexual exploitation was known to be taking place. The results were staggering. Along all of Brazil's principal haulage routes, there were 1,820 places where truckers knew they could stop and find an underage girl for sale and that was clearly those only identified by the truckers who they had spoken to. Of all the roads listed, the BR-116 was by far the worst with 262 locations. I did the maths: 262 places along a road 2,790 long. On average, children could be found selling their bodies every 10 miles.

The report went into further detail. The greatest concentration of child prostitution hotspots had been found in one of the poorest regions of Brazil, stretching from the south of Bahia state and the north of Minas Gerais state, and known as the 'corridor of child prostitution'. I looked at the map and saw Medina was right in the middle.

That area, I discovered, covered a region known as the Jequitinhonha Valley. Despite being rich in gold, diamonds and precious stones, it was one of the most impoverished areas of Brazil, punished by droughts and famines. Until recently, children commonly died from diseases associated with hunger and malnutrition. In fact, it was the mining of its precious resources that had brought about so much suffering as unscrupulous mine owners had poisoned the rivers and soils, leaving its population weak and its once fertile land barren. In the 1960s UNESCO named the valley as one of the poorest regions in the world. Brazilians still refer to it as the 'Valley of Misery'.

From there, I came across a series of TV reports about the

Jequitinhonha Valley broadcasted over a number of nights on one of Brazil's free TV channels, SBT, from a Brazilian journalist called Sérgio Utsch. The six reports looked at different aspects of the valley, its culture and people, but among them was one about the grinding poverty and how girls were having to sell their bodies to put food on the table. I recognised some of the towns he'd been to. One was Padre Paraíso, where we'd only stopped for refreshments while driving through. In another shot, the reporter did a piece to camera while walking past the terraced cottages of a street in Medina.

The interviews with several young girls were heartbreaking. One, her face obscured but her voice child-like, said, "I started out as a prostitute when I was 10. You know, because we didn't have food at home. So I began selling my body, for 50 cents, 10 cents…"

Another girl sobbed, her voice trembling as she spoke, "My dad, without telling my mum, asked me to start selling my body. So at the age of 15 I had to start working, giving over my body to anybody. Then a few days ago I found out I had Aids.

"My life will be this now, I'll carry on selling my body because I need to get money to give to my dad, so he can pay the rent and buy food for me to eat. I don't know how long I can take this life anymore."

It was a tragedy playing out thousands of miles away, but as Rita kept in touch, sending me distressing updates on the girls she knew, this distant world invaded my own. Mariana, the 13-year-old from the rocky hilltop, had gone missing. Rita had only found out when she called on the girl's house to see how she was and Maria casually told her she hadn't seen her daughter for weeks. Shocked at how little Maria seemed to worry about the whereabouts of her young daughter, what she was doing or if she was even still alive, Rita decided to do a video interview with her and sent it over so I could see for myself.

Mariana's mother was sitting on the same broken sofa Dean and I had perched on a few months earlier, in front of that crumbling mud-brick wall blackened with soot. Beside her this time was her own mother, Mariana's grandmother, who, she explained, the girl regarded as her mum because she was the one who had breastfed her and looked after her. Rita's chat with the two women revealed more about the scourge of child prostitution among the oppressed, impoverished people of the valley than anything I'd read or watched during my research so far.

Skeletal and trembling, her eyes dark and sunken, Mariana's mother looked more of a mess than the day I had met her. It was the grandmother who did most of the talking. Rita asked her what happened on the day Mariana ran away. "She said to me, 'I'll just go over there and buy something to eat and I'll be right back'. Well, that 'right back' never happened. She left in just the clothes she was wearing and a pair of sandals. A woman told me yesterday that she'd been to that place next to the motorway, in Pedra Azul…"

Rita described how the place, 40 minutes up the motorway, was a well known truckers' stop, where stalls lining each side of the motorway sold home-made regional cheeses, but behind was a row of bars and brothels where they knew they could find underage girls. The grandmother nodded her head as Rita described what Mariana was probably doing there.

"But you know what's the worst thing?" Mariana's mother suddenly interjected. "When she gets back home she doesn't bring any money with her, not even 10 centavos."

The remark seemed to take Rita by surprise. "She doesn't bring any money home?"

The grandmother joined in, thinking that Rita's shock was at what was being said, not the fact they were saying it. "Yeah that's right," she emphasised, shaking her head furiously. "She doesn't bring any money back, nothing at all…"

"That's the worst thing," repeated the mother.

"So the worst part of all this is that she doesn't bring any money back home?" said Rita slowly, spelling out what she thought she'd heard.

The two women, who were by now more animated than at any other stage of the conversation, both shook their heads and tutted. "Yeah," said the mother, her voice rising and falling. "Because they say she's out there prostituting. But then when she gets back home she doesn't have any money!"

What Mariana had told us was right. Her mother, grand-mother too, were only concerned about the money they could make from her, not the grave danger she was in, or the horrors she was being subjected to. But the exchange also hinted that Mariana's mother may have been just as much a victim as her daughter. The reason she wasn't around while Mariana was growing up was that she too had been expected to sell her body on the motorway, bringing home her earnings before heading off again. That tough life had taken its toll on her.

I was stunned to hear Maria say she was just 32. She appeared to be at least twice that. Perhaps the most revealing thing was when Rita asked Maria how old she was when she had done her first 'programme' and it was her mother who answered. "She was 13," Mariana's grandmother croaked. "That's when she began prostituting." It was staggering to hear; not only how families could see their daughters' bodies as legitimate sources of income, but just how far back that went, apparently spanning generations. I remembered Mariana's desperate cry for help that morning, away from her mother's earshot, how she wanted to run away and never come back. Wherever this poor girl was right now, I couldn't imagine how lost and unloved she must be feeling.

It was three weeks later when Rita called me to tell me Mariana had been found. Police in a town called Cândido Sales, 60 miles north on the BR-116, had raided an underage brothel masquerading as an ordinary home. "They found her in bed with a 12-year-old girl and an older man," she said. "The town's guardianship council brought her back in their car this morning." I imagined the reception Mariana probably received from her mother and grandmother, especially without any money to show for her weeks away, and I knew it wouldn't be long before she would run away again. Sure enough, two weeks later Mariana was gone again. When she eventually showed up this time, she was pregnant.

Accompanying each tragic twist and turn from so far away was agonising. This sweet, hurting young girl appeared to be free-falling towards destruction. She could easily disappear forever – or worse, lose her life in the dark world of brothels, bars and truck stops she was running to – and tragically, no-one, not even her own family, would care that she had gone. I knew now that the same was true for an untold numbers of other girls like her who were just as alone. One such girl, of course, was Leilah, who I still thought about often and wondered if I might one day find and help her. But I knew there was little I could do from thousands of miles away in a full-time, high-pressure job that demanded all my time and attention. I knew that if I really wanted to respond to what I had seen in the way it truly deserved, and to bring attention to this tragedy, I needed to be there. And that would mean leaving my job, uprooting my family and moving to Brazil.

These were the thoughts I tried to push back down each time they bubbled up to the surface. There were times they would stop me in my tracks, when what we'd seen in those two days in Brazil, and the stories that kept coming via Rita, would crowd my mind. Tears would catch me unawares, like when I was hurriedly writing up an article the news desk were screaming for, or while driving to the next breaking story.

I eventually decided to talk about it with my wife Dani who, to my surprise, didn't dismiss the idea out of hand, even with our son Milo just aged one. But I knew it would still be a massive move that could easily prove to be misguided, perhaps even disastrous.

Over the next weeks we engaged in hours of discussions, long walks, evenings going over every different scenario and private soul-searching. When we did finally decide to do it – dismantle the life we had constructed in the UK and start again in another country, another continent – it still wasn't with a complete sense of peace, more like an uneasy truce between the heart and the mind alongside a constant knot in my stomach.

In the meantime, I began to look for opportunities to speak about what I had seen and heard. During my research I'd failed to find any mention of child prostitution on the BR-116, or any of Brazil's motorways, in the international press or even by well-known NGOs dedicated to fighting abuse and injustice against children. The least I could do while I was still in the UK was to tell as many people about it as possible.

One of those meetings was at a women's conference in the Hertfordshire town of Bishop's Stortford. After the event a woman, her face mottled red by tears, came up to me. She almost hadn't come to the day conference, she explained, but reluctantly agreed to attend because a friend had asked her to help serve tea and coffee. From the back of the hall, Charlotte, a local teacher, had watched our presentation, which had included a video from mine and Dean's journey on the BR-116, set to a moving track Dean had recorded on his return, called *Leilah's Song*. The dramatic images and the girls' harrowing stories had left her shaken.

"I have to do something," she said. "I'm a teacher. I'm about to take on a new job and I have a day a week free. Please, I'm ready to do anything you need to help."

Having Charlotte on board was a real boost as we moved forward with our plans. Two months later, we held a 'Brazilian Banquet' where I'd lived in Blackheath, London, with typical Brazilian food, music and capoeira dancers performing the Brazilian martial art. Over 200 people came to the event where, between courses, I spoke about what I'd seen on the BR-116 and the girls we'd met. With word getting around and more people expressing an interest in supporting us, we arranged a conference, again in Blackheath, where more than 100 people from all over the country came to hear more about our plans and how they could get involved. Dean took a break from his hectic schedule in Canada to come over and retell his experiences in Brazil too. And with more and more people expressing a desire to invest what they could financially in the venture, we set up a registered UK charity, leaving Charlotte in charge of running it as we prepared to set off on this new chapter of our lives.

Nine months after we'd pulled up on the side of that Brazilian highway, I was sitting with the *Mirror*'s news editor, explaining why, after just 18 months in my new role, I was handing in my notice. My meeting with Chris Bucktin at The Crown Inn in Huntingdon was supposed to be for my yearly appraisal. He was taken aback when I told him I would be leaving, not for a better offer on a rival newspaper, but to pursue a story that was consuming me, on the other side of the world. When I told him about the journey I'd already been on over the past months, the girls I'd met, and something of the story, he nodded and smiled knowingly. "As a journalist you've just got to follow your instincts, even when it sometimes seems crazy," he said. "So go for it, you're doing the right thing."

There was a frozen sky over London on November 20, 2011 as we waited on the runway of Heathrow Airport, feeling an equal measure of trepidation and excitement, just like the calm before a rollercoaster sets off. Little did I know just how high the highs would be, and how low the lows would be.

4

TOO LATE

It didn't take too long to settle into our new home. We'd decided to move to Belo Horizonte, the capital city of Minas Gerais state, and rented a flat in the Buritis neighbourhood, a modern suburb of jutting high-rise blocks which crowded steep hills. The view from our window resembled a game of Tetris – still a very different world to the barren, empty panorama which had flashed past us for hour after hour as we drove up the BR-116. In a country of continental proportions, Minas is the size of France and Medina was further away from us than London is to Glasgow. It felt even more distant as we talked with neighbours and new friends, most of whom had never heard of those small towns and who were just as shocked as people in the UK, even incredulous, when I told them about girls being sold by their own families just a day's drive away.

Still, we felt it was best to base ourselves in the state capital, mostly because of the way Brazil is organised, with development often taking years to reach areas away from the big cities. First, I planned to pay the bills by freelancing for the British newspapers, so I needed to be able to access an airport at short notice. Mostly, though, I felt that it might be counterproductive to set up permanently in a region so cut off from the centres of knowledge and power. It might mean regular 10-hour journeys to get there, but in the big city we would be close to the institutions and people that could affect change.

Coping with Brazil's infamously insane bureaucracy was a different matter. Long days were spent waiting inside bleak government buildings and offices, or trudging along crowded city centre streets, to obtain identity documents, social security numbers, driving licences and other papers. A similarly interminable process was necessary for purchasing the simplest home appliance or furniture. The stress management techniques we had to learn in hours-long queues proved useful as we carried on waiting for delivery when the country ground to a halt for the month-long summer holidays, then again until after carnival in February. We spent two months having to eat out at the nearby buffet restaurant until the fridge and cooker we'd bought before Christmas finally arrived. On the other hand, we discovered that having a toddler in arms is a greater advantage in Brazil, getting you to the front of the queue everywhere from banks to the McDonald's ice-cream counter, and we made ample use of it. Milo also came in useful one day after we'd waited more than five hours in a bank for clerks to locate a missing transfer I'd sent from my UK account. After he'd done a smelly accident on the floor it didn't take long for them to find it.

Those first few months in a very different country took a harder toll on Milo, whose 18-month-old body took a while to adapt to the tropical climate and the incessant nighttime mosquitos. Soon after we arrived he spent two periods in hospital, once with pneumonia and soon after when his leg swelled and became infected after getting multiple insect bites around his ankles. Before long, though, particularly after the sweltering summer temperatures became milder, we began to feel at home and grew fond of the many appealing aspects of living in Brazil – the outdoor lifestyle, the vibrant colours and culture, the amiable, upbeat people.

I was also able to turn my mind to the reason I was there. Although I had a good idea of the tragedy playing out in the impoverished, far-flung towns of the BR-116, my journalistic curiosity wasn't satisfied with the online research I'd done so far. I still had too many questions. What was the true scale of the problem? Just how many children were caught up in it? Who were the abusers and exploiters and, perhaps most crucially, was anything being done to stop them and bring them to justice? I decided that, before anything else, I needed to conduct my own investigation, seek out the people who knew what was really going on and speak to them for myself. I would begin at the place we met Leilah a year earlier, and where I had seen that group of girls climbing into trucks four years before that, and travel north along the BR-116 right to the motorway's very first kilometre at the famous city of Fortaleza on Brazil's northeast coast. It would mean a journey of over 1,200 miles and probably months away from home, but I needed to understand all there was to know about this tragedy, no matter where it took me or how long it might take.

When I called Dean to tell him about my plans, he insisted on coming too, making a plan to fly to Brazil from Canada during breaks in his touring schedule so we could travel up the BR-116 together. We would make three trips in all, each time picking up at the place we had left off. As we set off from Belo Horizonte on our first stint up the motorway, we were much more prepared for what we might find, or so we thought.

We began back in Governador Valadares, where Dean was keen to look for Leilah again. The memory of our fleeting encounter with that lonely, waif-like girl on the side of the road had haunted him for months. The moving song he wrote about her — "Leilah, oh Leilah, the world has forgot you, but I know that I never will" — was now a track on his new album and he dreamed of being able to help her escape her nightmare. We arrived in the town late that night and decided to find a room for the night and get up early the next morning to start the search. While I didn't want to disappoint him, I quietly doubted we had any chance of finding that one child, whose real name we didn't even know, more than a year later in a chaotic urban sprawl of hundreds of thousands of people.

Following a town-wide search, full of twists and turns and more than a few disheartening false leads as locals tried and failed to help us locate her, we eventually did find Leilah again, just as night was drawing in and the withering daytime heat was beginning to wane. Dean spotted her first, standing in a concrete yard across the road from a different property we'd been directed to, and just moments after we had reluctantly decided to call it a day. She recognised us straight away, and at that moment we felt that this implausible encounter, like the first one, couldn't have happened by accident or chance. We were meant to find her again, so we could save her.

Our elation soon turned to anguish , and an awful realisation that we were too late. The girl, now just 12, was hopelessly addicted to crack cocaine. Initially attentive and playful as we walked with her to a nearby ice-cream parlour to chat, she became increasingly restless, irritable and aggressive, especially when we politely declined her requests for money. The drugs had changed her physical appearance too. Her face was gaunt and hollow, her teeth crooked and rotten and her hair no longer neatly combed and tied, but matted and scruffy. Leilah finally lost patience as we dropped her off outside her house again.

"You're really not going to give me anything? Well don't bother coming back," she shouted before storming off, spitting swear words as she went. She didn't head back to her house, but in the opposite direction towards the motorway, where she knew it wouldn't take long for a truck driver to stop with the cash she needed for her next fix, whatever she had to do for it.

That second encounter with Leilah was far more heartbreaking than the first. It was the last time we ever saw her.

"We left it too long, and we lost her," said Dean, wiping away tears as we drove back to the hotel. We were naive, of course. For a girl like her, with so much pain to numb and horrific memories to blot out, the path to drug addiction was perhaps an inevitable one, especially in the dark underworld where she spent most of her waking hours. It is that last memory of her, cussing and shouting as she marched away from us, pulled like a magnet back to the edge of the highway, which has remained seared in my mind, a constant reminder of how little time we have, that every day could be the day we lose them.

5

LIVING DEAD

The next day we headed north again, but this time stopping in some of the places along the route that we had driven straight through the first time. I was struck by the way in which the motorway sliced straight through the heart of many of these communities. As if a river of lava had carved an unstoppable path of destruction, the road cut through the middle of town squares and shopping precincts, passing just metres away from whitewashed colonial churches, food markets, schools and burger bars. The locals went about their errands, schoolchildren dashed to their lessons, shopkeepers carried out their wares, just inches away from nose-to-tail trucks trundling through.

One of those towns, at the end of a long, meandering climb where trucks struggling with the incline slowed to a crawl, was Padre Paraíso, built on the steep, red-earthed slopes of a mountain valley. Hundreds of tiny painted cottages rose up the hills on both sides, each one facing towards the busy motorway below. Welcoming visitors on a traffic island in the middle of the highway was a statue of a typical country peasant worker wearing a scruffy tunic and straw hat and carrying a pickaxe on his shoulder, next to his pregnant wife and pot-bellied toddler son. It was a curious scene of rural poverty and hardship, yet above it a sign proudly announced 'The Town of Precious Stones. Welcome to the Jequitinhonha Valley'. I remembered what I'd read about the region: rich in gold, diamond and jewels, yet its people lived in poverty and children were dying of hunger and malnutrition. We hadn't given it so much as a glance a year ago, but I'd also come across it during my searches back in England, on online marketplaces as the place of origin for rare and highly-sought gemstone specimens – aquamarine, topaz, heliodor – along with eye-watering prices. Padre Paraíso was the first town in the Jequitinhonha Valley, both Brazil's treasure trove, where many outsiders had made their fortunes, and its 'Valley of Misery', where destitute families sold their own daughters to stave off hunger.

The next morning we started to understand the depth and breadth of that misery. Sonia lived on a narrow cobbled street one block away from the BR-116 and just a minute's walk from the simple hotel where we'd spent the night. The closer a property was to the motorway, I later discovered, the greater its value, so central was the road to the fortunes of this isolated hilltop town.

Jovial and chatty as she welcomed two strangers into her home without hesitation, we soon discovered that Sonia, who ran a project for poor children, was as extraordinary a find as Rita in Medina – a rare gem in the Town of Precious Stones. Overweight, she hobbled and wheezed, but it was just as clear this devout Catholic, who was in her 60s, wasn't going to let irritations like health and mobility issues stop her responding to the need around her, taking food to hungry families, helping relieve their hardship, sometimes even bringing destitute young people to live with her in her home.

Sitting us down around her carved oak dining table, which she immediately filled with cake, tapioca biscuits and a big wheel of Canastra cheese, Sonia told us how, as the mining frenzy in her town had poisoned rivers, and killed crops and livestock, she saw babies and toddlers die from hunger and malnutrition.

"Every day we would lose one," Sonia recalled. "One day, five children from the same family passed away. It was terrible. So we decided to do something. We started a soup kitchen, we helped their mothers. It worked. The children stopped dying."

I smiled, but Sonia sighed. Yes, she had saved their lives, she went on, but had then watched as those girls, and their daughters after them, had fallen victim to the horrors of the motorway.

"My heart still breaks for them," she said, her eyes full of pain. "These days they're more dead than alive. I see them standing at the side of the motorway, selling their bodies to truck drivers. There's no life left in their eyes. I call them 'living dead'."

Some of the young girls of whom Sonia spoke so tenderly had literally lost their lives. Others had been missing for months, even years, after one day climbing into a truck and never returning home. The next few hours were some of the most heartbreaking of my life as Sonia brought us to the homes of mothers who'd had to bury their own young daughters and others who were desperately clinging on to a fading hope that they might one day see them again. Their homes – at the very top of the hillside, furthest away from the motorway – were sad, tear-soaked places and their mothers were broken and bereft, close to giving up on life themselves. Their daughters, when they last saw them, were aged between just 11 and 14. Cherished photos in frames on the walls and inside carefully guarded albums, showed bright-eyed, smiling children, full of life and promise.

In one simple house, a green-painted 'casa popular', one of rows of identical simple homes provided to the poorest by the local council, we found Roxa, the mother of a girl called Natiele. She gripped my hand tightly with bony, withered fingers when I introduced myself, explaining that we wanted to know more about her daughter.

"God sent you to comfort me," she whimpered quietly, her whole body shaking. "Because I can't take the pain anymore."

In fact it had been seven years since she last saw Natiele, aged just 14. She hadn't returned home after going down to the motorway to make money for her mother. She was found four months later, dead inside the cabin of an abandoned truck nearly a thousand miles north in the northeastern state of Rio Grande do Norte. The young girl had been brutally beaten over the head and shot through the chest. The news was so devastating for Roxa that she didn't speak for a year and for the next two years she was paralysed on one side and unable to walk. Grief had turned her into a shadow, who sat silent and motionless in a darkened home whose doors and windows were permanently shuttered. Dean put a gentle arm around her and I asked Roxa if I could see a photo of her daughter. Tears welled up in her vacant eyes. "I burned all of them. I can't bear to see her again. I'd die if I ever saw her beautiful face again." She dissolved in tears again and began to shake and wail. "Oh God, what am I going to do without her…"

The last house we visited in Padre Paraíso was also up a steep hill at the other end of the town, where we found another inconsolable mother alone with her grief. The woman, her peroxide-blonde hair matted and messy, squinted from underneath a blanket while her eight-year-old daughter answered the door to us. Sunlight flooded the darkened room. Her eldest daughter, Ana Flavia, had been one of the children Sonia had looked after at her project, but had drifted away as she started going down to the motorway with a group of friends, offering themselves to passing truck drivers.

One day, she, along with another young girl, barely escaped with their lives after a truck they were travelling in tumbled off a bridge into a ravine near the town of Cândido Sales, 100 miles up the motorway in the next state north, killing the driver.

Then, in May 2011, her mother was woken by a knock on her door and the devastating news Ana Flavia was dead. She had been found in the crumpled wreckage of a truck which had smashed into another which had broken down on the side of the BR-116, this time 50 miles further south. The driver had fled the scene, leaving the young girl trapped alone in the mangled metal and fighting for her life. Firefighters said she held on for nearly an hour but died before they could cut her free. She was only 11.

Like Roxa, Ana Flavia's mother was still in as much shock as she was the day her world came crashing down. Haunted by constant flashes of her young daughter, trapped and frightened as her life slipped away, she was barely able to drag herself up from the tattered sofa where she slept to be a mother to her other daughter. She hardly ever left her tiny rented house, or opened the wooden shutters to let in the light. Unlike Roxa, though, she guarded with her life the things that helped her remember her daughter, including two photos which were clearly her most treasured possessions. They were kept in a locked box, stored behind another locked door in her TV cabinet. She took them out carefully and held the old polaroids up for us to see, not allowing us to handle them ourselves. One showed Ana Flavia, aged four, beaming a smile in her swimming costume as she made sandcastles on the beach. In the other she was eight, just a normal, happy girl, giggling as she posed for a picture with her younger sister.

Seeing those pictures of her, so full of joy and life, choked me up. "She was a really good girl," she told me, seeing how I was fighting back tears. "She never wanted for anything. I gave her so much advice, I really did."

That advice, according to Sonia, didn't extend to forbidding her from getting into trucks on the motorway, even after her earlier brush with death. Like so many young girls here, Ana Flavia, like Natiele, was a valuable source of income for her family. Prostitution was something that mothers in the town had passed on to their daughters for several generations now. Supplementing the family income that way, even at the age of 11, was just what girls her age did. Even now, her mother would spend her nights touting for customers down on the road as it passed through the town, leaving her eight-year-old girl inside the house on her own. "I'm not ashamed, I have to put food on the table," she said. "Most single mothers in Padre Paraíso live on truck drivers' cash. I'm no different from anyone else."

If the pain of having to bury their own children wasn't enough, these mothers were also having to live with something even more debilitating – injustice. Neither the truck driver who left Ana Flavia to die alone, nor the one who brutally bludgeoned Natiele to death, had been caught and arrested, or even so much as brought in by police for questioning.

With their truck number plates, it would have been easy to find those men and make them pay for their crimes. But instead, they had been allowed to simply walk away and continue their lives, leaving behind them mothers who would never recover and siblings who would grow up believing they are just as insignificant and worthless, that exchanging their bodies for a few coins might be the best they can hope for too.

As we crossed over the noisy road on the way back to Sonia's house, I wondered how often these men still drove by here on their long journeys up and down the motorway, smug and emboldened in the knowledge they could do what they liked with these types of girls with no consequence or comeuppance.

It made me sick to the stomach. I wanted to stand up for the other young girls in this town who might be their next victims. We had to head on, but as we joined the motorway again early the next morning and drove out of Padre Paraíso, I knew I'd be back here again.

6

LOST

The green sign pointing sharp left to Medina was now so rusted it was hard to make out the name. Turning off the motorway, the town felt even more forlorn than the last time we were here a year earlier. Rubbish and rubble piled up on street corners, while potholes which had become craters turned the straight road to the main square into a slow-motion slalom course.

We'd been on the road for a week now and I knew we still had a distance to cover before I could get back to the comforts of home, and see my wife and young son again. I'd already collected enough information on Medina and its problems last time, but felt out of courtesy we needed to drop in on Rita again on our way through. From here, we would continue our journey north towards the state border, crossing over to the next state north, Bahia, and to Brazil's northeastern region, known for its high levels of deprivation and droughts. But what we had intended to be a quick 'hello' became a long and eventful week.

When we arrived, Rita had already laid a breakfast table replete with local delicacies – some delicious, like spongy local cheese, tapioca pancakes and fresh, sweet mangoes, and some considerably less so, such as mocotó, a foul-smelling thick brown jelly made from stewed cow hooves, which she assured us was full of nutrients. Over freshly-brewed, strong, sweet coffee, we chatted, chortled and caught up on the last 14 months since we'd last seen each other. We'd only been together for less than six hours in total, but that short time had left such a mark that our second meeting felt like a reunion of old friends without any of the polite courtesies of a year ago. Talk turned to the girls and Rita's cheerful demeanour changed.

"Oh, Matt, those girls you met, I'm afraid we've lost them."

The clatter of cutlery on plates stopped. "What... how?" I asked, aghast. "It's only been a year since..."

A year was a long time in the lives of these girls, Rita explained patiently. Already teetering on the edge of an abyss, it only took the slightest knock for them to topple over. Viviane, the younger of the two sisters from the house on the motorway's edge, had disappeared three months ago. Her older sibling last saw her getting into a stationary truck just metres away from her front door, telling her she would be back within a week. The horrific stories we'd heard in Padre Paraíso flashed through my mind. Viviane was only 13.

The second house we'd visited was the home of Leticia, now also 13, whose father had been so frantic about his daughter's increasingly wayward behaviour. During the last 12 months her troubled life had gone into free-fall. She had started spending longer periods away from home and now she too had been missing for weeks. Word had got back to her tormented father that she was in an underage brothel, somewhere close to Padre Paraíso. Rumours were also swirling that she had Aids.

Finally, Rita filled us in on the turbulent life of Mariana. The news was as bad as it could be. Just turned 15 and seven months pregnant, she had also not been seen for several weeks, not that her mother or grandmother had bothered to sound the alarm. She was last seen with another girl, ambling along the motorway's edge as it passed by the town. Rita assumed she was in one of the many roadside brothels along the motorway north of Medina, although she admitted no-one could know for sure where she was, or if she would ever turn up again. My heart sank. One of our hopes in returning to Medina was to see Mariana again and help her find a way out, but, like Leilah, and the other girls we'd met last time, we were too late for her too.

"Oh, they're not the only ones," sighed Rita. Almost all the girls she had known a year ago were now missing or out of her reach, she explained. Some had succumbed to the darkness swirling around them and fallen headfirst into the world of prostitution, drugs, or gangs, while others had simply walked out of their homes one day in the direction of the motorway and never returned. In their places were other young girls, in equally unbearable situations, confused, vulnerable lives that weighed just as heavily on Rita's mind.

That afternoon, she took us to meet one of them, a 12-year-old girl called Lilian who lived in a brick house in another poor district of town known simply as The Hill. Rita met her after her mother reported her to the guardianship council, complaining she wasn't obeying her and that she was spending most of her time on the streets. The dirt track up The Hill was too steep and treacherous to drive, so we parked the car at the bottom and trudged up the steps cut into the rust-red earth. As we did Rita explained what had caused Lilian to rebel against her mother.

"You see down there where we parked?" Rita said as we stopped to catch our breath. From here we could see the top of our car below us, a sprawling neighbourhood of red-tiled houses in front of us and the ever-busy BR-116 in the distance. "That's where the truck drivers would stop when they came here to abuse Lilian. They knew the way to her house by heart. They would park up, sound their horn and her mother would send her off down these steps, then wait for her to come back with the money. They would abuse her inside their cabins, right down there, literally under her mother's nose."

Dean was disgusted, especially when Rita added that most people in the neighbourhood knew of the arrangement but never alerted the authorities. "If this was happening in my hometown there'd be a posse of country boys banging on that trucker's door. It would be over," he fumed.

"That's the greatest tragedy," sighed Rita. "Most people here don't think there's anything remotely wrong with it. As soon as Lilian was old enough to get away from her mother, that's what she did. She told me she was only 10 when it started."

The few minutes we spent with Lilian were, like with the dozens of other girls we'd met so far, utterly heartbreaking. She spoke softly, with all the mannerisms and vocabulary of a child, but at the same time with a hardness she had learned from the streets. She was no longer being exploited by her mother, but it was clear the mixed-up girl was in just as much danger and not far off becoming yet another of Rita's lost girls. After what was done to her, Lilian quickly learned that her body was something that could be swapped and sold, so she continued to let herself be abused for money as, along with a group of other girls her age, she frequented Medina's back street bars and prostitution spots well into the early hours. Recently she had discovered she was pregnant, but a month ago she lost the baby in what Rita suspected was a dangerous DIY abortion, which the girls often carried out themselves. She showed us the scar on her back where, a month earlier, she had been stabbed during a fight in a bar. "I was terrified. I thought I was going to die. I passed out and woke up in hospital."

As we got up to say goodbye I asked Lilian what she wanted to be when she grew up. "A public prosecutor," she replied without hesitation, turning around and showing me the words printed on the back of her T-shirt: 'Let justice be done, though the world perish'.

****

The events of the last week had been physically and emotionally draining, so instead of taking up Rita's offer of dinner at her place that night, Dean and I decided to wander a short distance from the hotel to grab something to eat on Medina's town square. We found an empty table and ordered two X-Tudos, or 'Cheese Everythings', a burger packed with peas, sweetcorn, fried eggs and potato sticks which seemed to be one of the only evening snacks available in the small country towns we had visited. But this time there weren't the usual jokes and idle banter that we normally enjoyed on nights like this. Our hearts felt too heavy for that. Over the next half an hour we exchanged few words, mostly sitting in silence, lost in our thoughts which seemed to muffle the music and chatter all around us. At one point I found myself staring ahead at the road that wrapped around the square. Teenagers cycled along, overtaken by cars blasting Brazilian rhythms from booming loudspeakers while trucks trundled slowly round.

"Dean, that truck over there. What's he doing?"

Dean turned around. A mud-splattered dumper truck was

crawling slowly round the square, stopping momentarily, then moving on again. After one lap it passed us again, then slowly drove round another time, then again, and again, before finally turning off a dark side street and disappearing. Some minutes later there came another, this time a huge juggernaut that seemed too wide to navigate the cobbled road lined with parked cars. This truck also circled the square a number of times, hissing its brakes, sometimes stopping for a few seconds. They spent most of the time at the other end of the square where there were few people and no streetlights, where Rita had told us girls would wait on benches facing the road for 'clients'.

I remembered what Rita had told us on our first visit here, about how truck drivers on their long journeys up or down the BR-116 would turn into the town and drive around its dimly-lit streets, knowing that sooner or later they would find a child for sale. That's what we were seeing, predators on the prowl, just like those vultures we'd seen circling the town's slaughterhouse. And yet no-one else out on the square tonight seemed remotely bothered by it. They carried on without a care, laughing, drinking, dancing around their tables. I thought of Lilian, one of the girls whose life had been destroyed by these trucks and by the locals who let it happen. I thought of Mariana, Lidiane and Viviane, lost somewhere in the darkness of this cursed highway, frightened maybe, certainly feeling alone and worthless. I thought of Natiele and Ana Flavia, their young lives violently taken from them and Leilah, from whom the motorway had stolen everything before she had even reached adolescence and who I knew I would probably never see again.

It was all too much to bear. My eyes welled up and I found myself weeping. I caught Dean from the corner of my eye. Tears silently streaked from the corner of his baseball cap, which he'd pulled down low over his face. People sitting nearby looked over and talked amongst themselves. Our waiter approached cautiously, unsure of what to say. I smiled and waved him away, then dissolved into tears again.

We wept on that packed square without saying a word to each other as the emotions we'd bottled up over the past week finally poured out. Medina's town square was emptying, the waiters clearing tables and sweeping the floor when Dean looked up and broke the silence. "Matt, we need to do something. We can't just leave here and move on to the next place." I agreed. We hadn't been able to help – and in most cases even find – any of the girls we'd met just a year ago and the others we'd just met seemed so close to the same precipice. It was supposed to be a fact-finding trip, but it would take many more months before we could travel all the way up to the start of this vast motorway and that was too long to wait. We had to do something now.

So it was, our faces streaked with tears, that we began to sketch out a way we might be able to bring hope to the lost girls of the BR-116, starting in Medina. Maybe, we thought, we could open a house, where girls could come and know they were safe, where they would find people they could trust, who would fight for them and who genuinely wanted the best for them. A place where they would find the strength to take back control over their lives and find hope again, no matter what they had been through or what had been stolen from them.

As we thought about how we could bring the girls in, and help them discover their worth and potential, we both agreed on one thing – we could teach them to dance. It was what so many girls we had met had told us they loved most, one of the few things that had caused them to smile and their eyes to sparkle. Neither Dean nor I knew how to dance, but we both knew it held extraordinary power to empower and transform. And that was what these girls needed most, to dream again, to find the strength to take control of their lives, overcome the trauma of their pasts and find hope for their futures. I'll never forget that night. Those tears started a river that would become unstoppable.

* * * *

Rita's large oak table was crammed full again when Dean and I arrived the next morning. We'd already had breakfast at the hotel 10 minutes earlier, but pretended otherwise as we sat down and tucked in again. This time, though, we came straight to the point, and as we discussed our idea of starting a permanent project in Medina as soon as we could, a broad smile spread across her face. A safe space they could call their own, where they could be themselves and be helped to find a way out, was just what the girls needed, Rita said. It seemed such a simple idea – a house where girls could find a little respite from the disorder and turmoil of their lives, and hear positive, life-affirming messages for once – but she assured us for the teenagers she knew who had never had anyone so much as show concern for them, it would be a lifeline, something they would never have imagined could happen to them.

"Matt, no-one is going to believe it, not the girls, and certainly not the local people who see them as nobodies. That someone – two gringos! – are opening a house just for the motorway girls, and where they can learn to dance?! That's supposed to be just for rich girls!" she gasped, as what we were suggesting began to sink in.

Her eyes brightened. "Can you imagine," she said, touching my arm enthusiastically, "the girls going and dancing there on the town square, the place where men come to abuse them? Can you imagine them all dressed up in the same dance uniform, with music blasting out, showing who they really are and telling everyone to respect them?"

Rita continued to dream out loud as she imagined a house that was the opposite to everything the girls saw and heard in their own lives. "It should be full of music, colour, fun and laughter. We could paint phrases on the walls, telling the girls how precious they are… it should feel like a home, with sofas and bean bags to snuggle up in.. and their own space where they can keep their things safe… and times when they can all talk together about what they're going through…"

The project would need a coordinator, and it was abundantly clear who that should be. Rita already had a full-time paid job as an elected member of the guardianship council, and she was only a year into her four-year mandate. But when I mentioned it, she immediately offered to relinquish her position to head up our new house. "I knew when you knocked on my door all those months ago that this was meant to be. This is a dream come true. Of course I'll be a part of it."

7

FOUND

Dean and I were back in the pousada, packing our bags and preparing to hit the road again early the next morning. We still had a week left before Dean had to return to Canada, enough time to visit some other towns on the road north of Medina. In the meantime, Rita was going to start looking for suitable premises and for other women who could work with her when the project opened. That afternoon we had allowed ourselves to relax and unwind, spending time wandering around Medina's cobbled streets and getting to know a pleasant side to the town we hadn't yet seen. There were small boutique-style shops, a beautiful colonial-era Catholic church, a yellow-painted spire piercing a lush blue sky, and many snack bars where we sat on pavement tables eating deep-fried banana pasties, or bowls of ice-cold açai sorbet. It was now 9pm and we were waiting for a phone call from Rita who we'd arranged to go for a farewell dinner with her husband Max at the only pizza joint in town.

Suddenly someone was battering on my bedroom door. Startled, I opened it slightly and peered outside only to see Rita waiting impatiently. For a moment I wondered if I'd misunderstood the time we were supposed to meet.

"Matt," she blurted. "I know where Mariana is. She's in a

brothel on the side of the 116. It's between here and Pedra Azul, the next town north."

I opened the door. "How did you find her?"

"I just spoke to one of her friends. It's about half an hour away from here. Let's go."

Soon we were driving through the blackness of the motorway, following the twists and turns of the BR-116 in the remote hills north of Medina. Rita peered forwards in the passenger seat, anxious not to miss the opening, hidden in the darkness, where we were supposed to turn.

"Most people drive past without even noticing there's anything there," she said. "But truck drivers know. Last year we did a raid there with the police and found four girls aged 12 to 14. They closed the place down, but it reopened a few months later as if nothing had happened... Here it is, quick, turn in now!"

I swung the car round into what seemed like a dusty clearing amid towering eucalyptus trees. Rita was right, no-one hurtling by on this remote stretch of road would have noticed the bar, illuminated only on the inside, set far back in the thicket and, if they had, would probably have dismissed it as a herdsman's hut. But there were already two huge cargo trucks parked in the forest clearing. From inside the car we peered towards the small brick building and saw the silhouettes of a billiard table, beer bottles on tables, a number of men and what looked like another small girl holding a baby in her arms.

"I don't think I should go in there," said Rita. "They might remember me from the raid. I'll stay in the car, they'll think it's just you two."

Dean and I tried to hide our nerves as we got out of the car and walked along the pebbly ground towards the bar, the barking of drunken men and the decadent rhythms of forró country music growing louder with each step. Heads turned as we approached. The idea was to sit down at one of the tables, ask for a beer and make some discreet enquiries in the hope of finding out if Mariana was there. But the fact we'd arrived in a car, and looked very different to the bar's usual clientele, immediately raised suspicion. As we got closer, we could no longer see the girl with the baby and there was no sign of Mariana either. One man, his tattooed arms bulging from a sleeveless vest, pivoted around on his metal chair, following us with a piercing stare as we entered the bar.

I was wondering how we could abort the mission and get out of there safely when I caught sight of Mariana in a dark corner of the room. Wearing a pair of frayed denim shorts and a loose midriff top, she was dancing provocatively in front of a scruffy, unshaven man who held a billiard cue in one hand and a bottle of beer in the other. The man cackled as he ground his hairy bare belly against hers, unbothered about the baby bulge which showed she was seven months pregnant. I pointed at her jokingly and laughed to try to break the awkwardness. "Found you! I bet you never thought you'd see us again... Come outside, we need to talk." Recognising us, Mariana came straight over, leaving the man mumbling foul-mouthed protests as he took another swig of beer. My exclamation, and her reaction, seemed to settle the edginess of the other men, who turned back to their tables.

Dean, Mariana and I walked back down to the motorway's edge, past our car with Rita still crouching out of view in the back, and sat down on the concrete cover of an underground cistern. In that remote forest clearing, a long way from the lights of town, the darkness was overwhelming. We could barely make out our hands in front of our faces. The only time we caught a fleeting glimpse of each other was when a truck roared by, lighting us up for a few seconds. Without fail, the truckers would blast their horns as they caught sight of the young girl sitting on the roadside, clutching her bare legs.

Despite her inappropriate clothes and heavy make-up, Mariana was the same doe-eyed young girl we'd met in her home 14 months earlier. "What are you doing here?" I asked her. "This isn't a place for someone like you. I know it isn't the life that you want."

She sighed. "My mum never cared about me. She was just interested in using me to buy her cachaça. So I ran away. At least now I can keep the money for myself." Mariana looked up to a clearing in the towering trees where a clear sky was full of stars.

"So, is this it?" I asked her. "When we talked last year you said you wanted to change your life. And now you've got to think about your baby too. What happened to all those dreams, of being a dancer, and a judge?"

"What am I supposed to do?" she whispered, her voice faltering.

I couldn't give her an answer. Our plans to open a project in Medina couldn't help her. This girl needed a solution now… tonight. If she went back home, her mother and grandmother would belittle and berate her and send her back to the motorway with instructions not to come back again empty-handed. And if she turned around and went back to the brothel she would be at the mercy of drunken, violent men and who knows what other mortal dangers in that sinister underworld where teenage girls were just objects to be used and discarded.

A man in denim shorts stumbled out of the bar, urinated

on the front wheel of his truck, then climbed inside and drove off. The headlights passed over us and I could see tears silently streaming down Mariana's face. My heart was breaking. Sitting on that crumbling concrete block, she looked utterly lost and alone. I just wanted to take her away from there, to a place where she would never be in danger again. I took a deep breath.

"Mariana, come back to live with me in my home. We never forgot you, that's how much you mean to us. Please, leave all this behind and start a new life, a long way from here."

Mariana didn't react. She carried on staring ahead of her. There was a shift in the air and a chilling feeling came over me. We were being watched. A soft rustle of movement came from the shadows around us, footsteps in the undergrowth. Darting silhouettes of men circled us and the place felt extremely dangerous all of a sudden. Our hearts were beating furiously. Inside the car, Rita was slumped in the seat, undetected by the men with our blacked-out windows. No one had realised she was in there, or that she had watched two young men fetch revolvers from behind the bar and slowly come crouching in our direction.

"Look, let's get you out of here," I said, my eyes darting around me. "It will be easier for you to make a decision back in Medina. What do you think?"

Mariana nodded and we helped her up and made a break for the car where Rita implored us to get out of there quickly. I tore backwards and, glancing left and right, pulled out onto the motorway, spraying dust and loose stones behind us. Soon we were heading back towards Medina, just our lights illuminating the gloomy blackness ahead of us. It was only after five minutes of nervously watching my rear-view mirror in case anyone had followed us that we allowed ourselves to breathe a little easier.

However, while we had taken Mariana away, I knew there was another girl – whose silhouette we had seen holding her baby when we arrived – who was still at the mercy of those gun-toting men. Even Mariana didn't know her name, but as she told us about the illicit goings on at "the brothel at kilometre fifty-eight", and the types of men who frequented it, I regretted leaving before we'd met her, and wondered if we'd ever see her again.

With nowhere else for her to go until we had taken all the legal steps required to take Mariana away, we dropped her back at her mother's house, urging her to meet us at the guardianship council offices early the next morning so we could make representations to the local judge. As we pulled up in front of Mariana's house, her mother was sitting on a mound of earth outside, puffing on a rolled up cigarette, almost exactly as she'd been when we first met her. Seeing her daughter inside our car, she began to scream and swear. "Why did you bring this whore back here?" she spitted. "She's worth nothing. All she does is cause trouble. You should have left her where you found her."

That night I called Dani back home in Belo Horizonte, unsure how to explain that I'd promised a troubled girl that she could come back to live with us and our young son. But she had been following Mariana's story from afar too and while in the UK she had been just as moved by her plight. Her reply was simple: that I had to do everything I could to convince the authorities in Medina to let Mariana come home to live with us, recover from her years of rejection and trauma and start her life afresh. In the meantime, she started getting our spare bedroom ready and buying clothes for her and her baby, due in just a few months.

Our plans to travel north were put on hold once again, for a reason I had never in my wildest imagination considered when we left Belo Horizonte nine days before, to become the foster parent to a 15-year-old girl and soon her infant child. The next few days were spent visiting different offices of the council and judiciary, gathering the documents I needed to become Mariana's legal guardian, then waiting for the judge to examine the case and make his decision.

Thankfully, the town's public prosecutor supported our application to become Mariana's legal guardians, meaning the judge was much more likely to agree without any other complications. As expected, though, her mother wasn't going to let her go without a fight. When she was informed her parental rights had been removed in a document delivered by the court clerk, she turned up at the guardianship council building, drunk and incandescent with rage. "No-one's going to take my daughter away from me," she screamed. She turned to Mariana. "How dare you leave me! I'm going to get you and break your legs, you'll see!"

We booked another room in the hotel so Mariana didn't have to go back home, taking turns to keep watch outside her room. I was getting increasingly nervous being in the town and was counting down the hours until the judge signed the papers and we could leave. While Mariana's trembling mother was a pitiful sight, I knew she was also dangerous and unhinged, connected to the town's drug dealers who regularly dispatched bothersome types in a pool of blood. Now that we had succeeded in taking her daughter away from her – her only source of income – the town didn't feel safe anymore.

Six days after we arrived in Medina, we finally got word that the custody documents had been signed and we were free to leave. We immediately got into the car, which we'd already loaded with our belongings, and prepared for the long journey home. Just like we had the year before, we turned southwards onto the BR-116 and before long Medina's dusty sprawl was again just a speck in my rear view mirror. This time was different though. Back then my mind had been racing, my heart breaking for a girl who seemed so lost and alone.

This time she was in the back of my car, smiling and gazing out of the window, leaving behind her nightmare, about to begin a new start in life.

8

THE PINK HOUSE

My conversations so far with the girls I'd met had been fleeting, wary words snatched over the roar of trucks or amid tensions inside their homes. But now one of those girls was in my house, quickly becoming part of the family, eating with us, watching movies on the sofa with us, walking down the hill to the local ice cream parlour or bonding with our toddler son in the children's playground. It didn't take long for Mariana to realise that she was safe and the difference that made in her changed everything – her demeanour, her confidence, even her posture. The quiet and crestfallen girl who we had met in her home and outside the brothel, head down and shoulders hunched, quickly began to come out of herself. The real Mariana, unshackled from her fears, was funny and loud, sensitive and thoughtful. She laughed scandalously, gossiped, played practical jokes, would surprise us with touching acts of kindness, wept easily and little by little started to open up and talk about things she'd never in her life dared utter to anyone. What I saw happen inside our flat in a short period of time convinced me that every girl caught up in this tragedy needed the same safe space, the same chance to find people they could trust and who they knew genuinely cared.

I was also able to see more clearly than ever, in ways I would never have noticed outside the context of our home, how rejection, hardship and suffering had become entirely normal to her. For the first few evenings we would suddenly realise that Mariana wasn't around, then find her fast asleep in her bed. No-one had ever cared enough to wish her "goodnight" – she had never learned to say it – and would just take herself off to bed without a word. It was a poignant reminder of the loveless existence she had lived until now.

On another occasion, after a torrential tropical rainstorm, Mariana suddenly exclaimed, "Oh, the smell of wet earth. Whenever I smell it it makes me want to run out and eat it."

"Eat earth?" I laughed, assuming it was another of her pranks.

"Yes… why, don't you like it?" she said.

As the conversation progressed, it became clear that Mariana and her brothers really did used to dig up dirt and swallow it, something I would later discover was common among poor families in the region to stave off hunger pangs. Tragically, she just assumed it was normal and had even learned to enjoy the taste. It even took a while to convince her that eating earth wasn't something that most people did.

Most disturbing of all was hearing Mariana talk about prostitution as if it were something entirely normal for a girl her age. While she frequently rallied against her mother for not loving her, for calling her cruel names or for ripping up her precious notebooks to roll her smokes, she never expressed any anger towards her or her grandmother for forcing her to sell her body on the motorway. She believed it was what happened to every girl at a certain age. At first she would refer to the men who paid her as her "boyfriends" until we explained that having a boyfriend was something entirely different to what she thought. She also told us that the father of her baby was her "ex-boyfriend". In fact, he was a man she had met once in a grimy brothel bedroom and had never seen again.

Entirely unaware that she had been the victim of a sickening crime, she often came out with stories at the most inappropriate moments, like while chatting away at a pizza restaurant or sitting in the dentist's waiting room. But when she did start talking we didn't shush or stop her, wherever we were and whoever was within earshot. It was during those moments that we learned how she had lost her virginity aged seven, when she was raped by an uncle – Rita had already told me how abuse by a family member was a common way of initiating daughters into the life of prostitution which inevitably awaited them at puberty. How she had reluctantly done her first 'programme' on the motorway aged just 11 after her mother and grandmother had told her it was time. How her alcoholic grandmother would offer her to bar owners in exchange for shots of cachaça rum and how, again aged 11, her mother had handed her over to a gang of dealers for the night to clear the drug debts she had run up. Those conversations would leave me in pieces and when I got home afterwards I would often shut myself in my room and sob, my heart breaking for this young girl who had been so systematically robbed of her childhood she didn't even know what she was supposed to have missed.

So oblivious was she to the wrong that had been done to her, I would, in other moments, find her getting teary because she was missing her grandmother, who she called mother. Perhaps most tragic though was seeing how the cycle of rejection and lovelessness was being repeated in her feelings towards her own unborn child. She was rapidly approaching her due date, but never talked about her baby, never got excited when she kicked or moved and never directed a word to the little person growing inside her as other expectant mums would.

Once the day arrived and Mariana gave birth to a beautiful baby girl, there were few signs of the normal bond between a mother and child. She would change her nappies, pick her up when she cried and put her on her breast when she was hungry, but she never said a word to her and seemed to just be going through the motions, apparently devoid of any maternal feelings. After all she had told us, it was easy to understand why she didn't think becoming a mother was anything to be cherished. One day I sat down with her and asked her what she felt for her daughter, and she burst into tears. "I don't feel anything," she sobbed. "I don't love her, I never have. I can't. I want her to be happy, to never have to suffer like I have. But I don't want to be her mother."

A week later, at a meeting at Belo Horizonte's children court to discuss becoming the legal guardians of Mariana's baby until she turned 18, she unexpectedly told the social worker that she didn't want her daughter and wanted to give her up for adoption. In one of the most emotional hours of my life, the beautiful baby girl we had cuddled and cared for through the first weeks of her life was taken away there and then. Mariana's mind was made up, but she still sobbed her heart out as we drove home and as I took away the baby toys and dismantled the cot in her bedroom. The next morning, though, she woke up, got breakfast, and chatted happily as if none of the last 10 months had ever happened.

The Pink House

****

While I was grappling with the dramas happening in my home, I was also dealing with the more mundane aspects of setting up a non-profit organisation in Brazil, a process even more perplexing and bureaucratic than our experience of moving to the country. For us to begin any kind of charitable work the organisation needed to be officially founded with a legally acceptable written constitution and registered with several public bodies, authorised by Brazil's inland revenue and then approved by the local social assistance council in the municipalities we would be working. Every form and document needed to be signed by a lawyer as well as the seven board members and every signature notarised in different offices, which meant more long days crisscrossing the city in pursuit of paperwork, signatures and endless rubber stamps.

I decided to call the charity Meninadança, a word in Portuguese meaning 'Girldance', and with which I had a history. In my twenties, in what became an extended gap year after leaving university, I had travelled to Brazil, and lived for several years in Belo Horizonte, a vast but pleasant metropolis ringed by jagged hills, and where I had fell in love with the country's people, culture and language. While I was there, a group of friends and I had got together to help some of the girls we would see living on the city's streets, providing food and activities. The project, which the girls themselves had christened Meninadança, ran for three years before my visa expired and we all went our separate ways.

Meanwhile, I reconnected with one of those old friends. Warlei and I had been thick as thieves back then, but we had lost contact after I left. Life had swept us along in different directions and, with both of us occupied with work and family, our attempts at communication had slowed to a trickle, then stopped completely. I had thrown myself straight into a journalism postgraduate at City University in London before, thanks to a very fortunate exclusive about serial killer Harold Shipman, being hired by then-*Daily Mirror* editor Piers Morgan and finding myself at the bottom of a very steep learning curve in a newspaper newsroom.

Warlei, who had been teaching sport to disadvantaged teenagers back then, had also completed a postgraduate degree, in educational psychology, and was now helping train teachers and help state schools develop their curricula. He married wife Nahilla just before I left Brazil, but since then they had had a daughter, Vitória, who was born with cerebral palsy after her mother developed preeclampsia during her pregnancy. They chose the beautiful girl's name – 'victory' in Portuguese – after she was delivered three months premature, just 36cm long, but held onto life despite every expert telling her parents it was impossible that she would survive.

At first I was unsure about getting back in touch with Warlei after such a long time without speaking. We arranged to meet up a few days later, over drinks in a shopping mall bar. The years were quickly swept away as we remembered that time of our lives before kids, mortgages and bills, and laughed about some of the crazy adventures we'd had together. The conversation then inevitably turned to why I was back in Brazil, and I began to tell him the whole story, from the moment Dean and I had met Leilah on the motorway that night. Warlei seemed both stunned – as far as he knew I had found my niche in life, there was another factor we had to take into consideration: a gang turf war had broken out between three poor districts of the town, The Hill, on the west of town, Riverside, on the north and Lowland, in the south. Shoot-outs and murders were becoming an increasing part of daily life and anyone from one area wasn't welcome in the others. That really only left the town centre, which was considered neutral, to find a building, making Rita's task even more difficult.

Then one afternoon, she called me.

"Matt, I've found a great house. It's on the corner of my street. You can see it from the town square. It's not huge but it's got all the rooms we need and a big space upstairs which could be the dance studio. The rent's really cheap too…"

"Great! Let's take it then," I said, feeling a flush of excitement.

"Wait. There's just one problem."

The house, Rita explained, was right next to the town's jail which held political prisoners during Brazil's bloody military dictatorship between 1964 and 1986. Dissenters were tortured there and many were believed to have been killed and buried in the ground underneath it. People were so scared of that place that, once the prison was demolished, nobody was interested in buying the land and nothing else was built on it. It was the reason the house next door was so cheap – few people were willing to live there.

She continued, "I don't think the girls will be bothered. The owner said we could even plant a garden on the land next door if we dared disturb the soil. But I just wanted to know what you thought…"

I actually quite liked the symbolism of having our house –

where we hoped to bring freedom – in a place where innocents had once been held captive and where some never managed to escape. Rita said the town's older residents still recalled the haunting screams and wails that would echo from that jail through the night. Now, it was going to vibrate with the rhythms of dance and the sounds of life and joy. The house's sinister past actually made me even more convinced that we'd found the right place.

Once the contract had been signed, we had another decision to make – which colour to paint our new house. I already had a good idea: during my research into prostitution in the region, I'd read that in the past the houses that were bordellos were often ones that were painted the brightest. It had seemed wrong to me that those places of so much misery would be the most colourful and eye-catching and I wanted to turn that idea around. I told Rita and she laughed and told me to leave it with her. A few days later she sent me a photo of the house. It was painted the brightest, most garish pink imaginable. She'd taken another photo from the square, looking up from about the same place Dean and I had been sitting on that night, and the house stood out like a beacon. The main topic of conversation in town, Rita laughed, was what on earth was that bright pink house up on the hill going to be. From that moment there was only one thing we could call it – the Pink House.

raising descent, the asphalt finally started again, but by now we were hours behind schedule. It was 6pm by the time we finally turned onto the BR-116, an hour away from Medina – and Rita's meeting started at 7pm. We wouldn't even have time to stop at our hotel, freshen up and change.

"What happened to you?" Rita flustered as our mud-splattered car finally stopped outside the town's grand Catholic parish hall where the meeting was being held. "I thought you weren't going to make it. Everyone who's anyone is here: the police chief, the council president, the social assistance secretary.., even the mayor and his wife!"

Medinenses, we discovered as we walked into the packed room, really knew how to do special occasions. Everyone was dressed to the hilt, the men in flashy suits, huge shiny belt buckles and leather cowboy hats, the women on their arms in frilly floral dresses and impossibly high heels. Dean and I, on the other hand, were still in the clothes we'd spent a long day navigating scary dirt roads in in the sweltering heat. Rita, also dressed immaculately, and as always the perfect host, had arranged for a group of waitresses to greet guests with platters of finger food pastries and flutes of sparkling water.

Once everyone had taken their seats the room hushed and the presentation began. We started by showing a video with footage of motorway girls talking about their lives from the Brazilian news report I'd come across, followed by clips of girls dancing and smiling set to upbeat music. After the video, I took the microphone and tried to break the ice by joking that people needed sunglasses to walk past the new bright pink house before explaining how we'd arrived in Medina, met Rita, been moved by the plight of girls there and how we hoped the house would change many lives. But as I scanned the room, the faces I saw were stony and unresponsive. My stomach knotted and I began to wonder if this had been the right decision, to be so open with townsfolk about why we were there.

Finally, Rita brought the meeting to a close, inviting anyone who had anything to say to take the microphone. There was an eternity of awkward silence and I began to make throat-slashing gestures from my seat for her to wrap up. But then a chair scraped and a man walked through the audience to the front. It was the town's police chief. "I'd like to thank you for bringing this project to our town," he said. "I'm putting my police officers at your disposal, whenever you need us we'll make sure the girls are always our priority."

Next, a local grocery store owner took the microphone, saying how moved he had been and that he would donate a daily supply of milk and bread to the Pink House. The town's social assistance secretary was next, promising to put her team at our disposal. Before long, there was a queue of people waiting their turn to speak as, one by one, each made gushing speeches, ensuring us we could count on their full support. Finally, the room fell silent as a white-haired man with a moustache rose to his feet, removed his cowboy hat and shuffled slowly to the front. It was Joselio, Rita whispered, the mayor.

He leant forward and blew into the microphone. "I've also been touched by everything that's happened tonight," he started. "We all know how much the girls of our town need help. We will support you in any way we can. And to show you how much I mean it, in front of all these witnesses, I am pledging to donate… a horse."

Suddenly the room erupted in applause as the assembled

guests rose spontaneously to their feet. Clapping furiously, Rita turned round to me with a wide smile on her face as I mimed, 'A horse?'

"Senhor Josélio is a breeder of thoroughbreds," she shouted in my ear over the cheers. "The second-best in the whole of Brazil. People come from all over Brazil to buy his horses. Each one is worth tens of thousands of reals!"

I was thrilled, if somewhat bemused, by the mayor's generous gift and the apparently genuine outpouring of support for our plans. After what Rita had told me about the town, I hadn't expected such an enthusiastic reception. Once the event had ended many guests stayed, coming up to shake our hands and chatting cordially. After several months tangled up in infuriating paperwork and bureaucracy, this dream of ours finally felt within touching distance, especially now that we had the support of so many influential people – and most unexpectedly, had been gifted with a prize stallion.

One of the guests who had stayed behind was a man in his sixties called Evany. He hadn't been one of those who had come to the front to speak and immediately struck me as being different from the others in the room. Dressed in a scruffy denim shirt and threadbare brown trousers, he introduced himself as a local reporter and blogger. He made a point of taking me aside so we could talk without being overhead.

"This is a great thing you're doing," he said. "Child sexual abuse is this town's biggest problem. It's like a cancer that is slowly killing us, but no-one realises it. Good luck, and be careful who you trust…"

I was intrigued by Evany, both because I felt an affinity with him as a journalist, but also due to the way others appeared to be dismissive of him, even giving me discreet warnings not to pay him much attention. I asked him if we could have a further chat and, later that night after all the guests had already gone home and Medina's streets were quiet and empty, we met up at one of the roadside burger bars. Wispy-haired with a salt-and-pepper goatee and thick-rimmed glasses, he said people called him Owl, after his online blog, *Owl of the Valley*. Like an owl, he told me, he kept a sharp eye on everything that was going on, adding with a chuckle that he was virtually nocturnal too. He leaned in closer to me across the plastic table and went straight to the point.

"Matt, no-one here has any interest in protecting girls. Especially those people who were in that room tonight. Believe me, if they really wanted it to stop, they would have done something about it a long time ago."

"But... they all seemed so supportive. You heard them."

"Let me try to explain. What you spoke about tonight, it's this town's dirty secret. No-one ever talks about it. No-one wanted to hear about it. They know it's wrong, but they don't think it's that wrong... and many are involved in it."

"Now," he went on. "We Medinenses are friendly and eager to please, especially when foreigners turn up in town. So they clapped and made speeches and pledged their support. Because that's what they thought you wanted to hear."

"So... they didn't mean it?"

Evany smiled kindly. "They wanted you to feel welcomed and leave with a good impression of their town. But don't expect them all to be on your side once you begin. Especially if you start treading on their toes."

Evany seemed to be talking sense, and clearly knew much

more about this region and all its problems than anyone else I'd spoken to until then. I asked him why child sexual exploitation had become so normalised.

Medina, he explained, was built on the backs of slaves, African and indigenous people who were marched, shackled, to the region by Portuguese colonists in 1847. They were put to work building their houses and farms – including the Catholic church hall where the meeting was held. Slavery was abolished some 40 years later, but what replaced it was a feudal system where the rich noblemen owned all the land and allowed the poor descendants of slaves to live there in exchange for their labour. The town's gentry could do anything they wanted without fear of reprisals – including taking their poor workers' young daughters to satisfy their sexual desires.

"A lot of people in town can trace their ancestry back to that – their great-great-grandmother, probably of African or indigenous descent, being raped by a rich landowner when she was still just a child. The same might have happened to her daughter too. And so, over generations, it was buried deep into their psyche. Poor young girls could be used and abused by those with more money and power than them. It just became normal."

That was the reason, Evany explained, that when the BR-116 was built right next to the town in the 1950s and trucks coming from the wealthier south started to drive past, families began sending their young daughters to offer their bodies in exchange for money and food. Any cultural or moral impediment to child abuse had long been removed.

"You see what you're taking on?" he said. "Here, the rich people, like those who were there tonight, still think they can do

83

what they want and that the poor are their property. To make any difference here you'll have to reverse 150 years of history."

Evany's words, spoken in hushed tones on an empty street corner, have helped me understand the region and its people ever since. Over the next weeks, months and years, his confidence that we would encounter more resistance than support from the local leaders would prove correct too. And we never heard another word about the mayor's prized horse, pledged so passionately in front of that roomful of witnesses. A few years later it would emerge that he had been syphoning off public money to line his own pockets, desperately-needed funds which had been destined to help the poor families of his town. More than a century may have passed since entitled rich men took what they wanted from the less fortunate in their midst, but the truth was, very little had changed.

****

The next morning we drove out of town again and took the road northwards towards the state of Bahia. Half an hour into our journey we passed the brothel where we had taken Mariana from; the red brick building was innocuous and almost pleasant in the low morning sunlight. My mind darted back to home, where the girl who had seemed resigned to her fate as I spoke to her on that dark night was now enrolled in night school, beaming a smile every time she emerged from her bedroom in her school uniform, and everyday surprising us with her determination to not let her past destroy her future. The road then weaved upwards into an otherworldly landscape, where huge strangely-shaped rocks were strewn over a vast horizon. One of the jutting rock formations looked just like the front of an elephant, complete with a trunk, ears and eyes. Rita had told us to look out for this landmark when she waved us off that morning.

For the next two months Dean and I followed that motorway for 800 more miles until the BR-116 finally came to an end in the city of Fortaleza on Brazil's northeastern coast. What we found along the way convinced me that this wasn't a problem confined to the few towns we had visited up until then, nor specific to the notorious 'Valley of Misery'. In every town we stopped at, without exception, we found young girls – sometimes hundreds of them – trapped in a nightmare of sexual exploitation and abuse. Girls being sold by those who should have been loving and protecting them, betrayed by others whose job it was to defend them, abandoned by the state and its institutions. By the time we had reached the end of the road, it couldn't have been clearer in my mind – this motorway was stage to a child welfare scandal of colossal proportions, the worst road in the world for the sexual exploitation of children.

At the same time, Rita was getting our Pink House ready for opening. The house had been furnished with comfy sofas and bean bags, its interior walls painted bright colours and decorated with murals and affirming messages. One of the rooms had been made into a beauty salon with a mirror, styling chairs, hairdryers and nail polish equipment. Another room was full of costumes and props for our drama workshops and next to that was our dance studio, with a wall-to-wall mirror and rubber flooring, equipped with speakers and a sound system. On one wall there was a mural of a dark-skinned girl doing a ballet pose, flowers cascading from her head as she danced, while on another was painted the words: 'Don't be the girl who fell down. Be the girl who got back on her feet'.

By now we had also recruited a team of women who would be working at the house, three 'social educators' who would support and befriend the girls, as well as workshop teachers and a cook. Warlei had been helping with the recruitment process and trained the new team who had already started reaching out to girls they knew who were submerged in the dark work of exploitation. Meeting them wherever they were – on the side of the motorway, late at night on the town square, or in their homes – they would sit and talk, play cards, take them out for ice-cream or milkshakes or bake a cake together in order to get to know them better and build up trust.

By the time the Pink House was ready to open, the team had found and befriended 48 girls, aged between 11 and 16. We decided that we would open on the last Monday of January, the same day schools went back following the Brazilian summer holidays. During a week in December, the team visited each one of the girls in their homes, delivering a personalised invitation to be part of the Pink House. All were welcome unconditionally and regardless of their circumstances, they told them, but they did need to take an important first step towards change, by coming along themselves to register and show us they really meant it.

We needn't have been apprehensive about how many girls would accept that invitation and show up at the Pink House. Over the next few days every single one knocked timidly on the house's pink metal gate, clutching their invitations. Each girl was greeted enthusiastically by Rita and received their own tour of each of the house's brightly-painted rooms. Many gazed around them with a sense of disbelief – it really was like nothing they had ever seen in their lives. On the first wall they saw were the words, 'You are loved. You are special. You are worthy of your dreams' – phrases most had never heard directed at them. Next, in a room full of boxes where the girls would be able to keep their possessions safe, was the phrase, 'A winner is a loser who never gave up'. In a communal area on the second floor, scattered with pink, green and purple bean bags, was the Biblical verse which summed up everything we wanted to do there: 'I know the plans I have for you, plans to prosper you and not to harm you, plans to give you hope and a future'.

During these tours of the house the biggest reaction always came the moment they swung open the door of the dance studio. Seeing their reflection in the floor-to-ceiling mirror in front of them, some girls immediately ran out again. Their self-esteem was so shattered they couldn't bear to see an image of themselves looking back at them. Others hung around, intrigued by their reflection, giggling as they smiled at themselves or attempted a few awkward moves. It was immediately clear that this was where profound change was going to happen.

A week after registration we threw a big inauguration party at a ranch in the hills outside of Medina, inviting all 48 girls and their families. We kept the location secret, just telling the girls that a bus would be waiting for them at the Pink House at 6.30pm. On arrival, the girls were received like VIPs, walking down a red carpet and being shown to their tables by tuxedo-ed waiters. The lanterns hanging around them, the curtains of fairy lights, the pink tablecloths and columns of colourful balloons, increased the sense of magic. The excitement was palpable.

I also didn't know where the event was to be held – I had been busy travelling with Dean and arrived back just in time for the start of the party, following Rita's directions to the venues.

As soon as I saw the impressive entrance gate and the grand colonial buildings beyond it, a shiver ran down my spine. This was one of the original farms of the town's Portuguese founders that Evany had told me about, built by slaves, where rich men exploited the poor and stole their young daughters' innocence. It seemed right that our bid to reverse "150 years of history" would begin here. After Dean gave the girls a private concert, and Warlei and Rita spoke, I took the microphone and declared Meninadança in Medina finally open.

As the buffet opened and the girls excitedly queued up with their plates, waiters crisscrossed the tables with drinks, younger brothers and sisters chased and noisy chatter mixed with music playing from loudspeakers, I stood in the middle of the commotion, caught up in a mixture of pride and trepidation. Pride that we had gotten this far, less than two years after stumbling upon this remote town. Trepidation because in a month's time the real work would begin, and after giving these precious girls so much hope that their lives would change I knew we couldn't let them down.

10

NEUTRAL ZONE

Less than 24 hours after the elation of the night before, the reality of what we were taking on sent us crashing back down to earth. Rita and I were in the Pink House arranging each girl's forms in a filing cabinet when there was a rattling knock on the metal door outside. Rita went to answer. A man and a woman, both members of the town's guardianship council, marched in with a sober look on their faces. They explained that they had heard that we had invited girls from all three of Medina's poorest neighbourhoods to take part in the project and that they would be in the house at the same time.

"Yes?" I offered, trying to understand what they meant.

The man shook his head despairingly. We had naively overlooked an important detail, he explained. The turf war between those districts of town, controlled by rival drug gangs, was still raging, and had intensified in recent months. A week would rarely go by without someone from one of the areas turning up dead, followed by retaliation by another gang soon after. Innocent people who just happened to live in The Hill, Riverside or Lowland districts were getting caught up in the bloodshed, targetted in revenge attacks as they walked even though neutral areas. Many of the girls we had invited to the

Pink House were already either involved in the gangs, or had boyfriends or family members who were.

"It's crazy," the man exclaimed, throwing his arms up. "You'll have girls from each of the gangs in here. They hate each other. There'll be a bloodbath."

My heart sank. Keen for nothing to go wrong, we had been meticulously planning every detail, but it hadn't even crossed my mind that the girls we wanted to reach might be split along gang lines. In fact I'd never even imagined that girls might not be able to get on inside the house, let alone the possibility that rivalries could erupt into violence. We now had a huge problem, because all the girls had already received their invitations, and had even come along to our inauguration party – where, they suggested, the girls had probably tolerated each other for a few hours with so much excitement. How could we un-invite them now? The woman, who was more conciliatory, suggested opening the house at different times for girls from different districts. But that would be fraught with difficulties and just seemed to be the opposite of what we wanted to do, to help girls see themselves for who they really were and not what others labelled them.

Back in Belo Horizonte, I talked through the problem with Warlei, who had another idea. "During a war, there are often neutral zones, safe places where both sides agree they won't attack," he said. "Let's make the Pink House such a place, where hostilities are put on hold, whichever side the girls are on."

It was an admirable plan in theory, but we both knew getting the girls to leave behind their differences was going to be much more problematic in practice. As the clock ticked down to opening day, and as more news of Medina's gang turf war was relayed to us, our apprehension grew. If the guardianship councillors' predictions were correct, our dream of bringing hope to traumatised young girls could be over almost as soon as it had begun.

****

It was 11am when Rita finally answered my calls. The whole premise of the Pink House was to be an all-female space, so I hadn't intended to be there on the first day, January 28. But I was getting increasingly anxious as all my calls had been ringing out since 8am, the time doors had opened. When she eventually answered, I gasped as the sound of a rowdy commotion blasted through the receiver.

"Matt, we have a problem!" Rita shouted over the hubbub. "It's the girls… they're just… too happy!" before dissolving into giggles. Now I could hear that the riotous noise was that of elated girls laughing and shouting.

The girls had started to arrive in a trickle that morning, Rita explained. The younger ones came first, putting their heads sheepishly round the open door before being welcomed by the team. In the beginning, many were shy and awkward, unsure of where they could sit or what they were allowed to do. The older, more streetwise girls turned up last, hiding their own nervousness behind a loud swagger, arriving mostly in boisterous groups with their friends. By 9am, the house was already full of girls. But there was tension in the air, with girls from each of Medina's troubled districts staying apart and eyeing the others warily.

Before any of the activities began, Rita gathered all the girls together in the main room. As they slouched on the sofas and beanbags or perched on the sills of the open windows, she told them there was so much more that united them than divided them and that deep down each girl was no different than the next.

"You've all cried yourselves to sleep at night," she said. "You all know what it's like to feel alone in the world, you've all wondered if anyone will ever really love you for who you are." She watched as the girls' eyes widened. No-one had ever related to them in that way, or spoken to them so directly and yet so lovingly about their problems. But it would take a lot more than that to convince them to put aside their gang allegiances and mutual distrust and the truce still seemed like an uneasy one. One of the solutions we considered to avoid conflict in the house would be to not put girls from different districts together in the same activities, like dance, drama and art classes, and Rita decided, for the time being at least, that it was best to continue with that plan.

But it was precisely when the first dance class began that the tense atmosphere suddenly lifted. The first group were all from the Lowlands, but when the loudspeaker came to life and thumping beats started reverberating round the house, all the other girls excitedly ran upstairs to see what was going on. Our dance teacher was a bubbly young Yorkshire woman, Lauren, who had joined the team quite unexpectedly just a few days before the Pink House opened. After hearing about our work she had left a project she was volunteering at in Bolivia and diverted her planned flight home to help us. A Zumba teacher, Lauren's energy and positivity were infectious and within minutes of cagily stepping into the dance room, the girls were letting go of their inhibitions, leaving their pent-up negativity behind and surprising even themselves with the wide smiles beaming back at them from the mirrors. By the time all the girls had done their dance session – when Rita finally answered my phone call – they were euphoric.

The next day, we opened the beauty salon, allowing a number of girls to be treated to a special makeover. The team chose both girls who had arrived the most dishevelled, probably from sleeping on a dirt floor or a long, sleepless night on the streets, as well as those who seemed the most timid and lacking in confidence. One by one, they sat themselves down in the revolving salon chair, watching intently in the mirror as one of the team carefully washed, brushed and blow-dried their hair, while telling them how beautiful they were. For many of the girls it was their first experience of being pampered, or hearing someone compliment them, and the effect on their self-esteem was even more visible than their physical transformation. Those girls who had been quiet and sullen left the salon with their heads a little higher, more confident and talkative as they continued the day's activities.

Another part of the house which proved popular was the 'box room', actually a corridor between the main room and the kitchen, where dozens of plain brown cardboard storage boxes sat on a wall of wooden shelves. Their purpose was twofold. For many girls, it was the first time they had ever had their own place to keep their possessions safe and keep their writings, notes and drawings away from prying eyes. But the boxes were also a way for them to express their innermost feelings, something that would represent who they were and how they saw themselves. Every day the girls could take their box and personalise it by painting it or decorating it with stickers or magazine cuttings, changing the look of their box whenever they felt it no longer represented them. Again, the girls seemed amazed at the simple privilege of having a small space they could call their own. And as they set to work personalising their boxes for the first time, we got a glimpse of some of the sadness and turmoil going on under the surface. By the time they'd been put back on the shelves, most were dark and chaotic, smeared and splattered with blacks, purples and browns.

The more time the girls spent in the house, the more their hidden traumas began to bubble to the surface. One of the most important moments of each day was the 'conversation circle', when Rita or other team members would lead the girls in discussions of topics pertinent to their lives, which often touched on painful, personal experiences they had buried deep inside. Cagey at first, once they realised the other girls were hiding the same pain they became braver, talking even more honestly and candidly. Just as important were the impromptu chats the team had with girls on their own at different times of the day and in different parts of the house. One of the members of staff they most confided in was our cook, Cassilândia, a soft-spoken maternal figure who exuded kindness and listened much more than she spoke. As she prepared the girls' mid-morning or afternoon snack, or washed up and mopped the floor in between, the girls would come to her for heart-to-hearts, the details of which she would later pass on to the rest of the team.

After a few weeks, our initial fears about the local turf war erupting inside the Pink House had faded. They were replaced, though, with worries about the even greater danger many faced as soon as they left the house, especially when they were back in their own homes.

Top of the list were three sisters, Poliana, 13, Miriam, 12, and Paulinha, 11. I'd met them during one of my previous visits to Medina and was thrilled that all three had started coming to the Pink House after hearing Rita's grave concerns for them. Their mother, a foul-mouthed woman who spent most of her time drinking in a ramshackle bar on the corner of their street, was the sister of Lilian's mother, who used to send her 12-year-old daughter out to be abused by truck drivers parked in front of her home. They lived in a dilapidated mud-brick cottage just over the road from her on The Hill and Rita suspected that, like Lilian, their mother also used her daughters for financial gain.

Poliana, Miriam and Paulinha turned up every day at the Pink House, but they often arrived in a state, exhausted with their hair matted and bedraggled. Instead of taking part in the activities, we would often find them in a deep sleep, curled up together on one of the sofas. All three were malnourished and gaunt and when it was time for the mid-morning snack, they would gobble down their bread rolls or hot dogs in seconds.

Poliana, the eldest, was one of the girls who would hang around in the kitchen with Cassilândia, who would discreetly slip her spare morsels as they talked. During one of these chats, Cassilândia discovered why the sisters weren't getting much sleep – their mother had a new boyfriend, a violent drunk who would fly into late-night, booze-fuelled rages, terrifying the sisters. The three girls would often spend the night huddled together in the outside toilet at the back of their house – the safest place they could find.

As the days went by the sisters started to come out of themselves, losing some of their timidity and even managing the occasional smile. They quickly became attached to the Pink

House staff, who would wake them by gently stroking their hair, the kind of affection they'd never received at home. Each of the sisters was treated to a makeover in the beauty salon, and Paulinha seemed to love the attention from the other girls as they dressed her up and painted her nails. But halfway through the second week, Rita noticed that Poliana seemed quieter and more withdrawn. She didn't want to go home at leaving time, making any excuse to stay a little longer. She'd often be waiting with her sisters at the Pink House door early in the morning, even before the first member of staff arrived to open up. On Friday she was clingy and, unusually for her, spent much of the time with her arms wrapped around the Pink House staff, but when they asked her what was wrong she said nothing and just held them tighter.

That afternoon Rita got word that her mother's boyfriend had taken Poliana away for the weekend. They had gone "into the backcountry" according to family members – that could mean anywhere from a more remote town or village to a distant farm, or even one of the brothels we knew were hidden behind the tall trees and thicket in secret clearings off the motorway. We realised what had been terrifying Poliana and what she had been trying to tell us. Rita couldn't know for sure what was happening to the young girl, but she had a good idea, and knew there was no good reason why this man, who barely spoke a kind word to the girls, would take one of them away from town.

We spent the weekend sick with worry, desperately hoping she'd be there when we opened the doors again on Monday morning.

Poliana finally showed up, not on Monday, but on Tuesday morning. She was sitting on the kerb in front of the Pink House, clasping her bony legs to her chest and pressing her cheek to her knees, when Câssilandia, who always arrived first to clean and prepare the house, arrived. When Poliana saw her she threw her arms around her, buried her head in her chest and sobbed. Rita and the rest of the team were overjoyed to see her, but despite their gentle coaxing Poliana didn't want to say where she had been or what had happened. They continued to shower her, and her younger sisters, with love and affection, reassuring her that they would be there for her whenever she was ready to talk.

It was also becoming clear that a number of the girls were in abusive and exploitative relationships with men far older than them. Some, aged just 12 and 13, were living with older men, who they would refer to as their 'husbands'. They included Lilian, now aged 13, who was living with a man in his 40s. I had been thrilled when I saw Lilian at our inauguration party, but she never once made it to the Pink House after moving in with the man who, according to rumours, would beat her and barely let her leave his house at all. Other men did allow them to take part, but would come to collect them outside the Pink House at closing time, a scene I could never stomach. It was a clear example of child sexual exploitation happening right before our eyes, but such relationships had become so normal in town that most people would be genuinely puzzled by our suggestions that they were wrong.

Maria Lúcia was a petite 12-year-old with the body and face of a child, but who was already six months pregnant. She lived with a man in his 40s, the father of her unborn baby, in the Saudade district of town, a sprawling, sun-baked area of red-earth behind the fetid open-air slaughterhouse on the other side of the motorway. Saudade was by far the poorest area of Medina, inhabited by the town's most destitute in makeshift, mud-brick homes. Because it wasn't officially a neighbourhood, but had been built up from a squatter settlement, there was no sewage system, street lights or piped water supply. It was also the furthest away and Maria Lúcia would have to walk from her home up a steep hill to the motorway, cross the busy road before beginning her long descent along dozens of crisscrossing cobbled streets to arrive at the Pink House. She would always smile as she finally waddled into view, holding her huge protruding belly and our staff would stand at the front door, cheering and clapping her over the last 100 metres.

Rita had followed Maria Lúcia's story since her days on the guardianship council. The eldest of six children, she was left living with her father at the age of 10 after her mother left him for another woman. A granite miner, he had to go out to work and often left her home alone for several days at a time. It was during one of those trips that their neighbour lured Maria Lúcia into his house and raped her, then held her captive for several days. When her father returned and discovered what had happened he went straight to the police station and filed a report. But the man had already fled his home and left town.

There are many peculiar aspects of the Brazilian justice system which stack the odds absurdly against child victims of abuse and exploitation. One is the ability for police forces to archive crimes after 30 days if by then they haven't been able to track down the perpetrator. This is exactly what happened with Maria Lúcia's case. After 30 days her rapist emerged from hiding and returned to his home and, with the town's policemen as apathetic towards child sexual abuse as most other locals, nothing more was done. Soon after, however, the man convinced Maria Lúcia to live with him as "husband and wife". Traumatised, needy and probably already emotionally attached to her abuser, she ignored her often-absent dad's pleas and moved next door. Within months, she was pregnant, aged just 11.

Maria Lúcia was a sweet, softly-spoken girl, who so easily broke into a shy smile. Unlike some of the other girls who were rowdy live wires, she was calmer and happily went along with the routine of the house. There was almost no indication in her demeanour of the trauma and upheaval she had so recently experienced. Like the other girls, she spoke of her 'husband' – the man who had raped her – with the same ease as any wife and mother-to-be would. But she also played, coloured in pictures and acted out princess stories like the young child she was. Only on the few occasions when Rita's frustration at the situation bubbled over, and she told her she should be home being a child with her dad and not 'married' to a man her dad's age, did Maria Lúcia's placidity crack.

"I love him," she would shout, tears streaming down her cheeks. "I can't live without him, I want to be with him forever." Rather than risk alienating her from the house, we decided instead to refrain from trying to persuade her to rethink the relationship with words, and instead let what happened inside the house – the dance, the beauty therapy, the conversation circles – transform her feelings and thoughts independently.

Not all the girls were a pleasure to share the Pink House space with. Some were pent up balls of anger, moody, unpredictable and ready to lash out at the slightest provocation. The worst was a 14-year-old named Bia. Dark-skinned with tight afro coils and a beautiful smile on the odd occasion she let her guard down, I first heard about Bia just a few days after we opened.

"She's like a hurricane," Rita told me. "She's disrupting the whole house. She throws tantrums, shouts and swears. Sometimes all it takes is for one of the other girls to glance at her and she threatens to smash their face in."

Over the following weeks Bia continued to push the boundaries and unsettle the house. She would often arrive halfway through the morning, sometimes apparently under the influence of drugs, bruising for a fight. Staff would find her half-smoked cannabis spliffs or apparatus for smoking crack hidden behind the toilet in the Pink House bathroom. Clearly not used to being told what to do by anyone, she would constantly test our team's patience and resolve, refuse to take part in activities and storm out of the dance class if something irked her, often taking other girls with her. Bia, we discovered, was a leader figure amongst many of the girls in Medina. If she was in a bad mood, it affected the atmosphere of the whole house.

By the third week, the team were warning Rita that they couldn't continue working at the house with Bia still there. "I know what they mean," Rita told me. "But I can't expel her, not yet. Ours is the only door that hasn't been shut in her face. The whole town thinks she's a troublemaker, but I know she's really just a victim."

Rita explained how, four years earlier, she had stopped Bia, then a slight, shy 10-year-old, as she trudged sadly along a town centre street. She asked her what she was doing on her own, then noticed pieces of paper clasped in her closed fist. Unfolding one, she was horrified to read that they were offering the girl in exchange for a bag of rice or beans. Her older sister, who was looking after her while her mother was away, had handwritten them and sent Bia to deliver them to the homes of older men in the town.

"That was just the beginning," said Rita. "After that I'd often see her standing on the side of the motorway, waiting for trucks to stop, or hear that she was in a roadside brothel, or gone off with a group of men into the backcountry for the night.

"She fell deeper and deeper. Whenever there was any trouble, you could bet Bia was always in the middle of it. These days everyone looks down on her. She's been expelled from every school in town. She's seen either as a worthless whore or a hopeless case. I think we need to keep trying with her."

As we persevered with Bia we saw flickers of promise, times when she was more vulnerable and reflective, when she let down her defences and hinted that she wanted to live differently. But those moments were few and far between. We quickly realised that if the trauma behind her behaviour had been three years – and probably more – in the making we couldn't expect those wounds to heal overnight. Again, if the Pink House was fulfilling its purpose as a place of unconditional love and acceptance, the offer of living a different, dignified life would eventually become irresistible. In the meantime, though, it didn't make having Bia with us any easier.

For our team of local women, the first weeks after the Pink House opened were a huge shock, starting with the episode with Poliana, increasing as they got to know the harsh reality of the other girls' lives. One of our young educators, Cristiane, would later remember how she would sob herself to sleep at night, distressed and burdened by the girls' stories and knowing that many would be passing the night just trying to survive. She applied for the position because she enjoyed leading Sunday school classes in her church and thought a job helping teenagers would be suitable for her, but she never expected to be thrust into a world of tragedy she had no idea existed. It would be the beginning of a journey for Cristiane, still only 20, that would turn her into a passionate and tireless champion for girls' rights.

Some of our other staff members, however, reacted in a different way – with denial. They started to express resentment that the girls were talking openly about something which had always been hidden away and in staff meetings they appeared to object when we spoke of the girls as victims. It quickly became clear that even these women, who were outwardly kind and caring, didn't think there was anything much wrong – and certainly not criminal – with families using their daughters to supplement their income, or men paying poor young girls for sex. So, a month after we opened, we took the drastic step of dismissing half of our team. We carefully selected our new recruits, educators Nayara and Elisangela, and art teacher Eulina. They would have to get to know the girls from scratch, but if we were going to show these girls that what their community was telling them was wrong, then we needed to find people who truly believed it.

At around the same time, we made another change. Lauren, our volunteer dance teacher, had begun to notice that the girls were easily flagging during their dance lessons, some complaining of dizziness, while others had stopped taking part altogether, preferring to remain curled up on the bean bags and sofas. Other members of the team also noted that many of the girls were lethargic, inattentive and unwilling to get involved in activities, certainly with much lower levels of energy than other girls their age. We realised that most of the girls were arriving at the Pink House hungry. With hardly any food at home, many existed on scraps while breakfast was a luxury enjoyed only by richer families. The snacks we were providing midway through the sessions weren't enough to fill up and nourish them. We decided to start providing breakfast first thing every morning, then a balanced, nutritious lunch. The change in the girls was almost immediate. The day after their first Pink House meal the dance room was packed with girls, energetic and animated, many of whom didn't want to stop once the lesson had finished.

****

By mid-February, several weeks after the house first opened its doors, Warlei and I spent a few days in Medina dealing with these changes and overseeing the recruitment of new staff. One afternoon, as I was heading back to the Pink House for another meeting, I saw a slight young girl sitting on the kerb, her head resting on her arms and her knees pulled to her chest. She was whimpering. The girl's matted brown hair was tied back in a pigtail and she wore her white school T-shirt and pair of tattered plimsolls. A scruffy grey rucksack sat on the pavement next to her.

"Hey," I said, sitting down next to her. "What's the matter?"

The girl looked up, tears streaming from her brown eyes. "I didn't get invited," she sniffed.

"What do you mean?" I asked.

"I don't have a house, so when they went around giving the other girls their invitations for the Pink House, no-one knew where I was. Now the girls are saying there are no more places and I can't get in. I'm so hungry," she explained, dissolving into tears again.

"Wait there," I said, and fetched Cristiane, who helped the girl up and took her inside. With the other girls in their activities, she piled up a plate of food from the kitchen and sat down with her as she tucked in. Her name was Tainara, she said, and she was 12. Her mother had passed away unexpectedly two years earlier, leaving her and her two younger brothers on their own. One had been taken in by his godmother and the other by his father. But no-one wanted the sister, who didn't know who her father was and who had a reputation for being mischievous and difficult to control. Tainara had been reluctantly passed around by some family members, including two aunts, but each one had eventually kicked her out onto the street.

"So, where are you living now?" asked Cristiane.

"With anyone who'll have me. I've been staying with my friends, but I can never stay for long. After a few days their families make it clear I'm in the way, and I have to find somewhere else."

Cristiane gave Tainara a long, tight hug and told her the Pink House was her house too, and the girl let out an excited gasp. After that she started coming without fail, turning up every afternoon and always carrying her threadbare rucksack containing all her belongings. She would participate in all the activities, always with a smile and a spring in her step, despite carrying with her the heartbreak of having no-one in the world, not even knowing on whose floor she would be sleeping that night.

In the mornings she would take herself off to class, remembering that her mum told her she should never miss school, but mostly because the school provided an afternoon snack which was often the only thing she ate for the rest of the day. Tainara was yet another girl whose plight was a source of heartache and worry for our staff. But in her case it was difficult for them to see how the Pink House could give her the answer she needed. In a town like Medina, a vulnerable 12-year-old with no family and an ever decreasing number of options would quickly fall prey to abusers and exploiters. She needed a solution immediately and her situation was becoming more urgent with every day that passed.

A few days later, Rita called the girls together in the main room for a 'conversation circle'. With the girls settling into the rhythm and routine at the Pink House, and more accepting of co-existing with their 'enemies' without too many incidents, the daily conversation times had been proving increasingly fruitful. Rita had prepared another reflection, but before she could start one of the girls, 12-year-old Alicia, stood up and interrupted her.

"We've got something to say," she announced. The room hushed. Alicia was the self-appointed leader of the older girls from the Lowlands district, known to be friendly with dangerous gang members there.

"OK, go on then," said Rita, trying not to let her nervousness show.

Alicia signalled to the sofas where some of the other older girls were sitting, and a number of them stood up too. But they weren't all from the Lowlands. Among them was Vanesa from The Hill, and Bia from Riverside.

"Well," began Alicia. "We've been coming here for more than a month now. When we started here some of us hated each other, we didn't even want to see each other's faces. But we don't anymore. Being here has taught us that, deep down, we're all the same. It really doesn't matter which part of town we live in. So… I just wanted to say, we shouldn't let anyone keep us apart anymore. We're so much stronger together."

The room erupted in applause. Some girls smiled and wiped tears from their eyes. A few went over to their 'rivals' and offered a hug, which was accepted with more smiles and tears. Rita and the other staff members looked on in astonishment. In a town where gang rivalries had for years created hatred and division, caused communities to live in fear and claimed so many lives, what they were seeing inside that bright pink house was nothing short of miraculous.

Rita hushed the room again and the girls returned to their places. "So, what do you want to do?" she asked.

First, they told her, they wanted to take part in activities together and no longer wanted to be segregated according to the districts where they lived. They also wanted to create some house rules, based on mutual respect and cooperation, to which every girl would agree to adhere. The rules were decided there and then, from banning swear words and resolving disagreements to washing their cups and plates after they had used them. If the Pink House was their second home, they said, they had to ensure it was a place of order and peace, where everyone was equal.

Lastly, the girls said they wanted to let the rest of the town know that they had decided to be different. After they had learned to dance together, they wanted to perform together. Right in the centre of town, in the square, the place they knew everyone would see them. "We want to show them we're not the same anymore," said Alicia.

11
___

INGRAINED

The air was sweet and clammy and filled with excited chatter. A horseshoe of white plastic chairs arranged across the middle of the square was already full, with only standing room behind, in front of a blue floor mat and sign which read 'Meninadança: The Dream Come True'. As the loudspeakers clunked and whistled to life, a hush came over the crowd.

It was the middle of March and I had returned to Medina, this time on the overnight bus so Dani wouldn't have to do without the car back home. I thought not having to concentrate on the road would make the journey easier, but the opposite proved to be true as the bus hurtled through the pitch black, overtaking trucks at breakneck speed and screaming around blind corners. I spent the nine-hour journey keeping a tight grip on my seat in panic and didn't get a wink of sleep. As we rolled into Medina's bus station at 5.30 that morning, the driver proudly announced we'd arrived a full hour ahead of schedule. It was then I vowed to always be the one behind the steering wheel in future.

The day had been one of nervous anticipation in the Pink House, but now the moment had finally arrived for the girls to perform their dance in the town square. Rita tapped on the microphone and thanked everyone for coming, even though most had

107

just stumbled upon the gathering after making their customary evening trip down to the square for the bars and burger trailers. But as four girls, each wearing a different coloured tunic over a white dress, walked to the front and took their places, everyone stopped what they were doing and stared. Each of the girls was from a different one of Medina's warring districts.

As dramatic chords boomed round the square the girls swung round to face each other before reaching up to the sky in a statuesque pose, their fingers nearly touching. They froze like that for a moment and I looked around. Even the waiters serving tables around the burger trailers had stopped in their tracks. Others standing on the square seemed transfixed yet uneasy, unsure about what was going to happen next, perhaps even braced for trouble. Hip-hop beats burst from the loudspeakers as the four girls, now facing the audience, kicked and stepped, crouched and spun in perfect sync, beaming smiles as their performance rose to a crescendo. Finally, they faced each other again, linked arms and lifted them back in the air again in a powerful act of strength and unity, before the final beat echoed round the square. That was when the applause was supposed to start… but instead there was a stony silence. I looked around again, my pride for these brave girls suddenly turning to worry. A few more seconds passed before, from the back of the crowd, a hand began to clap, then on the other side, more clapping, before the whole square erupted in applause, whistles and cheers, with some rising to their feet.

The girls held hands and grinned widely as they bowed before filing off again, hugging each other and jumping with unbridled joy.

Other performances followed, with different groups of girls, each performed with the same gusto and received with the same enthusiasm. Then Rita, overcome with emotion, took the microphone again. What happened next was one of the moments on this journey which will be forever etched into our history... when the unwritten rule of silence was broken.

"These girls have asked me to say something... something important," she began. Her voice reverberated around the square. On the hill that rose up from the square behind her I saw a group of men, bottles of beer in their hands, straining to hear from the door of a street corner bar. Others chatting or playing cards on the square's low whitewashed walls stopped and looked up.

"They want you to know that things have changed. The girls you see here tonight were once used as objects on this square. No-one helped them. In fact many of you swapped them for money or drugs."

The whole square – the whole town – seemed to take a sharp intake of breath.

"Not any more," Rita continued, speaking defiantly into the still night air. "They're no longer on their own. Now they have someone to defend them. From this night on you need to look at these girls differently, because they know who they are and how much they are worth."

This time no-one applauded, but it didn't matter. I looked over at the girls, who were all looking straight at Rita, beaming confidence with their heads held high. I remembered the last time I had sat on this square, just over a year ago when Dean and I wept amidst puzzled locals as the business of child prostitution carried on as normal around us. I had no way of knowing if any of those young girls we had seen waiting in the shadows that night were here dancing today, but from the stories they had told I imagined some were. Our work with them had only just begun and I knew it was going to take more than six weeks to turn their lives around, and more than one evening to begin to bring lasting transformation, but that didn't make that night feel any less momentous. Most of all for the girls, who now had someone who was on their side and who would stand up for them.

There was another moving moment that night which I hadn't been expecting. When the girls had settled and the dances were finished, Rita read out a letter Tainara, the girl whose mother had died, had written about her life in the form of a prayer.

"God, will nobody hear me? Will I have to suffer for the rest of my life? Is it because I don't have a mother? God, help me to deal with this life and help me to get over the sadness. Thank you for my life. Amen."

I looked over at Tainara, who was sitting cross-legged on the floor at the front. Her eyes were fixed on Rita as she spoke, but streaming with tears. Cristiane saw her too and rushed over to her, holding her in a tight, reassuring embrace. As they did, the crowd, clearly moved by her words, burst into applause again. The evening ended with all 50 of the girls taking to the stage, along with dance teacher Lauren to perform a Zumba version of Shakira's *Waka Waka*. The night's success had left the girls on a high and they danced their last number with abandon, their nervousness replaced with smiles of relief. But my spirit dropped substantially when I saw Tainara in the middle of the group, doing the same moves as the others but with a look of melancholy and loneliness on her face. I felt overwhelmed by sadness and I knew what my heart was telling me to do — answer her desperate prayer for someone to love her and give her a family. But I also knew I couldn't make such a big decision in the heat of the moment. I knew I had a tendency to run away with my emotions and this time I had to properly think things through – talk with my wife! – and consider all the consequences.

My resolve to take things slowly lasted less than a day. Tainara was already at the Pink House when I arrived early the following afternoon, wearing the same scruffy pair of jeans and clutching her threadbare rucksack, looking like the weight of the world was on her shoulders. I called her into the office where she began to tell Rita and me more about how she had found herself without a home or anyone to care for her.

"Before my mum died me and my brothers were happy, we were poor but she loved us so much I never felt like I was. One day she was taken to hospital but no-one told us why. I never got to say goodbye. On the night she died my aunts just came and told us, and that was it. Then they split up me and my brothers. No-one wanted me."

Her life suddenly turned upside down, it was the start of two years of turmoil for Tainara, who was reluctantly passed around by family members, each of whom eventually tired of her and told her to find somewhere else to live, sometimes even kicking her out onto the street. One aunt was a prostitute who would take her with her to the gas stations where she plied her trade. "She'd leave me on my own while she went off with clients. We'd sometimes spend all night on the motorway. Even if I hadn't slept at all, I'd still get myself off to school in the morning. It's what my mum always told me to do," she said, gulping back a tear.

The last house Tainara found herself was with another family member who was living with one of the gang leaders on The Hill. "Of all the places I lived, that was the worst," she remembered. "I saw people being shot dead. There were always dangerous men in the house, carrying guns or doing drugs. I wondered what my mother would have told me to do, so I decided to get out of there."

"Where did you go?" I asked.

"I slept on the street for a week, I found a place next to the Catholic church. Then some friends let me stay at their house. But…"

Tainara hugged her rucksack closer as her eyes glazed with tears.

"What?" I asked.

"The family I'm staying with said I can only stay with them for a week. Last night was the last night. I don't know where I'll go after the Pink House closes tonight… I just wish my mum was here."

I put my arm around this sweet, vulnerable girl as she sobbed, my heart breaking. I knew the Pink House, which opened at eight and closed at six, couldn't help her, but I could. And at that moment I couldn't see any inconvenience or disruption too great to justify not taking away this child's inconsolable anguish and loneliness. She was clearly on the edge of the same abyss from which, even in this short time, I'd seen several other girls tumble into and, as I held her, shaking and whimpering, I knew I had to do everything I could to make sure we didn't lose her too. I went outside and phoned Dani back in Belo Horizonte, who didn't even flinch when I told her about another girl I wanted to bring home to live with us. "I'll go and prepare the spare bed," she said as we said goodbye, minutes after hearing about Tainara for the first time.

Several hours and a long wait in the town's courthouse later, Rita and I were sitting before the judge, explaining Tainara's situation and asking him to grant me temporary custody so at least she would have a place to sleep that night. She would then be able to stay at a house we had rented for volunteers to stay, close to the Pink House.

Peering over wiry spectacles behind a desk piled high with thick files, he listened intently. "Well, given her age and the fact she doesn't have a mother or father, you would have to apply to adopt her…" he finally replied.

Rita looked over at me. In Mariana's case we had been made her legal guardians, allowing us to have her live with us and do other things such as register her at school. Adoption would mean Tainara – who I'd only known for less than a month – would take my surname, become a permanent part of the family and become Milo's older sister. I decided to ask for more time so I could think it through properly. Then I thought of her again, the fact she didn't even know where she'd be sleeping tonight, and that permanently belonging to a new family was everything she dreamed of.

"Yes," I blurted. "We want to adopt her."

The adoption process, the judge explained, wouldn't be quick. First, their own social workers would need to ascertain that she didn't have any other family members who wanted her and compile a report, which would take at least a month. During that time he could grant me temporary custody, but I wouldn't be able to take her out of the municipality. I knew from my own frustrating dealings with Brazil's bureaucracy that a month may mean much longer. In short, I would have to stay in Medina indefinitely.

Armed with the freshly-signed custody papers, Rita and I raced back to the Pink House, which had already closed for the day, where we found Tainara waiting shyly alone at the front gripping her rucksack. When we told her she didn't have to worry about where she was going to sleep that night, she sank to the floor and let her rucksack fall from her grip as if she were suddenly relieved of the heavy burden of survival. There was less of a reaction when I told her we wanted her to be part of our family – her dream of a loving home had been snatched away from her so many times she wasn't ready to believe that yet. But later that night, after she had settled into her new bedroom at the volunteers' house, where dancer teacher Lauren was also living, the change in her demeanour was evident to everyone. She chatted, joked, showed off her dancing and made everyone her special milkshake, which consisted of throwing almost everything she found in the kitchen into the blender. That's how it tasted too, but I sensed this was her way of showing her gratitude, so I gulped it down.

That night, Tainara got ready to sleep in the bottom bunk in one of our guest rooms. But instead of changing into her night clothes, she had taken all of her clothes out of her rucksack and put them all on, with a pair of leggings under two pairs of jeans, and several layers of tops, all tucked into her belt. It was what she did every night, I later discovered – the way she had found during the last few years of staying at constantly changing homes to protect herself from being abused while she slept.

Having to remain in Medina for a much longer time than I intended helped me understand the town and its problems on a much deeper level. After a few days Dani arrived with Milo on the overnight bus after a friend agreed to give Mariana a place to stay while she was away. She stayed for a week with Tainara at our volunteers' house before getting to know Dona Geralda, an elderly mother figure who lived close to where Tainara had lived with her aunts in the years following her mum's death. Dona Geralda had a daughter and a granddaughter who lived with her in a simple terracotta-roofed cottage on a dusty narrow road at the foot of The Hill. Hearing how the arrival of Tainara, then Dani and Milo, had filled up the volunteers' house, she invited them to stay with her while the adoption papers were being prepared.

While I continued sleeping at our volunteers' house, I spent a lot of time at Dona Geralda's, where I got to know many of the other families living on this tight street of tiny terraced homes. Sometimes, as I turned into the narrow cobbled road, I'd give a polite nod to the lookout for the drug gang who was sitting at the corner, a revolver tucked in his shorts. I saw what it was like to live with the unrelenting grind of poverty, where everything else became peripheral to the daily struggle just to meet the most basic needs.

Most of all, I saw how prostitution was part of that cycle of poverty and had become ingrained in people's minds and lives. Both Dona Geralda's middle-aged daughter and granddaughter, who was 20, would often leave home at dusk in revealing outfits and heavy make-up, returning only after dawn, when they would slip bank notes into the matriarch's hand without a word before falling into bed. Twice I came across the daughter at well-known prostitution spots on the BR-116, clutching her handbag as she hobbled between stationary trucks. Both times she flustered that she was meeting up with a friend. Yet it was impossible not to like Dona Geralda, a sweet, kind old lady who would gladly cook her last spoonful of rice for Milo to eat than keep it for herself and who would fuss over everyone who stepped across her doorstep. I later heard that she was also once a 'woman of the night', like her mother before her. I found it difficult to see her as an 'exploiter' or someone who was to blame for the evil she and so many other mothers here were perpetuating.

Most disturbing, though, was hearing the subject of child sexual exploitation spoken with such triviality in the front door natter I overheard in the street. I'd often hear mentioned how someone had taken their daughter or niece on a trip with them, inferring that it was so they didn't need to pay for the ride, or could exchange her for accommodation or food. Mothers grumbling about how disappointed they were with their daughters, not because they hadn't done their school-work or had stayed out past their bedtimes, but because they weren't bringing home as much money as they were expected to. And it was common to hear men openly propositioning young girls in the street, promising everything from a ticket to the weekend music festival to a new pair of shoes in exchange for a 'programme'.

Most, including Dona Geralda, would be in church every Sunday morning, joining in the frenzied chorus of wailing babbling prayers or shouting 'Amens' as the preacher yelled and bashed his Bible. I'd often walk back to my bed in the vol-unteers' house burdened by the sheer enormity of the fight we were taking on. What was the point in trying to convince girls of their worth and dignity if people all around them still saw them as little more than currency – and worse, saw nothing wrong with that? If we wanted to bring lasting change, we needed to transform not just them but everyone around them, and from what I was experiencing that seemed just too colossal a task to get my head around.

12

AMBUSH

The more time I spent in the girls' community, the more I understood why they wanted to be at the Pink House. That bright building on the hill had become their refuge, a place where they felt safe, cared for and respected. Everything inside was different to what they knew on the outside – just as Rita had dreamed out loud on that first morning. With each passing day, absorbing the positive messages we were giving them, the girls became increasingly confident and self-assured, and began to discern for themselves how the society in which they lived was unfairly skewered against them. As a result, a sense of injustice began to stir in them.

Those changes could be seen in the box room, where the girls kept the boxes they personalised to reflect their changing feelings. A few months ago this room was dominated by dark, oppressive hues. Now the boxes were noticeably brighter, painted with vivid, bold colours. Perhaps most striking, many of the girls had also added their names to their boxes, proudly painted in bold brushstrokes or finished with glitter and sparkles, a sign that they were starting to value their identity and be confident in who they were. One day I sat in on one of the daily 'conversation circles' and was struck by how much more vocal and authoritative the girls were as they spoke together, encouraging, reassuring and affirming each other. It was incredible to see what was beginning to happen. Those girls who only months ago had few aspirations, no real idea of who they were and who mostly believed what those around them told them, were beginning to find their voice.

We decided it was time to have a logo, something the girls could rally around, which would identify the project and be adorned on the girls' dance uniforms as they performed. Our dance teacher Lauren's boyfriend Joel, who was visiting her from the UK, was an accomplished designer and generously offered to help. We wanted to involve the girls in the entire process, so Joel led design workshops in which they sketched what Meninadança meant to them and took part in the logo development. After several revisions he came back with one they all approved of – a ballet shoe design in a circle, along with our name written in bold pink brush strokes. It exuded hope, energy and life and the fact the girls helped create it gave them an even greater sense of identity and belonging.

In April 2013 we received our first team of volunteers from the UK. Nicola, Emma and Sara, from the EIC Dance group in London, arrived in Medina at just the right moment as the girls were anxious to perform in public again with a growing desire to show their community how much they had changed. The three young dancers spent the first week in the Pink House teaching new routines with dance styles they hadn't done before like ballet and jazz. Almost immediately, two girls stood out. Sacha and Marta, both 13, were best friends from the Lowlands district which sprawled between the town centre and the motorway to the east. Until now neither had made a big impression – they would join in the activities but never in a way that drew attention to themselves. They said little during the morning meetings and were always at the back of the room during Lauren's Zumba classes. But after a few days with the new team of dance teachers they began to shine. They quickly picked up the dance moves, executing them to perfection with a grace and lightness that showed real talent – so much so that the team was convinced they could pursue a professional career in dance.

What was most noticeable was Sacha's beautiful smile, which spread across her face the moment she started dancing. One day, after one of the dance classes, I complimented her on her smile, and she burst into tears.

"When I'm dancing I feel happy. It makes me forget about all the other stuff," she sniffed.

I asked what she meant.

"My life's a mess. I don't get on with my mum so I'm living with my aunt. But it's the same as living on the streets. She drinks and uses drugs. There's nothing at home, no beds, no fridge, and most of the time no food either. She doesn't pay the bills so often there's not even electricity or water."

Rita told me how Sacha's aunt would take her to the motorway to sell her body, but often used the money to feed her habits rather than pay the overdue bills. The teenager had also fallen prey to the local drugs gang who would use her as a 'runner' but also as bait for holding up trucks as they passed through Medina late at night. As if offering her body for sale, she would stand on the edge of the motorway, but after the trucker had come to a halt and opened his door to let her in, the boys would rob him at gunpoint. Whether it was deserved or not, this was not only pushing this vulnerable young girl into serious crime but also putting her life in real danger.

Her friend Marta's situation wasn't as bad, but her elder brother Diego had become involved in the same local gang and Rita was desperately worried that this talented, thoughtful girl could so easily be persuaded to take the same wrong path as her friends living nearby.

Sacha and Marta had impressed so much they became our lead dancers as, in the team's second week, we took the girls out to perform in venues around Medina. With each performance the girls' self-confidence visibly grew. But it was also clear that not everyone was so pleased to see these girls, from all of the town's different warring districts, dancing together in public. Not only were they showing that gang rivalries wouldn't stop them being friends, during the events they were also encouraging other girls to report abuse, and that clearly riled many who stopped to watch. During one show to local young people in a community centre in General Dutra, a village nestled in the hills 10 miles outside of Medina, they performed a powerful drama sketch depicting a girl having the courage to speak up after suffering abuse. Some of the older boys and men in the hall began to heckle, shouting out vulgar insults, some of them directed at particular girls they knew. But instead of intimidating them it actually made the girls more determined to carry on and despite the disruption they maintained their focus and made it to the end, standing together defiantly as they chanted together, "Don't be silent – abuse is a crime."

The next evening we were in another village, Comercinho, performing in the only venue we could find, the empty outdoor seating area of a closed bar, when men on motorbikes started to circle, roaring their engines menacingly and skidding their tyres on the dusty road. Comercinho was even deeper into the barren countryside than General Dutra, a remote settlement of simple brick houses at the end of a long road through the pitch black wilderness. With no police force and few street lights, the place had a Wild West feel about it and as more men started to appear, deliberately trying to drown out our presentation, the atmosphere grew tense.

After the girls had finished their performance, Warlei, who had come up from Belo Horizonte to accompany the events, made his way to the front and took the microphone. The girls stood behind him, refusing to let their nervousness show, as his voice boomed out around the gloomy streets.

"Listen up," he began. "Maybe once you thought you could abuse children and no-one would come to their defence. I want you to know that a group of people has arrived who are going to stand up for them. We are the strongest and we won't be intimidated!"

It was a bold gamble. We didn't know what the men were capable of or if they were armed. But as his words echoed out around the streets with the girls standing tall behind him, refusing to let their nervousness show, the bikes began to drive off, one by one, until they had all gone. The performance carried on as planned. Back on the bus, as we returned along the winding narrow road to Medina, the girls were ecstatic. They had stood up to their abusers and seen them off.

"Did you see them?" they giggled. "They were like dogs skulking off with their tails between their legs!"

Even more so than the first time they danced on Medina's town square, this week showed me just how powerful public performance could be in bringing change. The girls felt incredibly empowered by the fact they were all on one platform, united in their moves and their message, with a shared purpose and sure of how much stronger they were together. And it wasn't long before that new-found confidence began to spill over from their dancing and into their day-to-day lives. Just a few days after their performance in Comercinho, Sacha asked to speak to Rita, telling her she had decided to never again go with the gang to hold up trucks on the BR-116.

"I didn't feel I could say no before, but now I can," she told her. "I want something much better for my life and now I know I can achieve my dreams."

****

The night before Nicola, Emma and Sara were due to return home, they asked if we could show them something of the reality of the girls they had spent the last two weeks close to. Rita and I decided to take them in her car on a quick ride up the motorway heading north from Medina to show them some of the places where we sometimes came across the girls waiting for trucks. After leaving the edge of town, we drove up to the brothel bar where we had found Mariana just over a year earlier, and where we knew girls were still being exploited.

Ten minutes later, Rita turned into the forest clearing where we had been with Dean, and where we intended to point out the building, turn around and head back.

The bar, at the far end, was illuminated from the inside, but this time there was a group of men huddled on the steps outside. As we rolled onto the dirt driveway they looked up abruptly. They were clearly involved in something illicit, probably a drugs transaction and we'd interrupted them right in the middle. Ours was not the type of vehicle that would routinely turn in there, like a truck or farmer's pick up, but a black estate car with blacked-out windows.

Rita saw we weren't welcome there and quickly made a three-point turn, kicking up gravel and dust before joining the motorway again. But from the front passenger seat I could see through the wing mirror the men jumping onto motorbikes and furiously kick-starting their engines. At least one of them had a revolver in his hand. The English girls, sitting together on the back seat, had no idea what was happening and chatted together happily as we sped off.

Rita, who had now seen the motorbikes spilling out onto the road behind her, gripped the steering wheel with both hands.

"Just keep calm, but put your foot down," I told her, trying not to sound alarmed, but feeling my heart bursting out of my chest. Behind me I could see six headlights gaining on us. The motorway was twisting and turning so it was impossible to build up speed. It was so dark it felt like we were driving through a constant tunnel. The motorbikes were on our tail, with one edging closer towards the driver's window. Rita glanced over at me with a look of panic. I knew, like her, how common it was for people to be found shot dead inside a crumpled car on the motorway, especially on a deserted stretch like this. It rarely made news when they did; people just assumed the victims had been caught up in the drugs gangs themselves.

We were now hurtling down a straight stretch of the motorway, surrounded by the bikers. My heart was racing and sweat poured from my brow. Seeing the first man pushing closer to Rita's window, I inched my hand close to the steering wheel, ready to grab it if anything happened to her. Then I had a thought.

"Rita, roll down your window."

"What?!" she replied, incredulous, her voice shaking.

"They'll see who we are."

She pressed the button and the driver's side window whirred down. I knew the man coming up on that side could see there was a woman driving the car and could also make out other women sitting in the back. If they were pursuing us believing we were police, or from another gang, they might realise they were mistaken.

It worked. After a few seconds the motorbikes fell back until they were just specks in the distance behind us. It was only after we saw the lights of Medina in front of us that Rita and I allowed ourselves to breathe easy again, stopping as soon as we'd turned over the motorway into town, slumping in our seats and expressing our relief with laughter. Behind us, Nicola, Emma and Sara were still oblivious to what had just happened and were probably wondering what it was we found so funny.

The fright we'd experienced that night, however, was nothing compared to what some of the girls, especially Sacha and Marta, were about to go through.

I was in the office the following Wednesday morning when the metal door on the Pink House gate burst open, smashing backwards with an almighty clatter. Rita and I rushed out to the yard to find Sacha and her 12-year-old cousin Alicia, tumbling over each other to get inside.

"What happened?" I asked as they both landed on the sofa, distressed and scared. Rita put her arms around Alicia who was sobbing and shaking.

"They were waiting for us," jabbered Sacha between gasps of air. "They knew we go to the Pink House every morning, so they ambushed us. They started shooting. A bullet just missed me. I don't know how we got out of there alive."

The men who had tried to gun them down were gang members from The Hill, Sacha explained, wanting to exact revenge on the Lowlands gang for killing one of their own some days earlier. The turf war in Medina had become increasingly vengeful in recent weeks, but the different gangs hadn't before targeted teenage girls who just happened to live in their enemy's territory.

I drove Sacha and Alicia home that afternoon, and for the next few weeks they would call us whenever they felt brave enough to venture out of their district to spend the day at the Pink House. But it wasn't long before other girls found themselves in the crosshairs of the gangs too.

Days later, Marta was chased through the streets by several armed gangsters as she walked home from the Pink House, finally giving them the slip by ducking into an alley she knew was a shortcut to Lowlands after they cornered her in a dead-end street. Other girls from The Hill and Lowlands arrived at the Pink House with similar terrifying tales of being followed or shot at. One morning the front gate of one of the schools many of the girls frequented was peppered with bullets. While we didn't know for sure if any were being targeted because of their previous week's performances around town, or for the fact that the girls had refused to hate each other and the Pink House was the only place where those from each of the warring districts were together, the escalation of gang violence had suddenly made Medina a very dangerous place to be.

Nighttime felt especially uneasy, with the streets unusually quiet. One night Dani and I were eating a burger on the town's main square when there was a loud bang on a nearby street, after which all the lights of the town suddenly went out, plunging everywhere into darkness. It was a known tactic used by gangs before a rampage, and everyone – including Dani and I – immediately scattered, leaving food on the tables and bills unpaid. It turned out to be just a technical fault, but the reaction showed the extent to which the town was on a knife-edge. For a while the main road from the motorway into town, which separated the two warring districts, was referred to by locals as the 'Gaza Strip' because shooting could break out at any moment. The tension, though, didn't cause any of our Pink House girls to break their pact of friendship with girls from the other side. They continued to take part in activities together, leaving whatever allegiances they had at the door.

Early one Sunday morning I was woken at around 2am by what sounded like the loud pop of bullets being fired, one after the other. Four hours later I was woken again, this time by Rita battering on the door of the volunteers' house.

"Matt, it's Marta's brother Diego – he's been killed."

"What? But... when?"

"Last night. The gang from The Hill, they lured him and his friend to the square. They murdered them both right there, on the street corner next to the pharmacy. The place is still covered in blood. They were only 17."

Rita, Lauren and I immediately jumped into Rita's car and drove round to Marta's home, on a red earth road at the far end of the Lowlands district. In front of the house there was a large group of Pink House girls, all of whom were friends with Diego, many sitting on the dirt floor or holding each other, in floods of tears. One group of girls was gathered around an inconsolable Marta, hugging her tightly as she rocked backwards and forwards, sobbing. The scene, and the sound of girls whimpering and wailing, was utterly heartbreaking. Inside the house, we found Marta's mother, screaming hysterically as shocked members of her family held her. Losing a child is the worst pain for any mother, but today was also Mother's Day in Brazil, when she had expected to receive all her children to celebrate her special day. Instead she had been plunged into the worst situation imaginable for any mother.

We later learned more details of the murder and how it was carried out. The two boys had been caught in a type of honeytrap, using a 12-year-old girl who lured them to the square with the promise of a sexual liaison. It was incredible that in this town underage girls were used as currency even in the business of cold-blooded murder.

We returned to the house later that night for the wake, where we were served cabbage broth and made polite small talk around Diego's body which lay in an open coffin on the kitchen table. The following morning the bodies of both boys were brought to Medina's Catholic church for a joint funeral, where emotions erupted again. I watched from a side door as friends and family surrounded the two coffins, which were still open, weeping and wailing as they clung to the boys' hands and kissed their faces and hair. It was an alarming, turbulent scene, which seemed to convey the tragic inevitability that more would soon die to even the score.

That afternoon, we received an urgent message from Marta asking us to pass by her house again. We arrived to find removal trucks outside and family members hurriedly carrying out boxes and furniture. Marta rushed out and hugged us. Her mother didn't want to stay another night in the town, she told us, or risk losing any more of her children. They were going to start afresh in another city, Vitória da Conquista, 185 miles north in the state of Bahia.

Her life so unexpectedly and violently overturned, Marta was distraught. "I don't want to go," she whispered, welling up with tears. "There's no Pink House there. Meninadança was the best thing that ever happened to me. Just when my life was starting to get better, everything's been taken away from me."

An hour later, we stood on that dirt road waving Marta off, desperately hoping that the seed the Pink House had sown in her life would one day bear fruit. She wept again and kept waving until the truck reached the motorway far in the distance, turned and disappeared. As we wandered back to the Pink House, where a group of vulnerable, disorientated and frightened young girls were dealing with yet another blow, we wondered how we were going to set about picking up the pieces again.

13

OPEN YOUR EYES

It was the beginning of June when the papers finally came through allowing us to take Tainara home. We had become fond of this chatty, funny and sometimes stubborn girl. In recent weeks she had begun to lower some of her defences and was no longer the quiet, downcast 12-year-old I'd first met. It was only a trial period during which time we'd be accompanied by social workers from Belo Horizonte's children's court, but we were looking forward to helping her settle into our family and a very different life.

Brazil's sweltering summer had turned into winter, which meant the temperature had dipped from unbearable to merely uncomfortable, but at least there was some respite from the huge, ravenous mosquitoes which would attack with the fearlessness of angry dogs.

Medina was now in the midst of preparations for the month-long Junina country festival, the most important cultural event of the year for rural towns. Brightly-coloured bunting criss-crossed the streets, the smell of local delicacies like sweet hominy pudding and caramelised peanuts filled the air and traditional forró music blasted out from cars announcing the evening's show or square dancing event. The party atmosphere briefly assuaged the horrific events that had cast such a dark shadow over the town in recent months.

Dani was already back home with Milo, so I booked two tickets on the overnight bus to Belo Horizonte. But I wasn't leaving with the same positivity with which I'd arrived two months earlier. The trauma of losing someone so close to many of them had been a huge blow to the girls' new-found confidence and some seemed to have loosened their grip on the hope of a better life.

Without her best friend close by, and probably feeling she needed protection, Sacha, who only a few months ago had told us she had decided to live differently after her performances as lead dancer with Marta, had gone back to her friends in the drugs gang. Although she denied it we knew she was also putting herself in danger helping them hold up trucks on the motorway again. Other girls had also taken a step backwards. Some of them who had made a decision to keep themselves safe from danger had been seen wandering the streets in the early hours, or were rumoured to have gone back with their abusive boyfriends or older 'husbands'.

I hadn't expected that seeing one of their friends starting a new life a long way from Medina would be such a blow to some of the others. On the day we were due to leave, Cristiane found one of the girls, 12-year-old Alicia, curled up on one of the bean bags, sobbing her heart out. Alicia had also lost her mother to Aids a few years ago and she was now living with her cousin Sacha, in the squalor of their alcoholic aunt's house.

"Being someone's daughter is all I ever dreamed of," she told Cristiane as she hugged her. "I thought he might take me away from here too. Now I just don't know what I'm going to do." When Cristiane told me my heart sank. One girl finding someone who wanted her just brought home to the others how alone they were.

When closing time arrived, I stood at the Pink House door as the girls spilled out onto the street, waving them goodbye, knowing I probably wouldn't see them for a few more months. It was then that something caught my attention. On the other side of the road, a man, probably in his fifties and wearing a sleeveless shirt and baseball cap, was standing with a bent knee against the wall. Bia, the 14-year-old who had been such a handful during the first few months, crossed the road and went over to him, talking close to his ear as both of them looked over to the Pink House. The stubbled man was nodding and muttering something back. I followed their line of sight; they were looking at two of the girls, Nádia and Fernanda, aged 11 and 12, who had stayed put on the pavement outside the house while the others headed off home. They giggled awkwardly as Bia pointed them out.

"Hey, Bia," I called out. "Can you come back inside? And you two as well," I said to the two girls. "We need to talk to you."

Inside the office, my heart sank with shock and disappointment as Bia came clean and admitted to Rita and me that she had arranged the two girls for the man and was going to take a cut from the money. What's more, it was going to be the first time for the two ingenuous girls, which hugely inflated the amount she was going to receive. Bia had been a handful during the first few months, but she was becoming less disruptive and we thought we were seeing signs of change. To hear that she was pimping out younger girls from the Pink House was devastating. The girl, whose story of exploitation was the most horrific of those I'd heard, had become the exploiter, willing to destroy other girls' lives for financial gain. She wasn't just a bad influence on the other girls, she was a danger to them.

Cristiane, who lived near Nádia and Fernanda, walked the two girls to their front doors while Rita and I discussed how we should respond. Bia, now showing her childish side as she fidgeted on a chair where we had left her in the office, needed to learn her actions were utterly unacceptable. We needed to protect the other girls too. But at the same time, I knew that Bia was a victim and one I desperately wanted to rescue. I didn't want to slam the door shut on precisely the type of girl we had come to Medina to help.

We walked back into the office and Bia looked up sullenly.

Rita sat down behind the desk. "Bia," she began, with a caring smile. "We love you, but today you really let us down and there must be consequences. So we are giving you two months' suspension from the Pink House."

Bia stared straight ahead, blinking away the tears that were threatening to fall. As furious as I was at what she had done, it was heartbreaking to see her like this. She didn't react with anger or aggression, she just looked utterly dejected, as if her last vestige of hope had just been taken away and the only people who still believed in her were giving up on her too.

"We want to see you back here, two months from today," I tried to reassure her. "We know you can change and live a different life. We'll miss you."

A single tear trickled down her cheek and Bia swiped it away as if annoyed it had betrayed her emotions. Then, without saying a word, she slowly stood up, turned around and walked out without looking back. The metal gate outside creaked open and after a dramatic pause, crashed shut. Rita and I slumped in our chairs, staring solemnly at each other. It was one of the hardest decisions we had to make.

That night, the upsetting end to the day lingered in my mind as I took the long bus journey home with Tainara. She stared out of the window and chatted excitedly, visibly relieved and full of anticipation for what the future would bring – living in the big city, starting a new school, having her own bedroom, a little brother and older sister. Yet at the same time I knew that another girl was somewhere out there, probably feeling the opposite emotions, that the people she had perhaps dared to think genuinely cared for her had given up on her too.

I worried that we'd made the wrong decision pushing Bia away when we could have embraced her more tightly. But then I remembered young Nádia and Fernanda, who by now would have had their innocence stolen from them, and I knew we were right to act as we did. I also thought of heartbroken Alicia, who would probably be lying on the dirt floor of her aunt's house right now, feeling unwanted and hopeless, wondering if she would ever find her own happy ending.

Looking over at Tainara, who was now fast asleep and curled up on the seat next to me, I wished that every one of these girls could find their own way out. The simplest solution, of course, was to take them all far away from here, to a safe place where they would never feel alone or be in danger again. Doing this while they were still living in their homes and communities was much more difficult, but I realised it was the only way we could rescue most of them. And that would mean not just convincing the girls that they had worth and deserved to be treated differently, but also everyone around them.

My worries about Bia intensified as, over the next weeks, she fell completely off the radar. Rita scoured the poorly-lit streets of Medina at night and drove up and down the motorway peering at figures in the shadows in the hope they might be her. None of the girls had seen her either and neither had her older sister with whom she normally stayed in town, nor her mother who was looking after her young son in a straw hut deep in the bush. None of them knew – or seemed to care – where she was. As days stretched into weeks, the knot in our stomachs tightened as we began to wonder where her desolation had taken her and if we would ever see her again.

At the same time, the team were dealing with other cases which showed just how naive we had been in thinking that a week of public performances might have caused a significant shift in people's attitudes.

The first was that of Lilian, the 13-year-old who had started living with a man in his forties. Not only was he keeping her a virtual prisoner in his home, but he was also beating her up. On one occasion when Rita trudged up The Hill to her house on the off chance she might catch her alone, she appeared at the door with a black eye and a swollen jaw. Incandescent, Rita rushed down to the guardianship council offices where she'd once worked, bursting in with the news that a young girl was being held captive and subjected to physical violence by an adult man. The counsellor listened before replying, "You mean Lilian, who's living with her husband? Oh, we can't get involved with husband-and-wife stuff."

There was a similar situation with Maria Lúcia, now 13, the girl who was living with the man who had raped her, and who was already close to giving birth to his baby. She had turned up at the Pink House with bruises on her legs and arms, often looking upset. While she always claimed she'd had a fall or bump, it was obvious to our staff that her injuries were not accidental. One day, Maria Lúcia's father turned up at the Pink House, frantic about his daughter and asking for help to get her to come home. Rita went with him to the police station, where she knew the case against the man for rape of a minor had been filed away and forgotten.

Incredibly, the desk sergeant, after listening to the father's pleas, put a hand on his shoulder and tried to reassure him that there was nothing wrong with his 13-year-old daughter cohabiting with her rapist. "She's got a roof over her head, food on the table, and someone who likes her," he said. "You should be glad that she's not on the street causing trouble like so many other girls her age."

The close relationship we were building with the girls also allowed us to be more aware of situations which would otherwise have remained hidden and undiscovered. One day, Rita went to visit two young sisters, aged 11 and 13, who were regulars at the Pink House and had been living in a dilapidated shack at the far end of the Saudades district, the invaded land on the other side of the motorway. When she got there she discovered the wooden house empty and found out from neighbours that the girls and their mother had moved to a traditional neighbourhood, in the precincts of the Catholic church. That an unemployed woman who survived by selling ice pops from a cart on the streets, would suddenly have enough money to rent a spacious brick house in an upmarket part of town already, aroused Rita's suspicions.

It wasn't long before she discovered the truth. The mother

wasn't paying any rent. Instead, she heard that her eldest daughter had been seen around town, hand in hand with the landlord, a man in his forties who was also the proprietor of a children's clothes shop. For us it was clear – the mother was paying her rent by handing over her 13-year-old daughter to be abused, something the girl later confirmed as she opened up to Rita. But for other townsfolk, the boundaries were blurred. Back in Medina several weeks after leaving with Tainara, I mentioned the case to the pastor of the Baptist church I had got to know while staying at Dona Geralda's. His response was staggering.

"Oh yes, the man and the girl, they sometimes show up at church together. It's a bit strange, isn't it, I mean, the age difference. But he's an upright man who pays his tithe faithfully."

We knew that if we were going to bring lasting change to this town we needed to change the way people viewed and valued poor young girls. At the time we had an English volunteer with us called Kim, an incredibly talented artist who had been helping the girls express themselves through visual arts. As we discussed the challenge of convincing local people to look at girls differently, she had an idea.

"I was walking through town today and I noticed a derelict wall, right in front of the square next to the Catholic church. It's on the road down to the market, everyone walks past it. I wondered, what if we painted it, made it into an eye-catching piece of street art? It could engage people and give the girls a voice…"

I wasn't entirely convinced. After delving deep into this town's problems I knew we needed to find a way of confronting generational abuse and injustice and all its consequences. The public dance and drama performances we'd done with the girls had been moving, and had provoked a reaction on the night, but clearly not enough to change the way people behaved; it had been disheartening to see, despite our hopes, people carrying on with their lives, continuing to turn a blind eye to the business of abuse and exploitation happening right in front of them. Confronted with issues of life and death, and attitudes that were so ingrained, I'd begun to wonder how much of a difference art could really make. Even so, I agreed that we could give it a try.

We discovered that the land where the wall was belonged to the town council and used to be a leisure club before it fell into disrepair with only the front wall still standing. The mayor's office manager looked bemused when we asked if we could paint it, but had no objections. The next day Kim turned up at the unsightly wall, its faded yellow paint cracked and flaked, with her brushes, ladders and tins of paint, and set to work.

Over the next seven days, the wall underwent a dramatic transformation, right in front of locals who walked, drove or trotted on horseback past it every day. On the first day the wall's imperfections and faded painted letters were covered in whitewash. Then, little by little, starting with sketchy black lines, then abstract shapes which were filled with colour and gradually began to take recognisable form, the mural and its meaning was slowly revealed.

Kim managed to create a mural which was both eye-catching and full of meaning, especially for Medineses. Weaving across the 20-metre-long wall were three ribbons intertwined, red, green and white, the colours of Medina's flag. Underneath, small figures in colours that represented the town's different neighbourhoods held hands as they walked along the bottom of the wall towards the centre, where they were swept up to become jigsaw pieces that made two huge open hands, which also resembled Medina's map – instantly recognisable to townsfolk. Out of the hands flew four doves of peace into a sky painted at the top of the wall, which was almost the same deep blue as the real sky behind it.

Before long, the wall was the talk of the town. Instead of a passing glance as they walked past, people began to stop and gaze. The message – that everyone in town needed to work together for peace – was a powerful and unifying one which many could agree with, especially after the recent shocking murders of the two boys and the gangland execution of another teenage boy since. But then, halfway through the week, Kim subtly changed the focus. Instead of being about the town and its problems, the wall became about its girls, precisely those whose plight went unnoticed by most townsfolk. Inside the red ribbon, she had painted the white almond outlines of eyes and one afternoon the Pink House girls came along, each painting the iris of one of the eyes with their own designs. By the end of the day those who came to look at the mural saw 30 brightly-coloured eyes, clearly painted by teenagers, staring back at them. Finally, on day seven, a last ribbon, in the green and yellow colours of Brazil, was added along the top of the wall, with the words: 'Your look can transform our lives'.

During the week we had put posters around town, inviting people to a special unveiling ceremony on the Saturday night. Hundreds turned up, filling the rows of white chairs we'd placed on the cobbled road in front of the wall. Dusk had fallen by the time Rita and I walked up onto the platform to start the event. There was a real sense of excitement and expectation in the air.

"Sometimes we are so used to how things have always been that we don't think they need to change," I said, taking the microphone. "How many of you walked past this old wall every day but never noticed it? It's only now that it's been turned into something beautiful that we see it." There were nods and murmurs of agreement. "And it's not the only thing in town we need to start to look at differently."

Next, a video our team had filmed during the week was shown on a projector screen. It showed neglected corners of Medina – an open sewer in the Saudades district, a broken water pipe in Lowlands, a man showing how high flood waters reach with no drainage in his street. Other locals were shown holding up masks to their faces with the phrases 'Can you hear me?', 'I exist' and 'Speak for me'. People sat up in their seats, clearly in agreement and evidently impressed that someone was noticing them and their daily struggles. Many stood up and applauded as the video ended with the words, 'Open your heart. Open your eyes.'

None of them were expecting what happened next. A number of our girls had been sitting 'hidden' in the audience since the start of the event. One by one they got to their feet, shining a torch upwards at their faces and reciting a line of a poem they had written together. Again, the symbolism was powerful, inviting the audience to reflect on how girls were unseen and unheard in their community, with so many oblivious to their feelings and needs.

Alicia was the first to stand up. "We need you to look at us with new eyes. Not with indifference, or malice, but with respect."

At the other side of the audience a chair scraped as Maria Lúcia got to her feet and spoke, "Your look can change my life, if you could only see me differently. Not as a problem, but as potential."

Several other girls, who had been sitting silently in their midst, got up to say their lines as the crowd listened in hushed silence. The last girl was little Poliana. "Hey you, listen," she shouted in her high-pitched voice. "No-one's better than anyone else, we're all equal."

The evening continued with dance and drama presentations from the girls on the same theme until all the Pink House girls took to the stage for the final performance, flailing different coloured ribbons as they danced along the entire length of the wall behind them. The crowd rose to their feet in rapturous applause and the girls, beaming excited smiles, held hands and bowed in unison. As I scanned the faces of townsfolk, many of whom seemed genuinely affected, I wondered if, this time, it might finally have planted a seed of change.

14

THE GIRL AT THE BROTHEL

The Pink House was buzzing for days after the event. Girls arrived bursting to tell how someone had smiled at them in the street, or had even stopped to compliment them on their performance. One girl said someone had stuck up for her when a man made a lurid remark to her, another that her teacher had led a class discussion about how boys should respect girls. The mural and its unveiling had clearly provoked more than a fleeting emotional response, it had caused some people to reflect too. By the end of the week I was convinced that transformative art really could make a difference, a subtle yet powerful way of winning over hearts and minds.

I stayed on in Medina and the following week we decided to treat the girls by taking them for a pizza night in one of the local restaurants. Most of the girls had never sat down in a restaurant in all their lives, so there was palpable excitement in the Pink House that afternoon. It was 3pm when I went to answer the door after hearing a timid knock on the metal gate. In front of me a girl looked at the ground, her hair a tangled, matted mess. She looked up. It was Bia.

"It's been two months. I want to come back and I've decided to change," she blurted out before I had a chance to react.

I took her inside where the team members yelped when they saw her. It really had been exactly two months since we'd suspended Bia. She had counted the days and come back as soon as the time was up. Rita and I took her into the office for a chat.

"I'm sorry for everything, I know now that you were only tough with me because you want the best for me," she said before breaking into an embarrassed smile which she covered with her hands. "Not being able to come to the Pink House made me realise how much I missed it. I'd never felt loved or liked by anyone until I came here. I know I've got lots of problems, but I don't want to throw away this chance I've been given. Please help me."

Bia laughed and cried at the same time as Rita and I hugged her, telling her how brave she was and that we'd always be there for her. It was an extra reason for celebration as, later that night, we took over every table at Mr Uai, the town's best pizzeria on Medina's main street.

For girls who often went home to empty pans, and had to survive on other people's scraps, being served by impeccably-dressed waiters who indulged their every whim was something extraordinary. Bia was among them, savouring every second as she sat on a table with Sacha and three other girls from Lowlands, chatting excitedly between large mouthfuls.

After the evening was over the girls spilled out onto the street, said goodbye and started making their way home, with most walking off in groups to their homes in Lowlands or The Hill. Bia was the only girl from The River and was about to walk alone in the opposite direction until I offered to give her a lift home. She was still buzzing as we set off.

"That was the best night of my entire life," she gushed. "I never ever thought anything like that would happen to me. I still can't believe it!"

I smiled back at Bia. That she thought going out for a pizza was the best experience she'd ever had in her life was both sweet and tragic. She went on, "You know, I had a feeling something good was going to happen in my life the moment I saw you in the brothel that night."

I asked what she meant.

"The brothel at kilometre fifty-eight, when you came to take Mariana away. I…"

"Wait!" I braked and looked round at her. "That girl, holding the baby… that was you?"

I was stunned. On the night Dean and I had turned up at that roadside brothel, with Rita hiding in the back seat, we had seen the silhouette of a young girl holding a baby in her arms, but by the time we'd walked up the dirt hill to the bar entrance she had gone. We'd had to leave hurriedly after seeing men, who Rita later told us were armed, creeping up in the dark shadows and we never managed to find out who that other girl was. I'd often wondered about her, who she was, what kind of trouble she was in, if we'd ever find her again. After our terrifying experience on the motorway when we passed by the brothel again a few months earlier I knew I'd never be going back there and felt like I'd missed my chance of rescuing her. Now I realised that we had been rescuing her all along – embracing her despite her temper and tantrums, not letting her insults or bad language push us away and showing her that, whatever she thought or whatever anyone else had told her, she was loved and deserved a better life.

While dropping Bia off at her house, I got to know her better. Inside the tiny, terraced, mud-brick house the air was thick and black with soot from the open fire. Her toddler son and the young daughter of her brother who lived with her were asleep on a threadbare blanket on the dirt floor, along with two emaciated dogs, breathing in those fumes. In the kitchen there was a line of fizzy drink bottles filled with brown water – with no mains water this was what they used for cooking, washing and drinking, collected from the muddy stream at the end of their road, where Bia would also go to wash their clothes. My heart ached as I scanned that dark, dingy and dirty place... but when I got to Bia she was still beaming with a radiant smile.

The odds seemed impossibly stacked against her, but over the next weeks and months, Bia surprised everyone by stubbornly clinging to her new desire to live a different life. A few weeks later, she bravely took herself off to school, aged 14, starting the years she missed from scratch.

After her lessons she would come straight to the Pink House and empty her bag of books on a table so Cristiane could help her understand. There were bad days as well as good, sometimes more steps backwards than forwards, but little by little Bia began to change the cycle of exploitation that had been all she had known for as long as she could remember, even choosing to stay indoors when her friends knocked on her door calling her to cruise the streets with them at night.

One day Bia arrived at the Pink House looking pleased with herself. "Rita," she said, barely unable to contain her pride. "Last night I said 'no' to a man for the first time in my life." It was an emotional moment. The security and unconditional love Bia was experiencing at the Pink House was giving her the inner strength to finally take control of her life. It was empowerment in action.

As I got to know Bia better, I discovered she had a beautiful and caring spirit, always attentive to others' feelings and grateful to the point that we had to tell her to stop constantly saying thank you. It was an extraordinary transformation from that fractious, aggressive girl who had caused so much tumult in the house in the first few months. She also began opening up to us about her life, telling me some of the secrets she had kept to herself since she was a little girl. Her stories of unimaginable pain and heartache would leave me in an emotional state.

"My mother would send me to the motorway, and if I didn't come back with any money she'd beat me and send me back," Bia told me. "She'd even check inside my knickers to make sure I hadn't hidden anything. I was only nine years old. I was so scared of going home empty-handed."

The baby I'd seen her holding in the brothel was her son, who was now three, born when she was just 11 years old. "I got pregnant when I was ten. I don't know who the father is, he was just one of the men who paid for me," she said.

Bia became our friend and ally at the Pink House. Once an influential figure who would easily lead the girls astray, now she was bringing many girls back, urging them to take the same steps towards changing their lives. All the girls knew where she had come from and her reputation as the toughest girl on the streets, so they couldn't ignore her words of advice and encouragement. Because of her, more girls who we hadn't even known were out there started turning up at the Pink House, including four girls who, along with Sacha, were heavily involved in the drugs gangs and would spend their nights on the motorway, alternating between selling their bodies and helping the armed gang members hold up trucks.

Through Bia we also began to discover the worst that was happening in Medina's dark world of child sexual exploitation. She told us how policemen would stop the girls as they wandered the streets at night, demanding sexual favours in return for letting them go. How a group of businessmen in town were recruiting the girls, passing them around the group via WhatsApp. And how guards at the town's jail were letting in a group of girls, some as young as 12, so they could be sold to inmates.

Bia also told us about how one of the guest houses on the town square had a service they called 'Disque Novinha' or 'Little Girls Hotline'. Guests who wanted an underage girl would pay the establishment, who would make a phone call and get a girl delivered by mototaxi through the back entrance – just like they might order a pizza or burger. She also said that policemen who were patrolling town would go there, most Friday nights at 11pm, where they would snort cocaine for an hour before 'ordering' their girl, then leave to continue their night shift.

One Friday night when we were in Medina, Warlei and I decided to watch the guest house to see if Bia's appalling information stood up to scrutiny. We waited in the town square until 11pm when, sure enough, a police car pulled up on the side of the road and two officers got out, walked across the street and disappeared through the guest house entrance. They stayed there for an hour and a half – exactly the time Bia said they would – before reemerging, getting in their car and driving off. We had no way of knowing what they had done during that time, but it certainly seemed to tally with what she had told us. We went back to our own guest house – run by a Christian woman we knew well – feeling restless and overwhelmed. How could we show girls their true value and potential when the whole of society seemed to be conspiring against them? When so many seen as role models in the town – those in positions of authority and trust, whose job it was to protect them – were showing them that even the justice system was against them?

We also knew we needed to send an uncompromising message to the girls' parents, who were so often the ones who were to blame for their daughters' suffering. We decided to hold a mothers' meeting, using the excuse that, with Christmas approaching, it would be a festive gathering to get to know them. It worked – most of the mothers turned up – but as they filled the chairs we had placed around the Pink House yard we began to worry. They weren't going to like what we were about to say. How might they react to being told we wouldn't stand by and let them use their daughters as sources of income?

Rita welcomed the women with her usual charm, receiving smiles back as she launched into an eloquent speech about the joys of Christmas. There were more approving murmurs as she talked about the blessings of motherhood, the importance of family and the privilege of bringing a girl into the world. Then she paused for a moment.

"Here at Meninadança we want to help your daughters have the best start in life. But we know that many of them have already suffered more than most people do in their entire lives. Some have even been robbed of their innocence, and for many it was those who should have been protecting them, their family, who allowed that to happen."

I looked around, but the women just stared back expressionless. Rita went on, "So I'm here to tell you that we will no longer let your daughters be treated as objects, as currency, or as bargaining chips. We're here to defend and protect them and to give them back their hope for the future… whether you agree with us or not."

There was a stony silence. This clearly wasn't the Christmas party they'd been expecting. Then, on the back row, a woman in a red head scarf rose to her feet.

"I think you're talking about me," she said gruffly.

The other women turned around to see who was speaking. "My own mother sent me to work on the motorway when I was ten. I lost my childhood out there on the asphalt. All my dreams were extinguished. I never wanted my own daughter to suffer like I did, but… I thought that was just the way things were."

Another mother stood up. "For years it feels like I've been shouting into the silence. I couldn't bear to see my daughter being abused by my partner, then by her uncle, then seeing her drift away from me. I would cry for her at night, but I didn't think there was anything I could do to stop it. Bad things always happen to us, and there's never any justice, ever."

One by one, many of the other women told similar stories, opening up about their hardships, secrets they had never told and their feelings of powerlessness and regret. Many of those mothers fell pregnant when they were barely teenagers and most were now in their twenties, not much more than a decade older than their own daughters. As the conversation continued, and more women felt emboldened to speak, the mothers' meeting could easily have been one of our daily conversation circles with the girls. It was clear that they were just as much victims of exploitation and injustice as their daughters but, unlike them, were entirely alone as they grew up and never found anyone who told them that life could be different.

By the end the mothers were pledging to be partners with us, promising to be as open to change as their daughters. Then we really did have a Christmas party with food, games and laughter. The experience left me convinced that to really bring transformation to a girl's life we needed to reach out to her family too. Yes, they were often part of the problem, but they had once been the victims, and could also be part of the solution if we could get alongside them and show them that they too had more worth and potential than they had ever been told.

* * * *

It was approaching a year since we had opened the doors of the Pink House and so much had happened it was hard to take it all in. It was certainly a steeper learning curve than starting from scratch in a national newspaper newsroom a decade earlier. We had experienced the euphoric highs, unexpected breakthroughs and girls finding hope, but also the crushing lows of disappointment, loss and tragedy. Most of all, we were excited and optimistic about where this path would lead and confident we were heading in the right direction. We decided to throw a big party at the Pink House, inviting the girls and their families, for our first anniversary on January 27, 2014.

That party never happened. I was at home in Belo Horizonte the night before, packing a suitcase and about to embark on the long overnight trip to Medina when Rita called me. She was gasping for breath and choking on tears, in such a state I had to calm her down before she could get her words out. "Matt," she gasped. "The most terrible thing has happened…"

15

EMILLY

Emilly was a nine-year-old girl who lived with her mum and dad in a brick house on a patch of red earth on the outskirts of Medina. She was a year younger than our age group, but was due to start at the Pink House on her next birthday. Emilly's father José was a cattle hand at a ranch in the sun-scorched hills outside Itaobim, the next town from Medina following the BR-116 south. On Sunday evening his employer was hosting a summer party at the ranch and told him to bring along his wife and young daughter to enjoy the festivities.

Emilly had been excitedly running around the mango orchard and blood orange and lime plantations with other children and playing with the dogs, chickens and goats wandering around the ranch, while her mum and dad chatted with other guests. Every so often she would appear, breathless, at her parents' table to grab a strip of barbecued meat or take a sip of her fizzy drink before darting off again. But halfway through the evening, Emilly's mother, Edna, realised that she hadn't seen her daughter for a while and, when she couldn't find her, sounded the alarm.

Eventually they found her − raped and strangled to death, her lifeless body tossed into long grass close to a river dam a distance away from the party. The suspect, another labourer who had earlier been playing pool with guests, and who had been seen talking with Emilly before she disappeared, had already fled the property and was seen running along the side of the BR-116 towards Itaobim. Just weeks earlier the 32-year-old had been granted early release from prison where he had been serving time for killing a man in a bar fight.

News of the barbaric murder spread quickly in the region, leaving the people of Emilly's hometown enraged. A vigilante mob tried to lynch the man as police were taking him away and later attempted to storm the police station in Itaobim where he was being held. Emilly wasn't one of those girls who roamed the streets at night, offering their bodies to men, who were regarded as worthless and expendable. Indeed, if any one of those girls had disappeared, or even turned up dead, there would be no great outpouring of anger, as I'd already discovered while meeting the bereaved mothers of Padre Paraíso. Even so, I sensed that the town's justified indignation at the brutal rape and murder of an innocent child, and one of its own, might prove to be short-lived. As Rita poured out her own anguish over the phone to me, I realised we needed to find a way of making sure both Emilly, and the normalisation of violence against girls which was behind her brutal murder, were never allowed to be forgotten.

Needless to say, there was no longer an appetite for celebrating our one year anniversary the following day. Instead, the team spent the day comforting the girls and helping them to deal with the feelings this tragedy had brought bubbling to the surface. Most of them knew Emilly and were devastated by her death, but many also harboured their own memories of being violently attacked by men and knew the terror the little girl would have gone through. Still, over the following days and weeks, the anger that had taken hold of the town began to fade and life gradually returned to normal.

I arrived in Medina several weeks after the murder and went to visit Emilly's mother and father in their home where a rusty bicycle was propped against the outside wall and hens pecked at bare earth in the front yard. I wasn't prepared for how upset the meeting would make me. Clearly in the depths of crushing grief, Edna and José welcomed me into their home with such grace and kindness, leading me through to their living room with eyes puffed up with tears and feet that shuffled under the sheer weight of their loss. Emilly's little flip-flops were still lined up with others beside the front door, her dolls and cuddly toys lay in the corners of rooms and a frilly pink handbag dangled from a door handle.

I started to cry as soon as I opened my mouth to speak. Looking over at that young couple sitting utterly bereft on the sofa opposite me, in a room that should have been full of their beautiful young daughter's playing and chatting, was indescribably heartbreaking. I managed, through my tears, to tell them that I couldn't begin to imagine their pain and that they could count on us for anything they needed.

José was an empty shell, his eyes blank and emotionless, just how I imagined I'd be if such a tragedy had befallen my family. Edna, though, seemed stronger, emboldened by a mother's instinct to never stop fighting for her daughter. "I want justice," she said, her eyes immediately filling up again with tears. "But we're just a poor family, we're not important enough for that. Can you help me?"

She explained that Emilly's killer had applied to have the case against him thrown out using a plea of insanity. The family had been assigned a public defender for the case but had discovered, to their horror, that he was the same lawyer who had got the man early release from jail, an act which allowed him to murder their daughter. As Edna spoke, baring her heart with both a burning sense of injustice and a resigned acceptance that she was too poor and insignificant to matter, I remembered the women who'd turned up for our mothers' meeting a few months earlier. She was just like them, a young mother who'd learned that justice wasn't something she should ever hope for. Like them, Edna needed to know that she, and especially her daughter, were just as deserving of it.

After she had stopped I learned forward. "Edna," I said. "Please dispense with your lawyer today. We'll take on your case. We'll make sure justice is done, for you, and for Emilly."

As Edna and José watched from their front door and we made our way back down the cobbled road that led to their home, Rita made me aware of the challenge I'd just taken on. There had never been a single case of violence against a child in the town which had resulted in the perpetrator being prosecuted and jailed. If we made history and secured justice for Emilly, it could bring hope to other silent victims who were still too afraid and disillusioned to come forward. But if we failed, it would only confirm their belief that poor people should never expect anything except unfairness and impunity. Still profoundly affected by meeting this gentle, broken couple, I could think of nothing more important than getting justice for Emilly and making sure the memory of this defenceless young victim was never allowed to fade. "We'll do it," I said to Rita, that heartbroken couple filling my thoughts again. "And you know what? We'll do more. Let's get this road named after her… we'll get the town to name a day in her honour. We won't let her be forgotten."

It was just weeks later when, back in Belo Horizonte, a young lawyer called Tágory got in touch. He'd just moved from the capital Brasilia and wanted to volunteer some of his time on a pro bono basis for an NGO. I met him in a supermarket pizzeria and listened as he told me his background in human rights and his desire to get involved in something which needed his experience and expertise. It was incredible that he had contacted me precisely at this moment, I told him, as we were just wondering how we would find someone to get justice for this tragic young girl. I told him about Emilly's brutal death, the very real prospect that her murderer would walk free and just how significant the case was in the broader picture of violence against girls in the town. It would probably involve many hours' work, several long journeys to the region and we didn't have any money to pay him… but Tágory accepted without hesitation, immediately getting to work on the case.

****

Since arriving in Belo Horizonte I'd been paying the bills by freelancing as a journalist for the British newspapers. Now several months before the start of the 2014 World Cup, the attention of the world was turning to host country Brazil and my workload was increasing. I had travelled to the Amazonas city of Manaus to investigate how Haitian slave labourers were building the World Cup stadium there, reported from Rio de Janeiro's sprawling slums on brutal police crackdowns and had been embedded with Sao Paulo's military police in an operation to catch members of the city's notorious football hooligan gangs. I'd also travelled deep into the Amazon jungle for the *Sun* newspaper in perhaps my most bizarre assignment where on the Colombian border we met up with members of the Matis, an indigenous tribe known as the Cat People because of the 'whiskers' they attach to their faces. The tabloid, of course, wanted the Cat People to cheer on the Three Lions, who were playing their first match in Manaus. The picture of the tribesmen wearing England shirts was the *Sun*'s splash on the day Brazil's World Cup kicked off.

There were also times I was able to use journalism to bring much-needed attention to the subject that I was most invested in, the plight of young girls in Brazil, especially along this cursed motorway. I spent several weeks investigating child prostitution around the Itaquera stadium in São Paulo, where the World Cup's opening ceremony and first game was to take place and where in a nearby favela I met young girls forced to sell their bodies to construction workers building the venue. I also travelled to the town of Uberlândia, in the southeast of Minas Gerais state, to interview a 15-year-old girl who had been offered a chance to go to Rio de Janeiro to work at a snack bar during the World Cup. When she arrived there, she was locked up, drugged and forced to sell her body to tourists on the famous Copacabana beach and beaten up by gangsters if she didn't make her quota each night. Both stories were published in the *Sunday Mirror*.

In early 2014 Chris Rogers, a BBC newsreader I knew from my time in London, got in touch, asking me if I could help with a documentary he was making for the channel's flagship

Panorama programme. A respected investigative journalist, Chris had made several other programmes about children's rights around the world, including going undercover in Turkish orphanages with the Duchess of York Sarah Ferguson and investigating child trafficking in various countries in Africa and Asia. This time, he told me, he wanted to highlight the issue of children selling their bodies in the Brazilian cities that would be hosting games during the upcoming World Cup.

"Sure," I told him. "But you can't just go to the host cities. Let me show you a town no-one's ever heard of, somewhere along the BR-116. You'll see where the biggest problem is."

Chris agreed, and during several trips over the next two months we travelled all over the country, along with a cameraman and BAFTA award-winning producer Marshall Corwin. In São Paulo we filmed the tragic life of a 14-year-old, crack-addicted girl who sold her body near the World Cup stadium. Joice lived with her mother and young brother in a derelict tower block crawling with gangsters and addicts. There were some tense moments during our time there when, arriving back at the abandoned building late at night, men toting guns and high on drugs would stop us on the pitch black stairwells, checking our pockets and taking our passports. On another occasion, after we'd filmed in front of a seedy sex motel known for making money from underage girls, a man on a motorbike stopped in front of our car at a red light, making a gun sign with his hand and aiming it straight at us. We immediately sped out of the area, with our local fixer explaining that the sinister sign meant assassins were after us.

We also visited Rio de Janeiro, Recife and Fortaleza on the northeast coast, all well-known tourist resorts where brand new football stadiums were frantically being built to host the tournament. Chris and I would head out at night, pretending to be sex tourists, capturing on our hidden body cams the young girls who would appear out of the shadows, probably with pimps or gangsters not far away, offering their undeveloped bodies for a handful of dollars. In Fortaleza, we were shocked to see policemen patrolling the beachside promenade walk straight past as we talked with the girls, turning a blind eye to what they could only conclude was child sex tourism. When we later put this, and the girls' claims the tourism police officers were among their clients, to the city's police chief she angrily denied they could possibly have been involved.

From there, we took a plane to Juazeiro do Norte, a city in Brazil's drought-stricken backcountry, then a car for another two and a half hours until we reached Salgueiro, a remote town alongside the BR-116 as it cut through one of the poorest regions of Brazil, over 300 miles away from the nearest World Cup city, Recife. I'd been here before with Dean during our journey along the highway, and I'd asked the guardianship councillor we had met that time, a gentle, caring man called Sinval, if he could help the BBC crew understand the plight of girls in the town who sold their body on the motorway.

During one day, we visited the homes of young girls Sinval knew were caught up in the sex trade. In one neighbourhood, where wattle-and-daub mud houses lined red clay roads littered with rubbish and rubble, he seemed to stop at every other home, introducing us to girls far younger than any we'd met so far. One, 12-year-old Amanda, excitedly showed us the childish drawings in her colouring book, yet at night the tiny girl was selling her body to men in the seedy bars that lined the motorway just a few streets away. In another street, a shy 13-year-old called Jessica sat on a bed covered in cuddly toys and fiddled with her school exercise book as she admitted going out in the middle of the night to sell sex to truck drivers. She recently found out she was HIV positive. "Why do you do what you do? Because you're so young, and it's so dangerous…" asked Chris, clearly increasingly overwhelmed by what he was witnessing. "I think it's because I'm naughty. I think that's why," she answered timidly. We later discovered that Jessica had contracted HIV not during her dangerous late-night liaisons, but from her mother's partner, who would rape her in her own home after they had gone to sleep. It was no wonder this traumatised young girl would run away at night, letting herself be exploited on the many local truck parks and gas station forecourts.

That night, Chris and I met up in the hotel restaurant for dinner after a long, energy-sapping day. I asked him if I'd convinced him that, of all the child welfare scandals in this vast country, people most needed to hear about the tragedy of young girls on the BR-116.

Chris put down his fork and looked over the table at me. "I…" Tears welled up in his eyes. "I've never seen anything like it," he said, his voice faltering as the tears streamed down his face. "There are so many of them… and they're so young." Impeccably professional, it was the first time I'd seen Chris cry during the whole trip.

When the hour-long *Panorama* special, called 'Brazil: In The Shadow of the Stadiums', aired on BBC1 a week before the start of the World Cup – with, to my surprise, my name credited as 'field producer' in the closing titles – it was the first time any broadcaster had dedicated any airtime to the plight of girls on the BR-116. The documentary caused a huge stir. Even before it had ended it was trending on Twitter, with many expressing their shock at how girls were being sold for next to nothing while the government spent millions on white elephant stadiums for a one month-long tournament. The programme reached TV audiences around the world and would later be shortlisted for a BAFTA for best documentary.

Another trip reporting on child sexual exploitation ahead of the World Cup, this time on my own for the *Sunday Mirror*, took me to another remote town on the BR-116, Cândido Sales, in the northeastern state of Bahia. It was another place I had visited with Dean during our fact-finding trip, a town which appears suddenly as the motorway bends round a river valley past a long, vertiginous bridge. I'd immediately recognised the name: It was where Ana Flávia, from Padre Paraíso, had been headed when the truck she was in careered off the bridge at the entrance to the town. It was also where Mariana had been found during a raid on an underage brothel, back when I was back in England and she had gone missing for several weeks.

I'd kept in touch with Fábio, another guardianship councillor who had told us about the girls he knew caught up in child prostitution in the remote town. Two months before the start of the World Cup, he called me.

"Matt, you need to come here again. Trafficking gangs have been coming here to recruit girls for prostitution during the World Cup. I've just talked to two who say they're going with them to Salvador the day after tomorrow. You need to report this."

It was just past lunchtime on Saturday when my overnight

coach pulled onto Cândido Sales' bumpy cobbles, stopping in front of a row of corrugated iron-roofed snack bars, where Fabio was waiting for me. We headed to a district on the edge of town, where a red earth road, cracked and creviced by heavy rains and scorching sun, tumbled down a steep hill to the red-brown river. High above us, a constant stream of trucks passed slowly over the narrow bridge spanning two rocky outcrops.

Vanesa and Layane, the girls who had accepted the gang's offer of working in Salvador, were already waiting, sheepishly, by the river's edge. I was shocked when I saw them. For the last 24 hours since Fabio had called I'd been engrossed in trying to get back to Cândido Sales as quickly as possible and hadn't given a thought to the girls I would be meeting when I got there. Vanesa was 13, but looked no older than 10, and wore a frilly red skirt and matching crop top, while her friend Layane, 14, was taller but skinnier, her bony frame wrapped awkwardly in a white strapless dress. Both had bright eyes and innocent smiles. I was immediately horrified to think they were about to be transported like products to a big city hundreds of miles away, by men only interested in how much money they could make with that innocence.

More alarmingly, Vanesa and Layane had clearly been taken in by the gang and had no idea of the grave danger they were in. "They told us we'd make more money than anyone else here ever has," Layane enthused. "That it was an opportunity like this only comes once in a lifetime. We'd be able to afford everything we've ever wanted."

"Two of our friends went last week," Vanesa added. "I haven't heard from them yet, I think they must be really busy."

As they posed for photos it was clear they considered themselves lucky, girls who were leaving for the big city lights, who would be the envy of their friends on their return. We tried to convince them that they were about to fall into the hands of traffickers, probably wouldn't see a single centavo and may never return home at all, but the two friends soon made their excuses and had to rush off. Afterwards, I chatted to local people sitting idly on their doorsteps, who revealed a truly horrific picture of this far-flung place, to where gangs would travel for miles to snatch young girls from the streets.

"It happens all the time," one woman told us as she washed her smalls in a metal basin. "Last month two girls from this street went off with some strangers. A couple more the month before. They think they're going to make their fortunes. We never heard from them again." Just like in the towns of the Jequitinhonha Valley, where outsiders would make their fortunes taking off with their precious stones and metals, gold diggers came to Cândido Sales too, to steal away its young daughters.

As my bus pulled back onto the motorway, and I peered over that bridge down to the spot where I had been talking to Vanesa and Layane, I found my heart bursting. I thought of our fledging Pink House in Medina and the girls who had once also thought nothing of taking off into the night, even disappearing forever, but who were now experiencing the certainty that they were loved and valued and I desperately wanted the girls of Cândido Sales to find the same hope. The situation seemed so urgent – each day could literally mean a precious young life was lost – and from that moment on I knew our next Pink House would be there.

16

I WON'T BE SILENCED

Back in Medina, among those girls who were bravely taking hold of their own destiny was Maria Lúcia, now 13 and a mother to a newborn daughter. She had always been fiercely loyal to her 'husband', a man in his forties who had groomed then raped her, even after he had started beating her up while she was pregnant. Then, after the baby was born, he unceremoniously dumped her, kicked her out his house and brought in another 12-year-old girl to live with him. Once again, local people saw nothing criminal in the man's behaviour. Maria Lúcia was devastated and unconsolable, but continued coming to the Pink House every day, even if most of the time was spent curled up, crying into the sofa. Then, one day, she knocked on Rita's door.

"Rita, you're right," she announced. "You've been right all along. He took advantage of me because I was just a child. He abused me."

Rita got up from behind her desk and hugged her. "Yes, but that doesn't mean he has to destroy you. You're stronger than that."

"I know," Maria Lúcia replied, her assurance taking Rita by surprise. "That's why I want to tell others about what happened to me, so other girls might not have to."

The girls were getting ready for several days' performances in various locations around Medina, due to start the following week. Maria Lúcia hadn't been taking part in the dance or drama practises, but asked if she could tell her story at each of the events. I arrived back in Medina in time for the first event, in the open-air arena of one of the local secondary schools, and watched in astonishment from the back as, once the other girls had finished their dance numbers, this normally quiet, bashful young girl walked purposefully to the front clutching several sheets of handwritten notes and took the microphone. The audience hushed.

"I'm a mother, even though I'm too young to be one," Maria Lúcia began. "But that doesn't mean it has to be the end. And that's why I'm standing here, to warn you, to not take the same road as I did. I wish I'd had time to be a child, but someone took it away from me. Don't let the same happen to you."

As Rita gave her a reassuring embrace, Maria Lúcia went on, revealing the reason why her life had derailed at such a young age. As I listened I felt sick to the stomach – I had always believed that her father was one of the few good guys, who had fought to bring his daughter back home and been let down by the town's authorities. Now it appeared that it was he who had caused her life to disintegrate, seeing his young daughter, as so many fathers here did, as a source of income and favours. "My dad started bringing men home who I didn't know. That's when my sex life began and I soon felt dependent. It was only when I started coming to the Pink House that I realised that wasn't the way a child should live, that I could find a way out."

It was the start of a new beginning for Maria Lúcia who, imbued with a new boldness and purpose, continued to urge other girls at the Pink House to love themselves and avoid the pitfalls she'd fallen into. A doting, devoted mother, she promised she would give her daughter a double dose of love and protection, to make up for the lack of both that had blighted her own childhood.

But not all the girls in Medina had found the right path. Four worried us in particular: Sacha, her cousin Alicia, and their friends Laura and Patricia, all from Lowlands and friends of the district's drug gangsters, considered the most dangerous of the local factions. We knew the four girls were still selling their bodies on the motorway outside of town and also involved in something perhaps more perilous – late night armed hold-ups of long-distance truckers. The hold-ups, during which shots were often fired, had become so frequent that truckers drove with trepidation through the stretch of the BR-116 around Medina.

Often spending all night on the motorway, Sacha, Alicia, Laura and Patricia would turn up late at the Pink House, too exhausted to take part in activities. We continued to welcome them with the same warmth and affection as the others and gradually they started to open up about their lives, revealing the tragic reasons behind their wayward behaviour. "My mum doesn't care about me and just shouts at me all the time," Patricia told me once when I tried to warn her about the dangers of what she was getting involved with. "The gang is the closest thing I've got to a family. I haven't got anyone else who loves me." It was becoming clear that, while on the outside they were the loudest, toughest girls in the house, these four were actually lost, hurting young teenagers who were crying out for help.

At the time a filmmaker friend, Lytannya Shannon, and her

crew were spending time in the Pink House making a documentary for her final year project at the National Film and Television School. After already spending several weeks' filming, the girls no longer noticed the camera and microphone boom, and Lytannya was able to capture the girls, who had agreed to the filming, at their most candid and vulnerable. Perhaps the most heartbreaking interaction was between Alicia and Laura, two of the rowdiest, most volatile girls in the house, who seemed to revel in the fear in which they were held by many of the others.

We already knew that 13-year-old Alicia was staying with her cousin Sacha at their aunt's house after her own mother had died of Aids a few years earlier, and on the day I took Tainara to live with us she had broken down in unconsolable tears that another girl had found the happiness she had dreamed of. Laura, also 13, on the other hand, had only recently started coming to the Pink House, and even then quite sporadically. She hadn't let her guard down enough for us to know that much about her. Even more scandalous than her friend, when she did turn up she'd often be boasting about how she'd spent the night involved in crime. Yet as they sat together on a fallen log in a patch of wasteland in the Lowlands district, the deep hurt and loneliness with which each were living began to bubble to the surface.

Alicia remembered how, like Maria Lúcia, it had been a terrifying and unthinkably violent act that had first robbed her of her innocence and destroyed her childhood. The scene ended up being one of the most powerful moments in Lytannya's film, called *Esta Vida (This Life)*.

"I was at my cousin's house and I went to sleep with my sisters," remembered Alicia quite matter-of-factly. "Then some guys came in and raped me. Simply that. They burst in, raped me, put me on top of the oven… the oven fell on top of me… lots of stuff. I think there were three or four of them, I don't know… I think I was ten."

Their honest chat turned to the day Alicia lost her mother, who would prostitute on the motorway. "My mum died of Aids. I don't know who it was, one of them put Aids in her, and I have so much hate for them. That's why I rob these truckers. That's it, I hate them a lot. If it wasn't for the disease my mum would be alive today, she would be here with me and I wouldn't have to depend on anyone.

"After my mum died, everyone beat me up, everyone, Laura. Everyone despised me, I didn't have any of my own clothes, I didn't have anything. Everything's rubbed in my face, even when I eat their rice they rub it in my face that I didn't pay for it. It's like that, it's a tough life."

Tears streaked down Alicia's cheeks as she sobbed, "I just wish I had my mum to give me love, for me and my sisters. Today I'm in this life, I go with who I go with, I go into trucks, I sniff cocaine, I'm doing all this because I lost her. If I hadn't I'd be happy to this day."

In another moment captured in the Pink House office, Alicia and Laura sat with 14-year-old Sacha and 15-year-old Patricia as Rita tried to convince them of how perilous their late-night liaisons were.

"One day we'll take the chance and disappear from here, you'll see," said Alicia. "Me and Laura, we'll take a truck and get out of here, won't we Lau?"

"You know that you'll be prostituted?" replied Rita, her brow furrowed with consternation.

"Pros-ti-tu-ted!" repeated Laura flippantly.

"You're already being prostituted, girls!"

"Rita, we only prostitute when we want to. When we don't want to, we don't."

"But there are times when you crave drugs and so you do these things. Right, Alicia?"

The four girls fell silent, while Alicia nodded her head sadly and eventually murmured "Yeah". Only Laura remained seemingly unmoved, fiddling nonchalantly with a folded desktop calendar in front of her while the others fixed their stares on the ground.

Rita, sensing she had their attention, went on, "Guys, you're putting yourselves in danger, of picking up an illness, of being violated. What if, when you're high on drugs, three men arrive wanting to have their way with you..."

"I wouldn't have the courage to tell them to use a condom," said Alicia.

"You don't use a condom? My God, you'll catch a disease!" exclaimed Laura, again in a mocking tone, feigning shock.

"Yeah, and what about you? You can't speak," Alicia immediately retorted.

There was a pause before Rita asked, "Are you pregnant, Laura?"

"Me? No. I took medicine."

"Oh my God," said Rita, rubbing her hands on her face.

"Again, Laura?" said Alicia. "Two lives, Lau," added Sacha.

"And so you're going to just keep getting pregnant and aborting, getting pregnant and aborting..." asked Rita.

The conversation moved to their late-night antics robbing trucks on the BR-116 for the Lowlands gang.

"When you stop these trucks, how many do you rob?"

"Eight," replied Laura proudly as Rita gasped. "The other night I got home at five in the morning. I was so sleepy, but even then I still went on Facebook." She giggled at the others as Rita leant forward on the desk, trying to look her in the eyes.

"You're just a 13-year-old child, Laura!"

"If I die no-one will miss me."

"Yes they will," Rita pleaded. "Lots of people will miss you."

The room went quiet again, and this time Laura too dropped her bravado for a brief moment, a deep sadness in her eyes. Then she giggled again and, as if to distract from that glimpse into her heart, began to play with the calendar again.

"Don't you love anyone, Laura?" Asked Rita.

"No, nobody," she muttered without looking up.

"Do you only feel hatred?"

"Yeah," she replied with a smirk. "Only hatred."

****

A week later, I awoke from a deep sleep in my room in the town's pousada to find three missed calls from Rita. The last one, at 6.30am, had finally stirred me from my slumber. I called her back and she picked up immediately.

"It's Patricia," she blurted. "Last night she was knocked down by a truck. She's in a bad way in hospital. They said it hit her in the head and she's broken lots of bones. I don't know if she's going to make it."

I quickly got dressed and rushed round to Rita's house where, clearly beside herself with worry, she paced up and down her kitchen, getting breakfast ready for her two children as she told me what had happened. Sacha, Alicia and Laura had called her in the early hours, hysterical after seeing their friend ploughed down in front of them by a huge articulated lorry. They insisted it wasn't an accident – the trucker had changed direction after seeing Patricia in his headlights and deliberately ran her over, then sped off leaving her body crumpled and lifeless in a drainage ditch.

A few hours later, at visiting time, we arrived at Patricia's bedside in Medina's Santa Rita hospital. She was conscious, but upset, terror still etched on her face, clutching a rosary in her left hand which was wrapped around her forearm. She had broken several bones, including her right arm and leg and her nose. Her face, covered in black stitches, was swollen and bruised purple.

Patricia's mother was at her bedside, her own face swollen by tears as she dabbed her forehead with a damp cloth and fanned away the mosquitos from around her face. "She's my only daughter," she sobbed. "I thought I'd lost her. She knows that I love her. That's why I tell her off so much, it's because I love her." Patricia's eyes widened as she looked up at her distraught mother, who clearly did love her and was just as anguished as her by the fact she'd nearly lost her.

Rita placed a loving hand on Patricia's stomach. "This was a warning, Patricia. You remember at the Pink House, when we'd sit down with you all and try to talk to you about this, and you'd go, 'Rita, stop nagging!'. But look at what's happened. This is your chance to turn your life around."

Patricia, on the verge of tears herself, managed a painful nod.

Speaking close to her ear so her mother wouldn't hear, she added, "I spoke to the others, they told me what you were doing. Remember, Patricia, you're a victim. Don't think you can't get out of this, because you can. We're on your side, OK? You're not alone."

In fact her brush with death turned out to be a turning point for Patricia and some of the other Lowlands gang girls. Some days later, she was discharged from hospital, and as over the coming months her mother nursed her back to health, a special bond grew between them. The terrifying incident also affected Sacha and Alicia, who never again went to the motorway to help the boys hold up trucks. It appeared to have the opposite effect on Laura, however, who rather than distancing herself from the life of crime and gangs, became even more submerged.

A few months later, I went to visit Patricia at her home. Sitting close to her mother on the sofa as we talked, she seemed calmer and more content. "I'm kind of glad it happened," she smiled. "If it hadn't I might never have discovered who really loves me." The next day she enrolled back in school, leaving behind for good the gang life and the dangers that had so nearly robbed her of her life.

****

Nine months after Medina had been rocked by nine-year-old Emilly's brutal rape and murder, the day of the accused man's trial finally arrived. We had managed to replace the public defender who had been assigned to the family with our own volunteer lawyer Tágory, who had visited Medina several times in the past months and today was back, this time with Warlei. The trial reignited the anger that had taken over the town immediately after the murder and in the 24 hours before the courthouse opened the place was palpably on edge. With feelings running high, the arrival of Tágory and Warlei the night before had also been unexpectedly fraught.

For townsfolk, that tall, suited man with a neatly trimmed beard, driving a flash car with blacked-out windows and a number plate from the capital Brasilia, couldn't possibly have been there to represent the poor, downtrodden family of the murdered girl. Instead, they assumed he was a government official or federal attorney come to ensure due process was followed and her murderer's human rights were upheld. When they heard Tágory was staying at the only pousada in town, overlooking the main square, people began to gather outside, causing a noisy commotion. Rather than go for a wander around and grab a bite to eat once they arrived, they stayed put for the night. Warlei even had to give a backhander to the pousada staff in return for them being extra vigilant about who was allowed in during the night.

The next morning, a bigger, angrier crowd had gathered on the cobbled street outside the courthouse, some holding banners, many wearing Emilly's photo on their T-shirts. This time there was no suspicion about Tágory, as he and Warlei arrived with Emilly's parents Edna and José. Soon after though, they turned into a furious lynch mob as the accused, hidden under a blanket, was brought to the court gates in a police car. Guards managed to hold them back and bundle the handcuffed man through the gates.

But while those outside had already condemned him, inside all were well aware a conviction was far from certain, and perhaps even the least likely outcome. In a pre-hearing several weeks earlier, the man's attorney had made it clear he would be claiming his client was both schizophrenic and psycho-pathic and had no recollection of the crime. We knew that if we couldn't convince the jury, without any doubt, that he was mentally competent and completely lucid on the day of the murder, there was a significant chance the case would be thrown out. An uneasy, taut silence descended on the courtroom as the judge opened proceedings with a firm tap of his gavel.

Tágory, sitting on the judge's right alongside Warlei and the town's public prosecutor, was the first to stand up, followed by the accused man, in the dock next to his attorney on the opposite side of the court. On the front row of the public gallery, Edna and José clutched each other tight, their tormented faces blotchy and swollen with tears. José never took his eyes off the floor, while his wife fixed a cold, steely stare on the man who had so violently snuffed out her daughter's life.

Addressing the defendant, Tágory began by summing up what his lawyer had claimed in the pre-hearing, that he was mentally unstable and claimed to have been hearing voices in his head. "Tell me," he asked. "These voices, were they real, or just imaginary?"

"No, they were just in my head," he replied.

Tágory continued his interrogation. "And do you feel any remorse or regret for what you did?"

The man nodded. "Yes, I'm very ashamed of what I did. I would love to be given a second chance."

Some of those in the public gallery began to wonder what this lawyer was doing allowing the man to explain himself and express remorse. He went on, "Now, help me understand what happened on the day. You were at the party and you were having a beer, right?"

"Yes."

"Do you remember playing snooker?"

"Yes."

"Did you notice some young kids playing?"

"Yes."

Tágory's tactic was ingenious. With simple yes or no questions, beginning with some of the seemingly trivial details of that day, he gradually led the man towards the scene of the crime – and a full confession. By the end, the man who had sworn he couldn't remember killing Emilly had shown he could recall every detail, from the colour of the dress she was wearing, to putting his hand over her mouth to stop her screaming, to the feeling of her body under him.

Hearing him describing her young daughter's last seconds was too much for Edna, who suddenly jumped up from her seat, no longer able to control herself. "You took away my daughter!" she screamed, falling to the flood as tears streamed down her face. "Aren't you ashamed? You murdered my baby!"

After several warnings that she would be removed from the court if she didn't calm down, Warlei went over to her, persuading her to sit back down and staying with an arm around her shoulders as Tágory continued his questions.

Finally, Tágory turned to the jury of seven men and women. "Members of the jury," he began. "I asked this man if he could distinguish if the voices he was hearing were just in his head and he said they were, so I can tell you he's not schizophrenic, because schizophrenic patients cannot tell the difference between fantasy and reality.

"When I asked him if he had any kind of remorse and he said he did, he showed us that he cannot be considered a psychopath, because a psychopath is unable to feel remorse, regret or empathy.

"And when I began to cross-examine him, his answers proved

that he did not black out, he was entirely lucid and knew what he was doing."

The jury members looked stunned and even the judge sat up in his seat, clearly impressed at how this lawyer had so systematically destroyed the defence's arguments. When the defence attorney got to his feet, instead of questioning his client further he turned on Tágory in an extraordinary outburst. "Don't believe what this lawyer is telling you," he told the jury. "He's trying to trick you. He's a fancy lawyer from Brasilia, he used to work for the UN and now he has come here thinking he can pull the wool over your eyes. Don't let him fool you just because you're not from the city like him. Besides, he's just a lawyer, only a doctor can say whether my client is mentally ill."

Tágory stood up again. "I'd like to thank the respected lawyer for this contribution. We should always listen to a wise lawyer and he reminds us of something so important, that only a doctor can establish if a patient is mentally ill. I'm sure he will agree, then, with this psychiatrist's report that the defendant is entirely sane."

There was a collective gasp from the jury as Tágory waved a piece of paper, signed and stamped by a specialist doctor. It was a masterstroke. He had counted on the defence attorney, who had been brought in from Belo Horizonte after no local lawyers were willing to take on the case, not having properly studied the reams of paper in the case files, including that of a medical examination, ordered months back by the judge. Tágory had lured him into affirming that he would accept a doctor's report – exactly what he wanted him to say. When it came to the defence's summing up, he already looked deflated and embarrassed and had little to say to the jury.

Four hours later the jury returned with an unanimous verdict: guilty. The man showed no emotion, except for a contemptuous look towards his attorney as he was sentenced to 25 years and four months in jail. Those gathered in the public gallery erupted in cheers, followed moments later by the crowd outside, as he was led away. As Tágory and Warlei left the courthouse, the atmosphere in Medina had changed. Now, word was getting around that a lawyer had come from the capital to their small, remote town to get justice for one of their own and one of the least of their own. Uncomfortable with the attention, Tágory headed directly for his car, but stopped as he heard a woman calling out behind him. It was Edna. She ran and flung her arms around him, then held him tight, tears streaming down her face. "I owe you my life," she sobbed. "I don't know how to thank you. You gave me my life back."

It was a huge victory, and historic too – the first time anyone had been convicted of violence against a child in the town. But somehow it didn't feel enough. Emilly's murder was a tragedy foretold, something I'd feared myself as I'd heard both men and women speak of girls as objects that could be used and discarded without consequence. Yes, a child rapist and murderer was now behind bars, but actually that had changed very little in Medina. No-one saw a reflection of themselves in that monster, nor had it forced anyone to consider the way they themselves diminished and objectified young girls. I remembered how, right at the beginning, that one voice in the silence, journalist Evany, had warned me that if we wanted to change the culture of abuse in the town we'd have to take on over 150 years of history. I knew we needed to use this awful incident, which had momentarily jolted Medina from its slumber, I just had no idea how.

As I discussed the past week's events with Warlei when he got back to Belo Horizonte, he mentioned that Emilly's birthday would have been on December 9, just three months away, when she would have turned 10 – the age she would have been able to start coming to the Pink House.

"Warlei, let's do something on her birthday, to remember Emilly's life but also to tell people that things have to change," I told him. "It just needs to be something big, that will bring the town to a standstill, that no-one will be able to ignore."

With Edna and José's blessing, we set to work organising a march through the streets of Medina to protest about violence against girls, for which I imagined we could involve all 40 or so of the Pink House girls. Because we wanted to show that it was a bigger problem than most were prepared to admit, we decided to first get hold of the indisputable facts, requesting from the town's guardianship council, social services departments and police the numbers of reports they had received about children who had been victims of violence since the beginning of the year. When we got the figures back, they were staggering. In just 10 months, there had been 658 reported cases of violence against children in the town. With around 20% of inhabitants being under 18, that meant one in every six children had suffered violence at the hands of an adult… and those were just the ones which had been reported.

As the Pink House staff started to spread the word about our planned protest, it took on a life of its own. The girls told their friends at school, who went to their headteachers, telling them they also wanted to take part. Soon, every school in town had decided to suspend lessons on that afternoon so their pupils could join in and young people from all around town, and irrespective of the district where they lived, pledged to take to the streets with us.

A few weeks before the event, we held an open meeting in the Pink House, where girls from all around town packed the room as we discussed the message we were going to put across. Emilly's brutal rape and murder and the way the town had so quickly forgot and carried on as normal, had awakened something in the town's girls – and many of its young boys too. They wanted things to change. They too wanted to feel valued and cherished, not worthless and expendable. They didn't want to be the next Emilly.

There have been many significant days along this journey, but few were more momentous than December 9, 2014. It was a day I certainly never imagined I would see when Dean and I first rolled onto Medina's dusty cobbled streets years earlier. Now, along those same cobbles, over 700 young people came marching into view, having downed their books, walked out of their lessons and joined the procession moving slowly through town towards the Catholic Church square. They walked along in complete silence, their mouths covered in black tape, while holding banners and signs which screamed 'Sexual exploitation is a crime' and 'Break the silence'. Each of the teenagers wore a pin badge on their T-shirt which read: 'I won't be silent'. It was an incredibly powerful act of protest, deliberately non-confrontational, yet perhaps for that reason impossible to ignore. Townsfolk came out of their homes, shops, hair salons and bars and stood and watched, astonished, as the silent mass of young people walked past.

The protest came to a stop at the council chambers, overlooking the square. Again, there were no chants, shouts or speeches, just hundreds of young people standing in silence, their mouths covered, facing the place where lawmakers so often overlooked the young victims of violence and abuse. Next, they moved on to the town's police station and stood, silently, for another 10 minutes in front of the place inside which they knew there were people entrusted with the duty to protect, yet who so often turned a blind eye to the suffering of girls, or were even responsible for it. Lastly, they moved further up the road to the courthouse where three months ago Emilly's killer had been brought to justice, yet where they knew so many other aggressors, exploiters and abusers had been freed, their victims condemned to live with impunity. Again, they stood there for 10 long minutes, the black tape across their mouths showing how they had been silent for so long, prevented from speaking or shouting out.

Then the hundreds of young people were on the move again, this time towards the market square, the town's main meeting place and where everyone knew girls were bought and sold. When they got there the teenagers ripped off the black tape and began to shout "I will not be silenced!" as townsfolk watched in astonishment. Then each of the young people took a white rose out of their pockets and threw it down onto the concrete floor – 658 roses in total, representing the number of children who had been a victim of violence that year. Within minutes a white carpet of roses covered the market square, and more and more curious locals gathered around.

We had set up a sound system so the Pink House girls could give a performance of dance and drama. Rita took the microphone, "Today would have been Emilly's birthday. All of us were devastated by her murder. One of those white roses is hers. The others are all the other children who suffered violence at the hands of men in our town. We're here to say, this has got to stop. We will no longer stay silent."

Then, Emilly's mum Edna emerged from the crowd, walking over the white roses towards the front. Rita put her arms around her as, visibly shaking, she gripped the microphone. "I want to say that…" She burst into tears as for a moment the weight of grief overwhelmed her, but regained her posture as applause erupted around the square. "You might think I'm strong, but it's only God who's sustaining me," she sobbed. "Mums and dads, take care of your daughters. No other child should ever have their innocence, their lives, stolen from them. All of us, we all need to change."

That night, as I reflected on the day's events, I felt truly overwhelmed. I couldn't imagine, in Medina's 150 years of history, that there had been a day like it. The town's young people, those who had always grown up feeling powerless and voiceless, had come together to demand change. I imagined their shouts of 'I will not be silenced' echoing down the decades, from the days when the young daughters of slaves were dragged off to be abused by their rich masters to now, when trucks circled the town square and poor, powerless girls waited in the shadows. "I have no words for what happened today," I posted on Meninadança's Facebook page. "The silence which has left girls so vulnerable for so long is beginning to be broken."

17

RAINBOW IN THE SKY

The first thing I heard was on the local radio station news bulletin as I was driving back from a dentist's appointment in Belo Horizonte. A journalist had been tortured and murdered, his body decapitated and dumped at the side of a secluded dirt track. I listened more intently when the newsreader said he had been found outside the town of Padre Paraíso in the Jequitinhonha Valley. Then I heard his name: Evany Metzger.

I had tried to meet up with Medina's 'Owl of the Valley' several times since I spoke with him that night, following the event in which we had presented our plans to local people, but every time he had been out of town. Evany, I later learned, had started spending months at a time away from home, often not even telling his schoolteacher wife where he was or what he was doing, except that he was on an important reporting trip. His stories, sometimes about local concerns like potholed roads or hospital waiting times, but other times exposing drug gangs or corruption in local government, were posted on his online blog, where readers were greeted with a photo of an owl's piercing eyes.

Three months earlier, Evany had checked into a scruffy, cinder-block motel in Padre Paraíso, 73 miles south of Medina,

the town of Padre Paraíso in the Jequitin
181

from where he would leave early in the morning, often returning only late at night. Again, he gave his family no clues as to what he was doing, but confided to a friend that he was investigating a child prostitution gang operating in the next town south, an impoverished community on the BR-116 called Catují. A fellow blogger from Padre Paraíso later recalled how, a day before he disappeared, he and Evany had eaten barbecued meat and shared a bottle of beer at a roadside bar, when he'd told him he was about to publish a "bombshell story" without revealing any more details.

But whatever, or whoever, Evany was about to expose has never been revealed. Later that night, he left his motel room, leaving the lights and fan on and telling the receptionist he wouldn't be long, but he never returned. Five days later, farm workers spotted a headless body amid parched bracken ferns off a secluded track 13 miles from the town. His hands had been tied behind his back with shoelace and his bank cards and identity documents were strewn nearby. His head was found in a ditch 100 yards away, scalped and marked by torture. He was still wearing a black shirt with his yellow owl logo sewn on the breast.

I shuddered in horror as I read the details of Evany's murder, remembering that gentle, caring man who had generously spared me his time that night, who seemed to know more than anyone about what was really going on in this region and with a profound understanding of the reasons why. I couldn't bear to imagine what he went through in his last minutes or hours – no-one knows how long his torture lasted. Over the following days, his gruesome death made headlines around the world and was decried by human rights groups, with newspapers like

The Guardian and TV channels like Al-Jazeera even despatching their own reporters to the region. Many pointed out that he was the 17th journalist to be murdered in Brazil in just four years and how Padre Paraíso, with nine violent murders in just four months, had one of the worst per capita murder rates in the world. I remembered my own disturbing overnight stay in the town and Sonia, who had saved children from dying from hunger only to see the young girls become the 'living dead' as they fell into the clutches of pimps and paedophile gangs. Back then I was convinced that one day we would return there to rescue girls from those who were exploiting them. Now I wondered whether it would be safe for us to even set foot there again.

Of course, the police pledged to investigate and find those responsible. And, of course, within months, once media interest had waned, the case was quickly mothballed. But Evany's horrendous murder was so close to home that Warlei and I knew we couldn't just carry on. Not only had it happened in the same region as we were working, but Evany had apparently become a nuisance to the same people we were probably also starting to annoy, especially after our 'I won't be silent' march through Medina. It was a wake-up call for us, after which we treaded more cautiously, spoke with less candour and were more wary about those we crossed paths with. Sometimes we'd give fake names, and always false addresses, when checking in to a hotel while in the region; we wouldn't stay in town for longer than necessary and when discussing certain subjects always ensured we did so behind closed doors. While determined not to be cowed by those wanting to scare us into backing off, we began to weigh every action, every statement, every post on social media, against the possibility of retaliations, sometimes having to find other ways to communicate or resolve an individual girl's predicament.

We also agreed we needed to provide better support to our Pink House staff, who were working daily on the frontline and were most vulnerable. Emilly's trial, and the community's initial misunderstanding about Tágory's role, had also taught us that we needed to somehow separate the work of the Pink Houses with any future prosecutions or campaigns, to protect the women working daily with the girls from any threats or reprisals. We decided to open an office in Belo Horizonte, with a support team that would always be at the end of a phone line to offer advice and help, but from where we could also launch legal action and advocacy without others associating it with the Pink Houses.

In the Santa Amélia district, close to where Warlei lived and where I had recently moved, we rented a shop front with a mezzanine floor in a mini mall, between a hairdressers and a dentist's surgery. We also took on two new members of staff: Orlindo was a friend who, with decades of experience working in social projects in the city, had been a constant source of support and guidance for me since I first lived in Brazil in my twenties. A gentle giant who always had a pearl of wisdom or word of encouragement to impart at exactly the right moment, I knew he would bring that same serenity and security to our staff.

Lorene, on the other hand, was a young dance teacher with infectious enthusiasm, a sparkle in her eyes and an irrepressible passion for using the arts to empower young people and bring change. She had the gift of lifting your spirits and reigniting your passion with just a short chat.

Having our office 400 miles away from where we worked was certainly unconventional, and unlike any other project I knew, but it made sense and all the difference. While passionate about helping the girls, our Pink House staff, all local women who had been born and raised in Medina, were often having to deal with situations they were unprepared for, from deciding how to protect a girl who was in danger to navigating the bureaucracy of local government departments. Having people with knowledge and experience walking alongside them helped the staff feel more secure in their work, which in turn began to reflect on the girls' own confidence and self-belief. And although we didn't know it yet, over the coming months the women on the frontline were going to need more support than ever.

****

Dark grey rain clouds hung low over Cândido Sales as Warlei and I turned off the motorway after the hour-long journey from Medina. Curiously, the time we arrived was almost the same as the time we had left – Bahia was the only state which didn't adopt Brazilian summer time, so was already one hour behind us when we crossed over the state line from Minas Gerais. The foreboding weather, and the fact we seemed to have defied the law of time to get there, added to the uneasy sense of finding ourselves in a remote, forgotten place.

It had been nearly a year since I was last here, but I still remembered the knot in my stomach with which I had left, as well as the feeling that I would be back here one day for more than just another fleeting visit with a notepad and camera. Fabio had kept me up to date about the two girls we'd met that day. Days after I'd spoken with her, Vanesa had gone off with the gang, just as she'd said she would, lured by their promises of easy money in Salvador. No-one had heard from her since. Little Layane, on the other hand, had changed her mind at the last minute and stayed, although that didn't mean she was safe and well. While in Vanesa's case we could only imagine what horrors that young, naive girl was going through, Fabio would see Layane every day, flagging down trucks late at night on the motorway.

I had shared my desire to begin the next Pink House in Cândido Sales with Warlei and now, feeling more confident that the work in Medina was proceeding well, we decided to pay a visit to find out more about the town and the challenges we might face. We didn't know anyone else in the town except Fabio from my first visit here with Dean, when everyone else in positions of authority flatly denied there was any kind of problem. We wondered if we'd find anyone else who might support a new project here. Fabio had suggested paying a visit to the pastor of a church in town who he felt would be most open to the idea. Zeno, the leader of the Sião Baptist Church, was an outsider from Brazil's deep south and was known for encouraging his congregation to help the poor and needy. We needed to start somewhere and he was all we had, so decided to pay him a visit.

Zeno lived in a large house, by Cândido Sales' standards, behind a whitewashed wall on a quiet street several blocks away from the town centre hubbub. I recognised the area – it was just round the corner from the long dirt hill we had driven down to reach the river, and Vanesa and Layane. It was Zeno's wife, Ivanete, who opened the metal door. Her little Chihuahua scurried outside and started yapping at us.

"He's not in," she smiled. "He's gone away for a few days."

She went to bring the dog back inside as Warlei asked if we

could leave her husband a message. "We're not from town," he explained, "We've heard about young girls here, that they're being exploited, and that gangs come here to take them away. We've been helping these girls in Medina. We'd like to do something here too."

Ivanete, who was still trying to gather up the dog, suddenly stopped and looked up. She opened her mouth to speak, paused, then began to weep. Warlei and I exchanged a surprised glance – we had never expected a reaction like this.

"I…" started Ivanete, composing herself. "Those girls, I see them every day. It breaks my heart, but there's nothing I can do on my own. Every day for the last six years I've prayed for someone to come and save them. I was even praying this morning, just a few hours ago."

She was a midwife and worked night shifts in the town's hospital, she explained, and often saw young girls bring brought in in the dead of night, often badly injured after being attacked or violently raped on the streets. One of the girls who made regular appearances in the emergency room was a 13-year-old called Maira, who she discovered lived just round the corner from her.

She told us, "The last time was a few weeks ago. It was around three in the morning. She had been raped by so many men she couldn't stand up. She had horrific internal injuries. She stayed overnight but then when she had recovered enough strength, she jumped out of the window and ran away.

"A few days later I saw her, just over there, lying on the ground on the corner of my street. She seemed scared, curled up in a ball, just like an armadillo. I tried to get close to her, edging closer just like you would an injured animal, but she ran away.

I'm so scared that one day I won't be able to find her again, or worse, that I will find her, and it will be too late."

Living so close to the town's troubled Célio Alves district – the name, we discovered, of the rows of cheek-by-jowl brick houses crowded around that steep red-earth road – Ivanete knew of many other young girls like Maira, whose lives she feared were balanced on the edge of a scary cliff edge. Some she recognised from her late-night hospital shifts, where she would look on helplessly as girls the same age as the children she taught in her Sunday school classes would be brought in battered and bruised, or convulsing from overdoses. But with no experience, and fearful of the dangerous gangs she knew were preying on them and probably controlling them, she felt powerless to try to help. Warlei and I told Ivanete about how, in Medina, girls just like them were coming to understand their own potential and self-worth and how simply knowing that people would notice if they went missing meant none had taken trucks up and down the motorway for months. She wiped her eyes and smiled as we told her we'd like to begin the next Pink House in her town.

"Don't think there's no-one here who cares," she said. "There's me and I know others who feel the same. Whatever you need to bring these girls back to life, we'll help you."

As Warlei and I turned around to walk back to the car, both of us gasped. As we had been speaking with Ivanete a stunning rainbow had broken out across the gloomy sky behind us. From where we were, it appeared precisely over the corrugated iron roofs of the sprawling district of Célio Alves. It was a sign, if we needed one, that this remote place, in the deepest backcountry of Bahia, should be the next place we try to bring hope to the girls of the motorway. I took a picture and immediately posted it on our Facebook page, telling supporters our next Pink House would soon be opening here. It was hasty perhaps – we didn't even have the money to start a new project yet – but while convinced we had to do something to help girls in Cândido Sales, I also had a feeling that the kinds of challenges we would face here would far surpass those we'd grappled with in Medina. By making a public announcement it would be far more difficult to change our minds when the going got tough.

On the way back to Belo Horizonte we passed by Medina again and, over a burger in a roadside snack bar chatted enthusiastically with some of the staff about what had happened that day. Among them was Holly, a young Northern Irish woman who had been volunteering at the Pink House since the beginning of the year. A recently-qualified primary school teacher, she had grown up with a burning desire to help girls in Brazil and after hearing about our fledgling project decided to put her career on hold and come to volunteer for an indefinite period. She had brought her passion for education, her teacher's organisation and love of Lindy Hop dancing to the Pink House, while the care she put into homework classes, not to mention her home-made cakes and cookies, had quickly won over the girls. It was during a catch-up chat over Skype a few weeks later that Holly mentioned she'd be willing to move to Cândido Sales to help start a new Pink House there.

I was at first unsure about sending a single foreign woman to the town, especially knowing some of what we now knew, but she insisted she wanted to help pioneer our new project and was up for the challenge. We put her in touch with Ivanette and Fabio while we continued to get to know the town and study how we could find the money for a second Pink House.

18

RAFFLED

The opposition I sensed we'd come up against in Cândido Sales came sooner, and with more ferocity, than we'd imagined. Three months after meeting Ivanette, she and her husband Zeno invited Warlei and me back, to speak to their congregation about our plans, so we could garner support and find volunteers or even potential staff members.

Following the Sunday morning service we returned to their home for a barbecue lunch, where Ivanette had invited other people from town who might be interested in hearing more. One of them was a sympathetic council psychologist called Gleyce who worked for CREAS, the government reference centre which receives cases of child abuse. As we chatted, tucking into our paper plates balanced on our knees, I asked her more about the plight of girls in the town.

Gleyce reiterated the concerns we'd heard from Fabio, Ivanette and others, but then told me something more shocking than anything I'd come across so far.

"You know, recently we discovered that men were selling raffle tickets and the winner would get to abuse a young girl."

Stunned, I asked her to elaborate. "That's what it was, just like any other raffle, except that the prize was an underage girl.

The draw was a big event and eagerly awaited, that's what we heard. Each ticket sold for 20 reals."

That was less than £5. The image of men playing games for the chance to abuse a child, hoping their numbers would be pulled out of the hat, was utterly sickening. Maybe it was because this town felt so remote, hidden in a forgotten, inhospitable corner of one of Brazil's poorest states, that people thought their crimes would remain undetected. Unable to keep this information to myself, back at the hotel that night I wrote an email to our mailing list of supporters, telling them why starting a new Pink House in Cândido Sales was so important and so urgent.

The next day, I got an email from Dan Sanderson, the foreign editor at *MailOnline*, the world's most visited news website. I had worked with him on many Brazil stories since arriving here and he'd sent me on reporting trips all over Brazil, as well as Argentina, Venezuela and Honduras, but I hadn't realised that he also received the charity emails I was sending out.

"Hey Matt, could you get any more? Could we do it properly? They're really keen."

It was typical news desk speak, but I knew what he meant, and immediately set to work trying to find more details and people who would talk about it on record. I started by calling Gleyce, who put me in touch with a local lawyer who had been involved in investigating reports of the raffles for the town council. Michael Farias, based in the closest big city Vitória da Conquista, was more than happy to talk when I called him. The raffles were actually held in the neighbouring municipality to Cândido Sales, an even poorer, more cut-off place called Encruzilhada, he told me. They were organised by local gangs, and some of the girls were as young as 11. He also revealed that, as well as the raffles, one establishment organised weekly bingo nights, with the girls put up as prizes paraded before players before the games began.

"It was talked about for miles around," he told me. "Tickets were sold far and wide. When the girls were found to be virgins, the price of the tickets would go up significantly. The draw to find out which ticket holder would win the girl was a big event. The gang made a lot of money and the girls felt they had no choice."

I also managed to speak to the civil police chief in Encruzil-hada, who confirmed that an investigation into the raffles had taken place and the information passed to the town's public prosecutor's office. I had all I needed, quickly wrote up the story and emailed it to Dan in London.

The story went live the next morning, as Warlei and I were driving home, with the headline 'Revealed: The Brazilian town where girls as young as 11 are RAFFLED by paedophiles and the star prize is an underage virgin'. Over the next few hours the story was shared more than a thousand times. Then, as we were approaching Belo Horizonte, my mobile phone rang. It was Orlindo in the office, telling me the phone was ringing off the hook, Brazilian journalists who had seen the *Mail* story and wanted to speak to me. Warlei and I spent the rest of the day giving interviews to some of Brazil's biggest news outlets, as well as to reporters from local newspapers and radio stations around Cândido Sales. By nightfall, news websites all over the world were reporting the raffles, while in Brazil the story made headlines in many of the next morning's papers. *The Folha de São Paulo*, the country's most respected newspaper, carried a damning comment piece from the director of a state committee

see as worthless," I said in my last interview with well-known news blogger Rodrigo Ferraz. "Of course it's easier to deny it happened than to investigate and bring it to a conclusion. I'm seeing the authorities making a lot of effort to distance themselves from this case, but maybe they should put the same efforts into protecting the victims instead."

It was the following week when we received a phone call from the Bahia state's Human Right Secretariat, based in state capital Salvador. They had been following the succession of stories about the Encruzilhada raffles and, despite the repeated denials, decided to launch their own investigation. As a government department they had privileged access to police investigations in the state and the power to force local judiciaries to act to protect victims and bring perpetrators to justice. Just a week later, Admar Fontes, the secretariat's director, issued a statement saying that the investigation had so far discovered that the raffles did take place and that over 100 men took part from Encruzilhada and many other surrounding towns. "A lot of people are involved," he said. "We will find them."

****

Warlei and I decided to refrain from further visits to Cândido Sales until some of the dust had settled, but what we saw in the coming months in Medina made us even more determined to continue with our plans to open a new Pink House there. One incredible moment came when Rita went with Sacha and Bia to speak about their lives in a secondary school on The Hill. Both once members of gangs that were at war with The Hill, they had never before set foot on their territory. Sacha and her cousin Alicia had once nearly lost their life after being ambushed by armed gang members. Now they were standing in front of a packed hall of pupils, talking about their involvement in gang life, crime and prostitution and why they had now decided to live differently. By the time the girls had finished telling their stories, the school's headmistress and a number of teachers – who themselves remembered the two as some of Medina's most troublesome delinquents – were wiping away tears.

Sacha and Bia's lives were about to change even further. Knowing Sacha, now 15, wanted to become a hairdresser, our team in Belo Horizonte found a family who owned a beauty salon in the city and were willing to take her on as an apprentice, even offering to give her lodgings while she trained. She was wide-eyed and brimming with excitement as I met her off the overnight bus and took her to settle into her home for the next six months. Bia, who just turned 16, had also discovered a talent in the Pink House beauty salon, where she would pamper the young girls, doing their hair and painting their nails, while encouraging them to take the right path in life – advice the girls found even more irresistible because of her own powerful story. Although Bia was still very much a work in progress, we decided to take a chance on her and give her a job in the Pink House through the government's 'young apprentice' scheme. The day we asked her if she wanted to become the Pink House's new beauty salon teacher, with a monthly salary, she immediately burst into tears.

"This is the best day of my life!" she gushed.

It wasn't just the girls' lives where we were seeing changes. People's attitudes seemed to be changing too, accompanied by the stirrings of an acknowledgement from those in power that more needed to be done to protect their town's girls. On the day Rita and I had visited Emilly's grieving parents and, moved by their desolate acceptance that their daughter's brutal murder would change nothing, I had vowed that not only would be get justice for her, but that we would get a day and a road named after her, so the town would never forget. After her murderer was jailed, and following our historic silent protest when hundreds of young people came out onto the streets, we had petitioned Medina's council chamber to decree that the day of Emilly's birthday, December 9, be made a municipal day against child sexual exploitation. In their last meeting of the year, town councillors debated the motion and, to our amazement, voted in favour. It was something that had seemed impossible when we first opened the Pink House doors. Now, for the first time in its history, Medina would have a day, enshrined in law and on the town's official calendar in perpetuity, when its people and institutions would have to talk about the abuse and sexual exploitation of its girls and how to combat it. Coming at the end of the year when Evany, once one of the only Medinenses brave enough to call it out, had been taken from us for doing exactly that, I felt like it was his victory, too.

Soon after, Medina's council agreed to name, not a road, but a public building, after Emilly – the newly-built CREAS centre, a service provided by the federal government to offer support to victims of violence and human rights abuses. Emilly's mum Edna unveiled the plaque at the opening ceremony, after the Pink House girls put on a special performance. "This won't ease my pain, but it means Emilly stays in everyone's hearts," Edna said. "Now I know she won't ever be forgotten."

But it was what happened a week later that convinced me Medina was now a very different place to when we had first started working in the town. With Christmas approaching, the girls had formed a choir and been practising a repertoire of festive songs and carols. But this time they didn't want to perform as usual in the town square – they wanted to take a message of peace and goodwill to their own streets and neighbourhoods. That would mean all the girls going into all three of Medina's rival districts, The Hill, Lowlands and Riverside. Just a year ago that would have seemed like madness, but as the girls had shown they could be friends, and as the town had seen young people come together to fight for a common cause, this had begun to change.

There was something magical about that night, as the girls, dressed in red and white and wearing Santa pom-pom hats, stood together on the red dirt roads, swaying side to side as they sung songs of hope and peace.

One moment in particular left me choking back tears. For their last performance of the night they were in Lowlands, on the street where Marta used to live, and who just 18 months earlier we were comforting here after the violent murder of her teenage brother. Many of the girls who were singing today were there too, heartbroken and frightened as a seemingly unstoppable wave of violence rolled through their town. Now they were singing 'Hallelujah', beaming smiles, their eyes glistening in the Christmas lights as they looked out into the starry night sky. Locals came out of their homes and crowded round, clearly moved by what they were seeing and hearing.

Over the last few years we'd had so many ups and downs, moments of optimism and disappointment, but there was no mistaking it now. Hope and change really had come in this remote, forgotten town.

19

THE MAYOR OF TAIOBEIRAS

It was November 2015, Warlei and I had travelled to the UK for a speaking tour to raise more support and share our plans to open a new Pink House in Cândido Sales. We were in Saffron Walden, a chocolate-box town of cobbled streets and medieval half-timbered houses in rural Essex. That Sunday evening, I was about to get up to speak to a gathering at the town's baptist church when a Twitter notification pinged on my phone.

The tweet was from a newspaper covering the Jequitinhonha Valley, whose latest headlines would often appear first on my screen. This one caught my attention, describing how two girls, aged 10 and 12, had made allegations of sexual abuse against Joel Cruz, the former mayor of a town called Taiobeiras. The name immediately jogged my memory. Twelve years earlier, and still on my probationary period at the *Daily Mirror*, I had requested leave to travel to Brazil so I could get married. To convince the editor, then Piers Morgan, to let me go I'd offered to write a feature story while I was there and he was most interested in one of my pitches, following up a report that had appeared in the Brazilian press about a 12-year-old girl who, according to a police investigation, had been 'auctioned' for her virginity.

So just a few days before my wedding, I found myself in Montes Claros, the town in northern Minas Gerais where the grotesque auction was reported to have taken place. The woman accused of organising it had already fled, but I managed to meet up with an acquaintance who had showed me the names of men who had made bids on the girl. Among them was Joel Cruz, who she told me was a well-known local mayor. Running out of time, I filed the story and managed to get on the first flight back to Belo Horizonte the next day, arriving just a few hours before the register office appointment.

So many thoughts were swirling around my mind as I got up to speak that night in Saffron Walden. If this was the same man who had been accused of abusing young girls, then he had been doing so for at least the last 12 years, if not longer. Although I had made a report to the special state prosecutor's office dealing with crimes committed by mayors after seeing Cruz's name, I hadn't heard if it had led to any kind of action against him. As we showed a video to those gathered that night, I picked up my phone again and looked at the article properly, recoiling at what I read. The two girls had told police that they, and other even younger children, including the five-year-old sister of one of them, would be taken to the politician's house by their own mothers, who would receive cash in return. I searched for Taiobeiras on Google Maps – it was a town in the Jequitinhonha Valley, halfway between Medina and Cândido Sales, right in the region where we were working. I knew these girls would probably be entirely alone and that we needed to take on their fight.

A week after we got back to Brazil, Warlei and I drove to Taiobeiras to find out more. The town felt cut off from the outside world at the end of a 30-mile straight road through wild bushland and dense plantations of towering eucalyptus trees, surrounded on its northern side by a rim of rugged mountains. It was also unexpectedly attractive with wide tree-lined avenues, whitewashed colonial buildings and green lawned squares framed with towering coconut trees — a disconcertingly pleasant setting for the horrendous things I was about to learn about it.

Before the trip I had spoken to Dan at *MailOnline* who had commissioned me to write a story about the case. After seeing the effect international media attention had on the case of the raffles in Cândido Sales, I hoped that it might at the least help focus the minds of those who could bring Joel Cruz to justice too. We started at the office of the public prosecutor, who according to the reports had interviewed the two girls and brought charges against Cruz. Dr Andrea Duraes, it turns out, wasn't only being incredibly brave in indicting the former mayor, by a long way the richest and most powerful person in the town, but she also had personal reasons for doing so.

Andrea was younger than I had imagined, a recently qualified prosecutor who smiled genially as she welcomed us into her office, ordering freshly-brewed coffee as she apologised for making us wait. "They call him Big Joel," she said. "He's a huge figure here. He won four terms as mayor, starting in the '70s up until 2002. He was in control of the town for 16 years. Many people here still love him, they say he did many good things for the town. It doesn't matter to them that he was abusing children here for decades."

Most young public prosecutors we'd met in other interior towns were only there to serve their mandatory two-year placements in the provinces, after which they could leave to take up positions in the big cities. But Andrea told us, "I'm from Taiobeiras too, I grew up here. Joel's crimes were always an open secret here. Everyone knew that he liked young girls and that he'd give money, jobs, even new houses, to mothers who let him abuse their daughters. Some of my friends were his victims too. He destroyed so many lives here."

Andrea remembered how, during his tenure as mayor, every public telephone in the town had the mayor's mobile number scribbled inside, so young girls needing money could easily call him and arrange a rendezvous. How he would groom girls by pulling up in his car next to groups of them in the street and hand out 50 real notes, his way of enticing them to knock on his door. And how he would reward his victims by giving them a brand new pink 'Brisa' bicycle, the type that at that time all poor girls dreamed of owning. "Girls riding the pink bikes became known as 'Joel's girls'," she said. "It became so well known that he was handing out the bikes to the girls he'd abused that no-one else wanted to buy them for their own daughters anymore."

Andrea left her hometown to go to law school, returning only a few years earlier to take up her new role as prosecutor. When, a few months before, she heard that a distraught 10-year-old girl had turned up at the police station claiming the former mayor was abusing her, all the memories came flooding back – as well as the realisation that, 13 years since he was last in power, and now aged 75, Cruz was the same monster who stalked the streets when she was a child and still committing the same horrendous crimes.

"She said her mother would drop her off at Cruz's house. There were other girls there too. She said his house was full of toys, children's programmes were playing on the TVs and the fridges were full of sweets and chocolate. While they were playing and eating, he would take them into his bedroom one by one.

"The doctor who examined her was horrified. Her body was so small she now has problems with her spine, as well as neurological problems because of the trauma. He would pass her around his friends. She said she would be forced to have sex with up to eight men a night. Her mother would make her use drugs so she would tolerate the violent abuse."

I asked where the girl was now and whether Cruz, and her mother, had been arrested.

"The girl is in a children's shelter here in the town. Her mother confirmed everything her daughter said, she's in jail. But not Joel. As soon as he found out about the charges he fled town. He's considered a fugitive. I imagine he thinks he can disappear until it all blows over and then come back like nothing ever happened, like he did the last time."

"The last time?"

"Yeah. Didn't you know? About ten years ago, other girls accused him of abusing them too. But he ran away, paid the girls and their families to retract their statements and even paid a hitman to kill the social worker who had convinced the girls to speak out. The case fell apart, and after that no-one ever dared accuse him again. Until now."

I was astonished. This man, whose name I had read 12 years earlier in connection with another shocking case of abuse, was clearly a prolific paedophile who preyed on the poor and vulnerable, using his wealth and power to do whatever he wanted, confident he would always get away with it. I asked Andrea about the poor social worker Cruz had murdered. "Oh no, he didn't die," she said. "He was shot point blank in the head, but by some miracle he survived. His name's Ronaldo. Here…" She scribbled his address on a scrap of paper. "Try speaking to him. But don't expect him to tell you anything. He's refused to utter Big Joel's name for the last eight years."

Half an hour later, I was knocking on the door of a shabby concrete house in a less attractive part of town. The windows were shuttered up, while the stepping stone pathway was almost lost to view in a tangle of tall weeds. We were about to make our way back to the car when we heard the clink of keys and the sliding of a lock before the door slowly creaked open. A man, with a balding head of wispy black hair and red, glazed eyes, squinted at us in the sunlight.

"Ronaldo?" I enquired.

"Yes, can I help?" He asked. His mouth skewed noticeably to the left as he spoke, distorting his words. I introduced myself.

"We wanted to speak to you about Big Joel."

"Oh, no, no, no, not interested," he muttered, retreating backwards into the darkness of his house and starting to close the door behind him.

"Haven't you heard?" I carried on. "Two young girls have said he abused them. The judge has ordered his arrest, but he's on the run, again."

Ronald froze for what seemed like an age, his hand on the back of the half-closed door as he gazed down at the floor, lost in thought. Finally, he looked up. "Well, you'd better come in, then."

Ronaldo, we had discovered, had once been Taiobeiras' most vocal activist, a radio presenter and self-taught journalist, not unlike Evany in Medina. The only local voice on the airwaves in the '80s and '90s, the whole town would tune in as he called out everything from potholes to political cronyism on his pirate radio station. But the shell of a man sitting in front of me, hunched forward on an unmade bed in a dark, dusty room, seemed very different.

"Joel destroyed my life," he sighed, reading my thoughts as I looked around. "My wife left me, nobody in town wanted to give me a job, I lost everything. It's only because of a miracle that I didn't lose my life as well. In the end I decided it wasn't worth it, he would never be brought to justice anyway. I was wrong to think that someone like me could stop someone like him."

I asked Ronaldo if he could tell me what happened and he reached underneath the bed, pulling out an old shoebox, full of newspaper clippings. He unfolded the newspaper articles and laid them neatly on the bed, and for the next few hours meticulously recounted the full story. It all began in 1993 when, as he arrived at his radio station one morning, two 11-year-old girls asked to leave their bicycles in the car park.

"They said they were on their way to school, but I watched them walk down the road and straight past the school gates. I walked after them. A little further on the mayor's official car pulled up next to them and they both got in. I got on my motorcycle and followed. The car drove into a sex motel.

"I started making enquiries and discovered that the mayor had taken young girls to all three sex motels in the town. They were always very poor girls. Joel would get their families on side by giving them money or buying things for them. In some cases he would completely furnish their homes with everything from beds to TVs and fridges."

During his investigations, Ronaldo came across a butcher's shop in town used by Cruz which was a front for a child prostitution ring. Inside, there was a catalogue of nude young girls in pornographic poses for clients to choose. The mayor and his friends were dropping by the butchers not to buy meat, but to secretly choose the next girl they would abuse. Ronaldo contacted a national TV programme called *Ratinho* who sent a team to investigate. Their undercover expose of the butcher's was broadcast all over Brazil on the national SBT channel.

"When the programme went on air Joel cut off the TV signal for the entire town so no-one could watch it," Ronaldo said. "Even so, the exposure led to the owner of the butcher's being arrested and jailed. But although Joel was a client, nothing happened to him."

Undeterred, Ronaldo continued to collect evidence on Cruz's crimes, even once filming the mayor with three naked girls by the swimming pool of a rented house after getting a tip-off he was using the property to carry out his abuse. He also managed to win the trust of some of the girls, eventually managing to persuade them to make a police statement about their ordeals.

But Cruz was always one step ahead. "As soon as a girl went to the police station to testify, Joel would send one of his lawyers round the family's house," he said. "They'd offer them money, or even properties, to retract her statement. The family of one girl, who was considered a key witness, was given a whole farm in exchange for her silence."

One by one, all the girls changed their minds and pulled out, Ronaldo said. Then one day he got a call from the town's prosecutor, telling him her superiors in the state capital had asked her to set up a parliamentary inquiry into Ronaldo's claims that Cruz was abusing girls in the town.

Although most of the girls had retracted their statements, an inquiry meant that he could give evidence against the mayor before a commission of senators and congressmen with powers to bring charges. At the same time the local police chief unarchived Ronaldo's previous evidence and the statements from the girls he had brought and charged Cruz with crimes of child sexual abuse and exploitation. Suddenly it looked like the tide was turning.

"Wait," I asked, remembering the statement I had made to the prosecutor in Belo Horizonte after seeing Cruz's name on the girl's phone. "When did this happen?"

"Let me see… it was the end of 2003. It was funny because no-one had really taken me that seriously until then."

I gasped. That was just a few months after I had made my report. It seemed incredible, but also not entirely implausible, that my rushed visit to the state prosecutor's office had somehow caused them to look differently at Ronaldo's claims and trigger a parliamentary inquiry into the mayor's alleged crimes. Even more incredible how, 12 years later, a tweet on my phone on the other side of the world had led to me this brave man's front door and to him breaking a vow of silence that had kept him a virtual prisoner in his home for the past eight years.

"So, what happened?" I asked, even more eager to hear every detail of the story. "Did Cruz get convicted?"

"Ha!" Ronaldo replied. "This is what happened," pointing to a lacerated scar on the side of his jaw, then the skewed left side of his mouth.

"When the arrest warrant was issued Cruz fled town. Then when he found out I was going to testify against him he sent his men to try to persuade me not to. They offered me half a million reals, but I refused. Then they started leaving coffins outside my house. That's when my wife left me, she was terrified.

"Then one night I was driving back to Taiobeiras through the eucalyptus plantations into town. Another car behind me had been flashing its lights, so I stopped at a clearing, thinking there was some problem with my car. The next thing I knew I was laying on the ground, everything going black. Look..."

Ronaldo pulled out an old Kodak film case from the shoebox and tipped out two bullets into his hand. "I was shot six times. These two bullets were buried in my head."

Ronaldo had hit the ground just in front of the gunman's car. And incredibly, just before he lost consciousness, he looked up and saw the number plate and, after waking up days later in hospital, managed to remember it. Police ran the plate through the national database – it was a rental car and the person who had rented it was no other than the mayor, Joel Cruz. The driver, who police later charged with discharging the shots, was a close friend of Cruz's who was found to have travelled to carry out the assassination from one of his ranches in the far north of Brazil where the mayor was hiding out.

After miraculously surviving being shot twice in the head at point-blank range, it would be a long, slow recovery for Ronaldo. But surely being caught ordering the murder of the man investigating his abuse of children would finally put the mayor behind bars? Ronaldo shook his head.

"He was charged with attempted murder, but after several months the judge closed the case against him, saying there wasn't enough evidence! Clearly Cruz's men had got to him too. The abuse and exploitation charges rumbled on though, but on the day he was supposed to be sentenced another judge declared him innocent. That was the day I realised it wasn't worth trying anymore. He was just too powerful for someone like me to take on. That was the day I gave up."

That afternoon we found out that Ronaldo wasn't the only person in Taiobeiras desperately trying to forget what Joel Cruz did to them. On his directions, we knocked on other doors in the town and, on what seemed like every street found women, now in their twenties and thirties, who had been abused by him when they were young girls. After we introduced ourselves to one woman, Samantha, now aged 23, she quickly closed the front door behind her so her husband and daughter wouldn't hear. "They don't know," she whispered. "But I think about it every day. I hate him so much. I was only 10 when he raped me. He destroyed so many lives. From my time, just the girls I knew who he abused, there were more than 50. But I was one of the lucky ones because I managed to make something of my life, have my own family and be happy. But many didn't.

"He'd give us mobile phones, branded clothes, beautiful shoes, everything. Which poor girl who didn't even have money to eat could have resisted that?"

Samantha told us of another former friend who, after being abused by Joel as a child, had spiralled into drug addiction. Marta, now also in her early twenties, was squatting in a derelict house a few blocks down, on the other side of the same road. Closing Samantha's garden gate behind us, Warlei crossed the road, but as I followed a motorbike suddenly stopped in my path.

"What are you doing here?" the rider demanded in a gruff, menacing voice.

"Er, just visiting… some friends," I replied, taken aback. I hastily checked for traffic and began to cross.

"You've been going around, asking questions. What's it for?"

I pretended I hadn't heard and caught up with Warlei on the other side. The man deliberately revved his engine as he spun round and roared off, throwing a cloud of dust behind him.

We found Marta hunched on the pavement edge in front of the shell of a derelict building on the street corner, which appeared to have once been gutted by fire. She was thin and gaunt, her eyes sunken and appearing decades older than that of a woman in her early twenties. When I asked about Joel Cruz her face immediately contorted in anger. "I hate him," she spat. "My father, he still won't speak to me. He thought it was my fault. He blamed me for becoming one of Joel's girls.

"Look at me. He did this to me. He forced me to use drugs so I wouldn't fight back. By the age of 11 I was too old for him. That's when I started to use crack.

"For a long time I wanted to kill him. If I saw him in the street I would try to attack him, I didn't care that he might have me knocked off like he's done to some other girls. My friends said they wanted to chop off his penis, but I knew that wouldn't work, because he'd still have his finger. I wanted his head off.

"Now I just want to forget him. I've lost hope of him ever paying for what he did. Now I only hope in the justice of God, that soon he will die and face his punishment in Hell."

At that moment the motorbike growled past us, stopping on the far side of the road before turning around and riding by again, more slowly this time. He stopped just a metre from the kerbside where we were sitting, this time without saying a word. Marta became restless and lowered her voice. "Listen, you'd better go. His people, they get to know everything that goes on. They're everywhere."

It was already around the time we had planned to leave anyway, to allow us time to get back to Belo Horizonte sometime before midnight. We thanked Marta and walked back to where we had parked the car before finding our way through town and back to the long, straight road that had led us here.

The hour-long journey through the eucalyptus forest was an anxious one this time, with frequent glances behind us through the rear-view mirror, for we now knew that somewhere along this road Ronaldo had been hunted down and left for dead, two bullets buried in his head. Only when we were back on the motorway, joining the never-ending procession of trucks heading south, did we allow ourselves to breathe more easily and reflect on what had been an unexpectedly harrowing day. Joel Cruz, it seemed, was untouchable.

For over four decades he'd had Taiobeiras under his complete control, using his wealth and position to systematically abuse hundreds of poor girls, in complete impunity. Even as we drove away, it was difficult to comprehend what we had just witnessed, an entire town that was forever scarred by such a prolific and powerful paedophile. That so many had kept quiet for so many years for fear of this man made the bravery of two little girls, who had defied their own mothers to walk to the police station and speak out, even more extraordinary.

20

A THOUSAND LETTERS

Thoughts continued to crowd my head as the eucalyptus forests shrank into the distance behind us. I'd never imagined we'd find a place where there were so many girls – many now grown women – whose childhoods had been destroyed by one man. "We have to do something…" I finally said to Warlei. "But what? It's no wonder no-one thinks he'll ever be brought to justice."

Warlei, lost in thought himself, let minutes pass before he replied. "I know… The town, it's so cut off… it's as if no-one imagines that anyone else would be interested in what happens there."

We drove further in silence, keeping a steady pace as trucks snapped at our bumper or screamed past us. I remembered how this all began, in an English church, during a speaking tour when we met many people who were concerned about what was going on thousands of miles away. And we were also starting to get supporters from other parts of the world, such as Australia, New Zealand and Canada. An idea started to form in my mind. "What if we got people to write letters?" I suggested. "To the police chief who's in charge of finding him… telling him they know about it, that they are following the case, and they're counting on him to bring the mayor to justice?"

As soon as we were back in Belo Horizonte, I wrote up the story and sent it off, along with the photos we had taken in Taiobeiras, including Ronaldo holding the newspaper cuttings and the two bullets in his hand. It was published the following night on *MailOnline* and within a day had been shared over 1,000 times. Next, I wrote an email to our supporters, with a link to the story, asking for their help. We needed them to write letters to the police chief in Taiobeiras who was responsible for arresting Cruz, I explained, asking for him to redouble efforts to find and catch him. I included the words in Portuguese which they could copy onto a letter or postcard, and the address to post them. It was the first time we'd asked those on our email list for anything except a monthly donation, so had no idea how many might actually do it, but figured that even a handful of letters was better than doing nothing.

***

In January 2016 Holly kept her word and moved to Cândido Sales to begin laying the ground for our new Pink House in the town. She rented a tiny flat next to a clothes shop in the bustling town centre, with tiled floors and cast iron barred window frames, at the top of a narrow flight of concrete steps. It was an incredibly brave thing for a single 25-year-old woman to do and, although she never showed it, quite a culture shock for the primary school teacher from Bangor. During our phone conversations we'd often have to pause while a loudspeaker car passed by on the street outside, drowning our voices with booming announcements about low prices or unmissable events over the bouncing sounds of forró songs. She would also always know when it was time to take her rubbish bags out – the bin lorry blasted out the *Mission Impossible* soundtrack as it came up the street, even while people were still sleeping. And at 6pm without fail every day the Catholic Church would invade everyone's homes, playing a synthesised version of *Ave Maria* at full volume. The middle of the night wasn't peaceful either – the rumble of trucks passing through town on the BR-116 a few blocks away was a constant soundtrack to life there, anytime of the day or night.

Holly began her work by linking up with some of the women from Zeno and Ivanette's church who had expressed an interest in helping us. Among them was a woman called Claudia, a nurse who worked nights at the town's hospital and lived a block further up from Holly on the same street. Holly and Claudia began meeting up in the afternoons, walking the streets until late in the hope of finding girls who needed help, or visiting the ones they already knew about in their homes. Early on, Holly realised she already knew two other them, sisters Luiza and Liziane, who had moved there from Medina where they had sometimes frequented the Pink House. They were now living with their old infirm grandmother, but with hardly any food at home and their gran, who was blind and deaf, incapable of properly taking care of them. The pretty sisters, aged just 14 and 15, had quickly fallen into the ever-present world of sexual exploitation. Holly was alarmed when she saw them again for the first time. Swapping their bodies for money or food had already become second nature. But the fact the girls already knew and were fond of Holly helped her and Claudia win the trust of other girls in the town.

It was during one of their long walks that they came across a thin, pale girl with messy bleached blonde hair, standing motionless on the green metal footbridge that arched over the slow-moving parade of trucks on the BR-116. As they got closer Claudia recognised her – it was Maira, the girl Ivanette had told us about when Warlei and I saw her for the first time, and who Claudia also knew from her frequent admissions to the hospital emergency room in the small hours of the morning. She looked uneasy as the two women approached her, but didn't turn and run as she had often done when Ivanette had tried to speak with her, intrigued both by Claudia's calm, reassuring voice and Holly's bouncy enthusiasm and strong foreign accent. Before long, Maira, now 14, was tripping over her words as she chatted about her life, then accepted their offer to walk her back home so they could get to know her better.

They entered a simple brick house and the women began to understand why Maira would spend so much time roaming the streets. Her grandfather, grandmother and older sister, cradling a newborn baby, sat on a threadbare sofa. All three turned and glared at her with a look of unconcealed disdain.

"What's she doing here?" her grandmother barked. "That lazy piece of work never lifts a finger in here. All she wants is to bum around the streets all day getting into trouble. She can stay there as far as I'm concerned."

"She's a waste of space that one," boomed the grandfather, an intimidating man with a potato-shaped nose and a bushy moustache. "We've tried everything with her, but it's no use. Her mother would be ashamed."

The cheery demeanour with which Maira had led Holly and Claudia to her home disappeared in an instant. For all the time she was inside, she didn't say a word and looked no-one in the eye, her whole body flinching every time her grandfather spoke. Maira, the women soon discovered, had lost her mother to a drug overdose when she was 11, but felt unloved and unwanted by the grandparents who had reluctantly taken her in. This neglect pushed her towards the pimps and traffickers on the motorway, who always showed an interest in her – although only for the value she had as a marketable product.

Back on the cobbled hill outside her house, Maira wiped a defiant tear from her eye.

"All they do is shout and curse me with swear words. That's why I hardly ever sleep at home. They don't like me."

As their friendship with Maira deepened, Holly and Claudia, alongside the other women who began to join them on the streets, got to know other girls, including her best friend Tábita, and Sofia, who lived opposite her house on the same street. Both girls were 13 and both, they discovered, were being taken by their own mothers to sell their bodies on the BR-116.

Often when they came across Maira and Tábita standing on the edge of the motorway late at night, her mother was not far behind them, while Sofia's mum would drag her out of bed and walk her to one of the roadside brothels whenever she needed extra cash. Regularly spending all night in bars, brothels and truckers' cabins, the girls would often fall through their front doors after sunrise, spending the day sleeping instead of going to school. Yet in moments of candour they would all talk of their dreams of studying to become a lawyer or doctor. After several weeks, Holly persuaded Maira and Sofia to return to classes, enrolling them in night school, partly because it was a way of keeping them off the streets, but also because they had missed so many years that they would have been in classes with five and six-year-olds in normal daytime school. Holly and Claudia began taking it in turns to collect the friends from their homes and walk them to their classes, meeting them later to walk them back home. The plan worked, but not always. On some evenings they would see the girls jumping out of their bedroom windows and fleeing when they saw the women walking down the hill to collect them.

It was when she sensed resistance from the girls she was trying to reach that Holly would bring out her secret weapon – her home cooking. One day, she came across Layane, the girl I had met a year earlier with Fabio while writing a story about World Cup trafficking gangs, who was with her two sisters, aged 13 and 17. Back then, Layane had changed her mind about joining her friend Vanesa travelling to Salvador but, now 14, she was even more deeply involved in exploitation. Tough and temperamental, she was now known by her nickname 'Little Fire' and spoken of by locals with a mixture of loathing and fear.

Perhaps for that reason she wasn't interested in reciprocating Holly's attempts at making friends. So when Holly invited all three back to her flat for cake, the three sisters were taken aback – they were more used to being looked down on, or looked over, and certainly nothing as civilised as being invited to someone else's house for cake. They hesitantly accepted. Back at Holly's they sat together awkwardly on her sofa, glancing at each other, as she rattled around in the kitchen before bringing out her speciality banana and chocolate sprinkles cake with a pot of fresh coffee. Just as she'd hoped, once they began to tuck in the conversation finally started to flow.

Before long, girls began finding their way to Holly's flat on their own, knocking on her door when they were in trouble or just needing someone to talk to. It meant that, much sooner than we had expected, we knew we needed to find a building that would become our new Pink House in the town – even though we didn't yet have enough monthly donations to fund a new project. Warlei and Orlindo travelled up to Cândido Sales and found a good-sized property at the end of one of the roads leading from the motorway, not far from the poorer districts where many of the girls lived.

There were no plans yet to officially launch Meninadança in the town, but the house – not yet painted pink, and still unfurnished – soon became a place girls knew they could run to. Holly, Claudia and new volunteer Zilda would bring in board games to play, dance to music on their mobile phones and take turns to bring in cake, bread and – with the water company yet to connect the property – bottles of water. It didn't matter that they had to improvise, or sit on the floor in bare rooms. For girls like Maira, Sofia and Layane, the house was already a place they felt safe and where there were people who loved them for who they were.

It was during a trip to visit Holly and the team in Cândido Sales, while tucking into her homemade tikka masala, that my phone rang, a number with the area code 38, which I didn't recognise. It was Andrea, the public prosecutor from Taiobeiras and there was a glow of delight in her voice.

"Matt, they caught Big Joel!" she exclaimed.

"Whoa!" I gasped, causing the others in the room to cease chatting and look over. It had been four months since we asked people to write letters to the police chief and we hadn't yet heard whether they had even reached their destination and, if they had, if they had made any difference. "How? Where?" I asked.

"The police, they tracked him down to the Amazon rainforest. He was hiding out in a ranch in the jungle. He's under arrest and being flown back."

It wasn't much of a detour to pass by Taiobeiras on the way back to Belo Horizonte, so Warlei and I decided to pay the town's police chief a visit to find out more about the operation and thank him for his efforts. Dr Alessandro Lopes was a bearded man in a crisp shirt and tie who bounded up and shook our hands vigorously after we arrived at the town's civil police station. Back in his office, he emptied a tray of around 20 letters onto his oak wood desk.

"These are just the ones that arrived today," he said. "We've been getting dozens every day. Every day I would arrive at work and those letters reminded me that Cruz still wasn't behind bars and that I needed to do more."

"How many letters have arrived altogether?" asked Warlei.

"Oh, a thousand, maybe more. When they first started arriving I was astonished, I had no idea who was behind it. But I knew what I needed to do with them."

Alessandro explained how he opened all the letters, then attached every single one to Cruz's case file, before sending it to his superiors in the nearest large town, Salinas. Equally impressed, the police chief there forwarded them to the regional police headquarters in Montes Claros, an important city in the north of the state. There, they were sent to state capital Belo Horizonte, where the pile of letters arrived on the desk of the most important police chief in Minas Gerais. The letters, and the sheer number of them, moved him too, so much so that he assigned a team of his best investigators just to find Cruz. When they tracked him down to his remote ranch in the dense rainforests of the state of Pará, 1,500 miles north, they sent a team of five agents to raid the hideaway with heavily-armed local police and arrest him. Alessandro seemed in no doubt that there wouldn't have been the will or urgency – and certainly not the resources – to hunt Cruz down if it were not for those letters arriving from around the world. We were astonished at how this simple act of writing a letter, multiplied hundreds of times by ordinary people who wanted to make a difference, could have succeeded in bringing about such a breathtaking result.

"I'm so glad we caught him," Alessandro said as we got up to leave. "I interviewed the 10-year-old girl. Every time she tried to say anything she began to cry. She told me he had ruined her life. I had to stop the interview because I began to cry too, it was so hard to hear. Cruz is a monster. Hopefully now this town will begin to heal."

Two weeks later, Warlei and I were invited to join the civil police at a press call in Montes Claros, when the captured mayor would be presented to the media. We arrived by plane the next morning, and found that we had been allocated our spaces on the press conference desk, along with plates bearing our names, between Alessandro and the civil police's chief investigator. Once members of the press had filled the room each person was introduced, with the police making clear that he wouldn't have been caught if it weren't for Meninadança and our hundreds of letter writers around the world. "I was surprised, it was the first time in my career I'd seen anything like it," Alessandro replied to a journalist's question. "I felt very motivated to see that we were not alone and that people around the world also wanted justice."

Once members of the press were assembled, Joel Cruz was

brought out, handcuffed. Shuffling slowly in flip-flops, he didn't say a word as cameras flashed and journalists lobbed questions. Once he had sat down in a plastic chair beside the press conference table, I went over and took some pictures of him on my mobile phone. Up close, unshaven and doddering, the monster who had terrorised his town and destroyed the lives of hundreds of young girls cut a pathetic figure, although his refusal to speak, but still look me and others in the eye as we took his photo, still carried the sense of arrogance of someone who thought he would have the last laugh.

This wasn't the end of the story, of course. He was yet to be convicted in court and he had every reason to believe he could still buy his way out of this one like he'd done the other times. But for now at least, Big Joel, the man who thought he was too powerful to ever be held to account, would be going back to a prison cell. I couldn't resist a last word – one I can't repeat here – in his ear before he was led away.

21

PINK RIBBONS

I was already feeling a little flushed when I got up to speak to those gathered at our annual conference, this year held in Kingston, southwest London. Warlei, Rita and I had only gotten off the flight the night before, so I put it down to the long journey and stale aeroplane air. As the day wore on my muscles started to ache too, but I kept going, promising myself I'd get an early night and sleep it off. There was so much to share – the successes we were seeing in Medina, the beginnings of a new Pink House in Cândido Sales and the capture of Joel Cruz just weeks earlier. We had hoped the event would persuade more people to get involved, helping us raise the funds we needed to maintain the new project. Many of the 150 people who had turned up were visibly moved by what they heard.

That evening, I fell straight to sleep as soon as I hit the Premier Inn bed, only to wake up hours later, sweating so much the sheets and duvet were completely drenched. For the next few hours, hot flushes and cold shivers would come in waves as sweat poured off my body to the point of dehydration. I decided to get some water from the vending machine down the corridor, but after a few steps my legs were buckling under me and I had to return to bed. The next morning I woke with an excruciating headache, pain behind my eyes and aching limbs.

We had planned to stay in the UK for a week with a number of other meetings organised around the country, but with no let up from the fever and chills I stayed in my room for the next two nights. I wondered if it was one of the diseases that were common in Brazil like dengue or malaria. It was only after the third day, when a red rash began to engulf my entire body, my joints began to seize up and my feet and hands became red and swollen, that I realised what I'd been struck down with – Zika.

Brazil was the epicentre of the new mosquito-borne virus which was causing alarm around the world, especially with just months to go before the start of the Olympics in Rio de Janeiro. Zika had been linked with birth defects and other serious illnesses and was being reported as a 'killer virus', with a number of prominent athletes refusing to participate in the Games. I'd covered the story myself for several newspapers and just a few weeks before our trip to the UK had travelled to the town of Goiana, Pernambuco state, which had the highest infection rate in the country. *The Daily Mail* headline read: "The world's most infected town: Inside the tiny Brazilian 'death zone' where 500 A DAY are struck down with deadly Zika virus". I remember standing in a hospital waiting room packed by hundreds of Zika patients coughing and spluttering. It now seemed entirely possible that while I was there it had got me too.

While I knew this was a horrific virus for pregnant women, having held babies born with 'shrunken head syndrome', I knew that for me it would most likely just be a rough week, although that didn't make it any less bearable. Halfway through the week, I felt as if I had aged 50 years; my knees, ankles and toes were stiff and aching. Once the rash had subsided, my whole body began to itch. My skin felt like it was crawling with thousands of tiny ants and as much as I scratched and scratched, nothing relieved it. These were all symptoms of Zika, but I decided not to visit the doctor. I hadn't heard of another Brit who had caught it so didn't want to end up being prevented from catching my return flight, or on the newspaper front pages.

Almost a week after the symptoms had started, they stopped almost as suddenly, just in time for the journey home. The following week I was well enough to travel to Rio de Janeiro to do a story about the so-called 'rat kids' who earned £1 a day sifting through rubbish pouring into the city's bay, which would be hosting the sailing competition during the Olympics in just two months' time. While I was there, one of the editors of the new national newspaper *New Day* called me about another story and I happened to mention that I'd just recovered after coming down with Zika. She asked me to write an account of what happened, which I obliged, thinking it would be a first-person feature somewhere in the health section. But to my shock the next morning the story was the newspaper's splash: 'Brit's Zika battle after he catches disease on maternity ward'.

One of the first messages I got was from Chris Rogers, the BBC newsreader with whom I'd done the *Panorama* special who found out about my 'plight' as he was reading out the front pages live on the BBC News channel. I later saw the footage of him losing his train of thought as he saw my photo while reading the headline. "Oh, it's Matt, he's a friend. I hope he's alright. I must give him a call," he worried.

I assured everyone that I was fully recovered, but it didn't stop the barrage of requests to appear on British TV, including from

BBC Breakfast and *Good Morning Britain*, causing me to delay my flight home from Rio so I could do the live interviews from my hotel at four in the morning. That afternoon, as I strolled along Copacabana's beachside promenade, I reflected on the crazy last few days.

I knew why there was so much interest in me getting Zika, the same reason why newspapers wanted to publish stories about youngsters wading through the Rio sewage to help their families pay the bills. In just a few months, Brazil was about to be the stage of the greatest show on Earth, the Olympic Games, when over two weeks the world's best athletes would descend on this city and the whole world would be watching.

I thought of some of the girls whose paths had crossed ours in recent months – the 10-year-old drugged and sold to Taiobeiras' most powerful man, Maira, Tábita and Sofia in Cândido Sales, or the girls sold as raffle prizes in nearby Encruzilhada, then blamed by those who were supposed to protect them when word got out. Of course, Brazil will want to show only its best side to the watching world. How could we also shine the spotlight on the plight of its most vulnerable?

Back in Belo Horizonte, I gathered the team together in the Meninadança office.

"The Olympics begin in a few months and everyone will be talking about Brazil. We need to get them talking about the BR-116 too," I said. Everyone nodded their agreement.

"It has to be something that will catch people's attention. So I've been thinking, what if we walk along the BR-116, from Medina to Cândido Sales, carrying a flame, just like the Olympic torch? We can say we're carrying a torch for the girls of the BR-116…?"

Warlei, Orlindo and Lorene looked at me in astonishment, but were too polite to dismiss my idea out of hand.

"Okay…" said Lorene, finally breaking the silence. "It's a long way, maybe a hundred kilometres. And it might be quite dangerous – have you seen how trucks hurtle around those corners? So, who are you thinking will do it?"

"Well, at least me and Warlei. The others can be our support team."

Warlei spat out his coffee comically. "Well, I was happy when they awarded us the Olympics, but I didn't realise I'd have to compete as well!" he joked. The others, more relaxed now they knew they wouldn't be expected to walk themselves, started discussing how we could make the scheme work. It would probably take four days of solid walking, bringing us through one town, Divisa Alegre, and several other small communities or gas stations where there would probably be a place to sleep for the night. We would have to average around 30km a day – quite achievable, except we knew that much of the terrain between Medina and Cândido Sales was mountainous with steep climbs and descents. We also had no idea what walking along a badly-maintained highway pummelled by heavy trucks would look, how we might be affected by the hot sun beating down and soaking up the asphalt underneath us, or what other dangers we might encounter in some of the remotest parts, which even while driving through seemed wild and treacherous.

In the following weeks, the plan started taking shape. It soon became clear that it wouldn't be practical to carry with us an Olympic-type flame – there weren't any similar ones available to buy and anything else would be too heavy to hold aloft for a long period of time. Instead, we decided we would tie bright pink ribbons on each of the numbered kilometre signs we passed, another way of lighting up the highway – a ribbon tied to a sign every kilometre along that 100km stretch would be unmissable to anyone driving along it and to the local communities around. We also decided that, as Warlei and I walked, a team would do outreach events on gas station forecourts and truck stops, as well as town squares along the same route, making others aware that child sexual exploitation was a crime.

We never intended for the walk to be a sponsored event, until one of our supporters replied to the email I sent out about our plans asking if they could donate for each kilometre we walked. The offer started me thinking – why not ask people, instead of sponsoring our walk, to adopt one of the 100 kilometres between Medina and Cândido Sales by giving a small amount per month? In return we could write their names on the pink ribbons that we were going to tie on to each kilometre sign and in the process guarantee the monthly funding we needed to run our new Pink House.

I imagined that stretch of the BR-116, which according to that Federal Highway Police report was the worst stretch of the whole highway for child sexual exploitation, lined with pink ribbons, each bearing the name of someone living on the other side of the world. For supporters it would be a way they could speak out for the girls and show them and their communities that people around the world cared about them and wanted to see change.

****

Back in Medina, Rita had decided to leave as coordinator of the Pink House to concentrate on her ambitions to go into local politics. One of the young members of staff, Cristiane, had over the past months shown leadership qualities and an ability to win over the girls and, reluctantly at first, agreed to take over. At the same time, more and more girls were knocking on the door of the Pink House as, following our courtroom victory for Emilly and the 700-strong protest march through town, a flicker of hope had been lit in many lives.

The two-storey house on the corner of Rita's street quickly became too small, so we moved to a more spacious building on the main road into town from the motorway, just before the wide tree-lined avenue arrived at the town centre square. The new Pink House had more rooms, a large outside space and even a swimming pool, much to the girls' excitement.

What was most pleasing was seeing many of the girls who had already spent some time with us now bringing in others that needed help, encouraging them towards the right path once they were inside.

One day, a group of girls arrived holding the hands of a friend who had never been inside the Pink House before. Fifteen-year-old Samara was timid and wary at first, but soon settled in as she felt the warmth of welcome and realised it really was the safe place they had told her about. As her confidence grew, Samara began to lose her inhibitions, especially during the dance lessons where she would break into gleeful, involuntary smiles as she found her rhythm and poise. During the daily conversation circles she seemed less willing to open up, but instead listened intently to the often animated discussions.

One day, Samara asked if she could speak privately with Cristiane, who she'd grown closest to in the past few weeks. Seeing her eyes filling up with tears, Cristiane immediately gave her a reassuring hug, then took her into the Pink House office to talk in private.

"Before I started coming here I thought it was normal. I had no idea…" Samara started, her voice faltering.

"What do you mean?" Cristiane asked.

"I didn't know it was wrong. I didn't like it, but I didn't know it shouldn't happen. I just thought that every girl… had to do those things with their dad."

Tears cascaded down Samara's face as Cristiane held her tight. It was the first time she had told anyone about the abuse, which she had endured every day for the last 10 years. Gripping Cristiane's hands tight, she told her how her father would summon her to his bedroom and lock the door while her mother and brothers carried on as normal outside, doing their chores or watching TV, clearly aware of what was happening but apparently entirely unconcerned.

It was all she had ever known, and all she could remember, until she stepped inside the Pink House and began to hear a different story: that it was in fact a crime, that she had a choice and that girls like her had as much right as anyone else over what happened to their own bodies. Samara sobbed for over an hour as Cristiane cradled her gently in her arms, stroking her hair and telling her everything would be alright. They were tears of unconsolable heartbreak, of a decade of pain and broken dreams – but also of relief, the hope that her nightmare might finally end.

It was already mid-afternoon and it wouldn't be long before Samara's family would be expecting her. Cristiane's head was spinning. What this young girl had confided in her was the most horrific thing she had ever heard and she knew she couldn't allow her to return home. After speaking with the team in Belo Horizonte, she asked Samara if she felt able to repeat what she had told her to someone else – a policeman. Unwilling at first, Cristiane managed to persuade her that it was the best thing to do. Half an hour later was holding her hand as Samara made a formal report of her abuse at the police station. Later that night, her dad was arrested, and casually confirmed everything his daughter had said. However he wasn't expecting to be handcuffed and read his rights, and struggled and shouted as he was led away by the police.

But if Samara had believed she would find solace and support in her family after bravely speaking out, she was wrong. She found herself an outcast, berated and bad-mouthed by her mother and brothers who were furious that she had got her father arrested for something they saw as, at its worst, just a minor misdemeanour. Disowned by those who should have reassured her of their love, and even shunned in the street by other family members and friends of her father, she had to stay with a more sympathetic aunt and uncle in another part of town. Fortunately, they lived behind Cristiane's grandmother's house, where she knew she could always find her, along with a sympathetic ear or a shoulder to cry on.

Over the next few months, Cristiane and the other Pink House staff did what they could to ensure Samara was never alone, often taking her out at weekends, staying with her in the evenings and accompanying her to further interviews with police or social services. At first, we were all impressed by Samara's unwavering resolve and her belief that she would get justice, empowered by what she had heard in the Pink House conversation circles. But as time went on, and weeks turned into months with little progress on her case, the young girl began to crack under the strain. One day, Cristiane turned over her hand to find her forearm criss-crossed with deep red lacerations where she had slashed herself with a knife. Despite their continued love and support, she slowly began to drift away from the Pink House team, turning up less often and no longer answering Cristiane's phone calls or messages. After hearing disturbing reports from some of the other girls that she had started to use drugs, Cristiane would walk the streets at nights, hoping she might find her and convince her to come back.

That moment came when Cristiane least expected it as she was walking home from a Sunday evening church service. When she saw the silhouette of a girl's thin body, hunched up in a dark corner of a patch of wasteland, she knew immediately it was Samara. She ran over to find her clutching her legs and sobbing silently.

"I can't take it anymore," she whimpered. "I just want to die."

Cristiane cradled her in her arms, rocking her as she tried to calm her trembling body. "You can't give up," she whispered in her ear. "Come back, you're not on your own."

"I was stupid to think he'd face justice," she sniffed. "Who'd ever do that for someone like me? There's no point anymore. I don't want to keep on living."

Cristiane shushed her lovingly. "You will get justice," she assured her, wiping away her tears. "You will be happy again, I promise."

A month later, the date for the trial of Samara's father finally came through. Samara, now back at the Pink House, listened calmly as Cristiane sat her down and read her the court papers, but she didn't show any emotion or excitement. She'd given

Cristiane the benefit of the doubt, but still wouldn't allow herself to believe she might get justice. As the days counted down to the trial, we knew that what happened on that day – October 2, 2016 – would either revive her hopes and dreams, or bury them forever.

22

WE ARE AGAINST IT

Two weeks before the grand opening ceremony of the Olympic Games in Rio de Janeiro, Warlei and I stood next to the kilometre 76 sign on the BR-116, opposite the entrance to Medina. Looking ahead at the winding motorway as it disappeared northwards into the distance, we were apprehensive about what the next four days would bring. We'd be pounding every inch of that asphalt, over the mountain range and the vast backcountry wilderness we'd often driven through, past those eerie truck stops and isolated hamlets that appeared out of nowhere, all the way to Cândido Sales. Black clouds swarmed the skies above us – it was relief in a way that the usual hot sun wouldn't be scorching our backs, but it also raised the possibility of a tropical downpour as we navigated the narrow hard shoulder, which was even more concerning.

Starting on number 76, we tied a pink ribbon to every kilometre sign we passed – odd numbers on the left side, even numbers on the right – each bearing the name of the person who had adopted it. It seemed an even more powerful gesture while we were doing it, as if we were claiming each remote kilometre, showing that people thousands of miles away knew and cared about what was happening to girls there. As we posted photos of the signs we had tied ribbons to, more people signed up, until every single one of the hundred kilometres had been adopted. Once we finished, we had the monthly funding to fully fund the new Pink House in Cândido Sales. And anyone driving that notorious stretch of motorway would see a ribbon every 40 seconds or so, the so-called 'corridor of child prostitution' threaded with a line of bright pink.

Warlei and I started off from Medina with a spring in our step, but began to flail about five hours in as the road undulated up and down through endless parched bushland. We had aimed to walk until the tiny hamlet of Cariri, the next habitation of any kind after Medina, around 30 miles north. But it was already nearly 6pm when, with five miles to go, we were climbing painfully up a steep incline when first Warlei's legs, then my own, seized up in protest and simply refused to carry on. Finding ourselves unable to take even one more step forward, we sat down on the kerbside until our support van, driven by Orlindo and Lorene, passed by to rescue us and take us the rest of the way to Cariri. There, in a simple truckers' hotel, Warlei, who had been feeling the most pain as we'd walked, took off his shoes and carefully peeled off his socks, revealing both feet covered in a dozen blisters. Later on that night, after we'd decided to find something to eat and hardly managed to hobble over the road to the kerbside burger van, we wondered if we might have to admit defeat after just one day.

Thankfully though, the night's sleep did enough to rejuvenate us and get our bodies cooperating again. The next morning we set off from the exact spot from where we'd been picked up and, albeit at a slower pace, managed to complete the next day's goal of reaching a huge sprawling truck park called Faisão on a flat plateau of red earth on the highest point of our journey, a thousand metres above sea level. There, our aches and pains seemed rather pathetic when we met two men coming in the opposite direction, wearing worn out flip flops and pushing their belongings on the back of a wheelbarrow. They couldn't afford the bus, so had set off from Garanhuns, a town 800 miles north and were walking all the way to Vítoria, 500 miles further south, joking, singing and swigging cachaça rum as they went.

Our walking was just a small part of our overall campaign. A team of 15 young volunteers who had come up from Belo Horizonte were marching ahead of us. Each wore a T-shirt emblazoned with the campaign slogan 'I Am Against…' – a reference to the climate in Brazil at the time of declaring your political position – with the added words 'Child Sexual Exploitation'. They would stop in truck parks, gas stations and village squares along the way, handing out leaflets, advice cards and bumper stickers and doing street theatre and musical performances, communicating to locals, as well as those passing through, that child sexual exploitation was a crime. By the second day, some trucks began to sound their horns as they passed Warlei and I trudging along the motorway shoulder, wearing the same bright pink T-shirts as the team. Some had our 'I Am Against' stickers in their windows or bumpers, which we knew would soon be taken to far flung places all over Brazil. As the message began to filter through in the region, people started coming up to us as we passed through their communities. Some congratulated us for shining a light on the problem and seemed relieved to offload what they knew about the murky world of sexual abuse and exploitation in their midst. They included two young boys, aged around 12, who caught up with us as we walked along the motorway on the outskirts of the town of Divisa Alegre on the afternoon of the third day.

"You're the ones putting the pink ribbons on the signs, aren't you?" one said.

"That's right," I said. "Have you heard about us?"

"Yeah we saw those people performing in the town square. Hey misters, you need to do something to help girls here. Our sister, she's being abused by a man here. I don't think it's right, but whenever I say anything everybody tells me to keep my mouth shut."

We'd heard about Divisa Alegre from people in Cândido Sales, the next town north. Just over the state border into Minas Gerais, truckers often had to stop for several days while their cargo and papers were inspected and that inevitably meant the young daughters of poor families were particularly at risk. We congratulated the two brothers for thinking differently and standing up for their sister and gave them Meninadança's WhatsApp number so we could help them report the abuse to the authorities.

It wasn't long before our trek caught the attention of international press, who were already gathered for the Olympics 600 miles south, to cover the scandal of child prostitution along its longest road. *Fox News* published a story headlined 'Just outside Rio's Olympic Village, girls as young as 9 recruited for sex', pointing out that the BR-116 also passed just a few miles from where one of the event sites. Australia's biggest news website, *news.au*, also highlighted the plight of young girls "just a few kilometres from the glittering new stadiums where the world's elite athletes are gathering to battle it out for Olympic glory". Describing our protest walk along the BR-116, it went on, "As the final preparations are made on Rio's thirty-two sporting venues, Meninadança is tying pink ribbons along the highway." And the *Huffington Post* also ran a report on Brazil's forgotten girls, quoting me saying, "You should not underestimate what they are really going through. They are treated as nothing, as objects, and men have no qualms about harming them."

It was around midday on the fourth day when we finally reached the long bridge just before Cândido Sales and carefully edged our way along the narrow concrete edge between the trucks thundering past us and the dizzying sheer drop to the river 15 metres below us. At the other end were Holly and Claudia, who walked with us for the last stretch to the new Pink House, freshly painted bright pink and ready to open its doors.

We showered and changed, then, as the light began to fade, made our way to the main square where a special event was about to start in front of the town hall to officially inaugurate our new project. Intrigued, townsfolk were starting to gather and by the time the loud speakers screeched to life, hundreds had come to find out what was going on. More wandered over from the burger bars and popcorn carts on the other side of the square as pounding music began and the girls who Holly and the rest of our fledging team had been getting to know did their first public performance, bravely dancing and beaming excited smiles. They included Maira, the the girl who would once curl up 'like an armadillo' whenever anyone tried to get close and Layane, or 'Little Fire', who I thought I'd never see again after the last time I met her; she was going off with a trafficking gang to Salvador. By the time Claudia passed over the microphone to me, I could hardly contain the emotions bubbling up inside.

My voice echoed around the square as I explained how Warlei

and I had walked for four days on foot to arrive in the town. "We did it to show girls that they are not alone, that no-one has the right to treat them like objects to be bought and sold… and now we've arrived in Cândido Sales, we're here for good and that's what we'll be doing here too.

"This is a new chapter for this town, where the voices of those who shout 'We Are Against' the sexual exploitation of children will drown out those who do it or profit from it. So let's shout it together, 'We are against it! We are against it!'…"

I hadn't planned on leading the crowd in a chant against sexual exploitation, especially in that place where we knew so many were involved or complicit in it, but after I'd started I had to run with it. At first the Pink House staff and girls in the front row shouted with me, punching their fists in the air, then other onlookers nearby joined in. Perhaps it was more out of kind sympathy for me than anything else, but soon hundreds of locals gathered in that square were shouting 'We Are Against It!' I then declared our new Pink House open, still buzzing at the town's warm reception to our arrival. I had no idea of the battles we were still to fight, some involving some of those very people standing on the square that night.

****

A week later, still with sore legs and feet, I stood amongst another multitude – the tens of thousands of people gathered inside Rio's Maracanã stadium for the opening ceremony of the Olympic Games. Below me, thousands of performers danced in flamboyant costumes, perfectly choreographed on a massive digital floor before the roof exploded in fireworks and confetti in a spectacle beamed around the world. This was a very dif-

ferent Brazil to the one I'd just been in, where girls were forced
to sell the only thing they'd been told they had of value and
authorities pretended there wasn't a problem. It was the only
Brazil the outside world was supposed to see.

I remained in Rio for the next four weeks, covering the
Olympics for *MailOnline*, although I didn't actually go to a single
event. I was there to report on everything except the actual
sports events. With Alex, a Brazilian photographer friend, we
spent long days fighting the city's gridlocked traffic as we chased
stories, from climbing a labyrinthine hilltop favela in search of
the family of a Brazilian synchronised diver who had become
a surprise star, to being the first on the scene after the Russian
ambassador pulled an armed robber through his windscreen
and shot him dead. We visited every gas station in Rio's south
zone looking for CCTV footage of American swimmer Ryan
Lochte on a secret alcohol-fuelled bender with fellow athletes.
My last assignment was successfully beating *The Sun* to the
story everyone was after – an exclusive interview with the local
woman who claimed she'd had a 'lightning' fling with Usain
Bolt.

Once it was all over and the rest of the world had packed up
and left, my mind turned back to the other, unreported Brazil
and particularly to Medina, where the trial of Samara's father
was drawing nearer.

Things were getting tense. Not only was this the first time
anyone in the town had been brought before a court for child
abuse, what he was accused of was no more than what many
other fathers in the town had been doing, in impunity, since
anyone could remember. Many locals were indignant that a
daughter could have conspired to put her own father in jail.

Worse, Samara's father had a violent reputation in town and was known to associate with drugs gangsters. Two weeks before the trial day, Cristiane called the office, her voice vexed with worry.

"Matt, Samara's saying she doesn't want to go ahead with the trial. She's frightened, she's been getting threats from her family. I'm scared too. I'm afraid they'll come after us as well."

We decided that Orlindo, our lawyer, should travel up to Medina as soon as possible, to help them through the coming days and accompany Cristiane and Samara to the courthouse. That succeeded in calming Samara, who bravely gathered her resolve again. Even so, the situation had worsened by the time he arrived, with a fretful Cristiane making sure she was by Samara's side wherever she went, even at night when she brought her home to sleep in her house. It seemed ludicrous that a town could turn so dangerously against a young, fragile girl, just because she had found the courage to name her abuser.

On the day of the trial, Samara hardly loosened her tight clutch around Cristiane's waist from the moment they walked into Medina's courthouse. Cristiane later told me how the pounding of the girl's racing heart seemed louder than what was being said by the judge, prosecutor and lawyers. Samara's extended family were there too, all in support of her father. They refused to even acknowledge her as they walked past her to their seats, but shot daggers at her from across the wood-panelled room. When her father was brought in, handcuffed and surrounded by prison guards, the family burst into loud shouts and applause while Samara just squeezed Cristiane tighter.

As is often the case in court cases in Brazil, there was no jury this time, just prevarication and attempts at finding loopholes from the man's state-appointed lawyer. Because he had initially confessed, no doubt thinking there would be no consequence, possibly even boasting to whom he thought were like-minded police officers, it was clear there was little they could do to wriggle out of a guilty verdict. But most in that room were still confident that if he were sent to jail at all it would be for just a few years, less considering the time he had spent on remand awaiting trial. As most prisoners were released on licence after just a third of their sentences, that could mean he wouldn't need to return to jail at all. It was mid-afternoon when the court clerk announced that the judge, who had retired to consider the case, was ready to deliver his verdict and those inside hurried back to their seats.

The judge read out a lengthy statement recapping on the circumstances of the crime before declaring the man guilty as expected. Next, he moved onto delivering his sentence. Turning towards the man without looking up from his thick-rimmed spectacles, he reeled off his long name again then, after a pause, declared, "I sentence you to twenty-two years in jail."

Samara's father contorted in his seat as if he'd received an electric shock. There was a collective gasp from the right side of the public gallery, followed by frantic whispers. Samara clutched Cristiane's hand – this was more than anyone had expected.

The judge cleared his throat and the murmuring faded. He continued, "That is the maximum sentence established in the law for your crime. However, I consider there to be aggravating factors with your case, namely that you committed this particu- larly heinous crime repeatedly, for many years…"

Apprehensive silence suddenly fell in the courtroom.

"I will therefore be adding two and a half years to your

sentence for every year that you abused your daughter. That is, from the age of five to fifteen, 10 years. An additional twenty-five years and eight months. I therefore sentence you to forty-seven years and eight months in jail. Take him away."

The man was too stunned to get any words out as the guards bundled him to his feet and out to the waiting prison van. There was commotion in the gallery as they shook their fists, hurling angry words at Samara. "You're worth nothing!" yelled one man. "I hope you're pleased with yourself," taunted another. Guards herded them outside while Cristiane and Orlindo stayed behind with Samara, leaving only once they were sure her family were well away.

Half an hour later, back at the Pink House, Cristiane called me to tell me the news. In the background, I could hear Samara, laughing and singing gleefully. The change in her was instant, as if an unbearable weight had been lifted from her, that she could finally allow herself to believe all that she'd been told since arriving at the Pink House. It was the clearest confirmation yet that if we wanted to truly change girls' lives, simply helping them overcome their traumas wasn't enough. We needed to take away the weight of impunity from their shoulders and bring them justice.

The ruling also had an immediate effect on other girls in the Pink House, many of whom had themselves been cautiously waiting to find out what would happen. Over the following weeks, several girls came forward to tell how they too were being abused or exploited. Some mums too began to knock on the doors of the Pink House, ready to pour out their own traumatic childhood experiences. Then, several weeks later, something even more unexpected occurred. Samara's mother turned up at the Pink House, expressing remorse that she had allowed her daughter to suffer so much and asking her to return home. We were wary at first, wondering if her mother was only saying that because she knew police were considering charging her too over Samara's abuse. It was, nevertheless, the beginning of a journey towards reconciliation between mother and daughter which, entirely because of Samara's willingness to forgive, would eventually lead to them rebuilding their relationship.

Two months later, we got more good news. Joel Cruz, the paedophile mayor of Taiobeiras, had been found guilty on all counts with a judge sentencing him to 26 years in jail for abusing girls in his town. I remembered, just a year earlier, walking around that town, all the time tailed by Big Joel's henchmen and listening to the whispered anguish of scarred young women who assured me they would never see justice done. He was far too powerful, far too wealthy and well connected, they believed, to ever have to pay for his crimes. Ronaldo, the brave guardianship councillor who nearly paid for his tenacity with his life, called me that night. "Everything's suddenly changed," he told me. "Today I saw women who I'd never seen looking happy, strolling down the street with big smiles on their faces. It's like a huge weight has been lifted off their shoulders." I wondered how many young girls in that town were now feeling empowered, affirmed, ready to believe in themselves again, just like the Pink House girls after Samara's court victory.

It was from then on I was certain: we couldn't bring hope and lasting change to girls' lives without also fighting to bring them justice. We would soon find out, though, just how hard that part would be.

23

WORTHLESS

Someone was knocking impatiently on the steel door of the Pink House in Cândido Sales. Claudia went to answer. It was Edinilda, the mother of Sofia, a 14-year-old who had been coming along every day, but a day earlier had slipped while trying to do a somersault on the shiny tiled floor and broken her leg. The team had transferred the screaming girl to Claudia's car who had rushed her to hospital.

Edinilda wasn't in the mood for niceties and ignored Claudia's questions about how her daughter was coping. She came straight to the point.

"Sofia's leg is in plaster. The doctors said she could be like that for a month. We haven't got any food or gas at home, or any way of paying the bills. That's your fault, so Meninadança should give me compensation."

Taken aback, Claudia asked what she meant. Wasn't it obvious? the mother signalled. For at least a month Sofia wouldn't be able to make any money for her. It was because of us that her source of income had stopped and so, in her mind, it was more than clear that we should make up what she would lose until her leg had healed.

Claudia made an excuse that she would call the office and

quickly shut the door, aghast at what she had just heard. She knew Sofia, like Maira and Tábita, was seen by her own family members as little more than a meal ticket – the team had patiently been coaxing more out of her, especially on the mornings when she would arrive with only enough energy to collapse on one of the sofas and sleep. We also knew that her mother was a drug user who cared more about how she would pay for her next fix than protecting her girl from harm. But Claudia never thought she would hear the girl's mother speak so directly about how she was pimping out her own daughter, to the point of demanding that we pay for lost earnings when she had so inconveniently got herself injured.

Sofia's leg was in plaster for 30 days, during which time we got to know her more as she hobbled around the Pink House, making the most of the team's eagerness to spoil her. But once it was off, her appearances became more sporadic, and when she did turn up she was once again exhausted and quiet, and increasingly withdrawn. Claudia reported our concerns, and the mother's demands for compensation, to the town's guardianship council, but they told her that unless the mother was caught red-handed selling her daughter, or Sofia herself reported her, there was nothing they could do. And over the following weeks, despite the team's attempts to make her feel safe and convince her to talk, even taking it in turns to watch an old man's house where they believed her mother was taking her, they had to witness her slowly drifting away.

The episode horrified Claudia and the team, but as they got to know the other girls coming along to our new Pink House in Cândido Sales, they were faced with the awful realisation that many others in the community wouldn't have thought the mother's demands shocking or unreasonable. The more they reported back to me the more I understood how much darker and more dangerous the town was compared with Medina.

The place was in the grip of criminal gangs whose business was drugs, arms, robbery – and especially young girls, for the simple reason that they yielded the greatest financial return. The girls our team were getting to know were in constant, mortal danger and hadn't known anything different since their earliest memories. They thought it was normal to be awake all night, being passed from man to man in squalid brothels or street corners, falling into their beds when everyone else was waking up. Most horrifying of all, the gangs weren't just made up of local mobsters and the fugitives who flocked to the remote town to escape the law – but often also of members of their own families, sometimes their mothers and fathers.

The sense that Cândido Sales was especially lawless and dangerous became stark one week when fear gripped the region as a heavily armed gang held entire towns to ransom. First, the group of bandits rode into Medina on pick-up trucks late one night, encircling the police station and spraying the building and police vehicles with bullets. Then, while some of the criminals drove around the town's streets, firing indiscriminately at people's homes to terrify them into staying indoors, the gang exploded the ATM machines inside the three banks on the town square, then looted an electronics store. Throughout the night our Pink House staff sent frightened messages to our in-house WhatsApp group and in the morning posted pictures of the streets littered with bullets.

The next night the gang brought the same terror to the next town north, Divisa Alegre, where they again exploded the banks and fired warning shots into the police compound. It was only logical, then, that Cândido Sales, 18 miles further on, and with several bank branches around the town square, would be their next target. But while many shop owners shuttered up early and townsfolk kept away from the central area – including Holly, who slept at Claudia's house that night rather than in her town centre flat – the local policemen didn't seem to share their concerns. And sure enough, there was no late-night terror. The gang appeared to ignore Cândido Sales, instead continuing their audacious raids in towns further north. It was further evidence of just how organised crime appeared to have permeated the town and its institutions.

One of the girls regularly coming to the new Pink House in Cândido Sales was Maira, now 14, who, far from the girl once known for not letting anyone near her, was affectionate, even clingy, possessive of Holly and the team who had invested so much time and energy in her. She was also hard work, throwing tantrums and dissolving into rages of envy and tears, but we saw this as evidence of her trusting us with her emotions too, still a huge step forward.

The international coverage we got during the Olympics was still generating interest and during a week I spent in Cândido Sales with a documentary film crew from Denmark's national TV channel DR, I was able to get to know Maira better. She took us back to the home she hated so much, to her favourite place – the secret stream through an overground forest path where she would go to play with her friends – and to the place she visited the most – her mother's gravestone, in the middle of the town's crowded cemetery. One night, after going out under darkness to film, we came across her and her best friend Tábita standing on the motorway's edge as it passed by the filthy makeshift wooden bars at the entrance to town. Their pimp, Tábita's mother, was watching them from a distance, sitting on a concrete bench on the other side of the highway.

Happy to see us again, Maira, wearing tight leggings and a blue crop top, was friendly and chatty. As we stood with her and Tábita and trucks rattled by just centimetres away, the two girls began to describe, matter-of-factly, lives entirely devoid of any kind of value or meaning, where death was always just around the corner.

The reporter, Kristian Almblad, asked what happened after a truck stopped and they climbed inside. "We get in and he asks where we want to be dropped off," Maira replied. "That's where he pays us. So we take the money and get off. Then we have to wait for another truck to bring us back."

"Or we have to come back on foot," completed Tábita.

Maira went on, still scanning the lines of trucks making their way through town, "These truck drivers do really cruel things to us, they're perverts." Tábita nodded.

"If we don't do it with them, they'll kill us, or they might rape us. They might murder us and chop us up. They're capable of anything, believe me." Still, the two friends continued to try to catch the drivers' eyes, flashing expectant smiles if one slowed down or flashed his lights. Violence and danger had become completely routine for them, as had their late night shifts flagging down trucks, under the sinister gaze of Tábita's mother just within eyeshot. Eventually, after a signal from her, the two girls said goodbye and crossed over to the other side of the motorway – the beginning of another long and perilous night neither were certain they would survive.

Kristian and his crew were also interested in filming the work of law enforcement in combatting child prostitution, so I'd contacted the police chief in Medina, Alexandre, a young, enthusiastic inspector who'd recently taken the post and seemed decent and sincere. He'd agreed for us to join his unit on an operation against child sexual exploitation on the motorway – but the late-night blitz ended up revealing something even more concerning.

We met at the regional police headquarters in Itaobim where Alexandre had worked before his promotion. Wearing dark glasses and touting a mean semi-automatic, the police chief had gathered his team together, showing them a crime report they were going to investigate, an anonymous phone call that a motorway bar in the next town south, Ponto dos Volantes, was a front for an underage brothel. But when he handed me the paper I could see that the call actually came in a full two years earlier, and no action appeared to have been taken. I pointed it out to Kristian – it looked like they had only dug out the report now so they could stage a dramatic raid for the TV cameras.

Minutes later, we were hurtling down the BR-116, lights flashing and sirens blaring, as the armoured Chevrolet Montana weaved through heavy motorway traffic, overtaking on blind bends and swerving past oncoming trucks with a screech of tyres. The two police cars skidded to a halt outside the address, a drab, sun-bleached building like so many others on a patch of earth behind the motorway's edge.

"It's the police! Open up," shouted Alexandre as he took out his pistol dramatically and edged around the side of the house, using his mobile phone to light up the darkness.

The door opened, revealing a startled father, mother and adult daughter, the man shirtless, the women in their nighties.

Their house was a canteen serving the mother's home-cooked food during the day, the man explained. "We moved here a year and a half ago," he said. "I think it was a bar before that." Alexandre apologised and we got back in the cars, while he explained to the camera that whoever made it was obviously mistaken. I knew differently of course; the report came during the time the building was a roadside bar, and thanks to officers' apathy the culprits were long gone, the damage to young lives already done. I wondered how many girls had met the kind of fate Maíra and Tábita had described to us because no-one had been bothered to follow up the crime report as soon as it was made.

****

There was another time when the indifference and inertia of those who were supposed to protect young victims was caught on camera. Joseph Campos, a young British filmmaker, and son of a British woman who had worked in the favelas near Belo Horizonte, spent several months at the two Pink Houses documenting the new project's first months. One afternoon, he had been filming life inside the Pink House in Cândido Sales when, just as the girls were leaving at the end of the day, a loud commotion erupted on the street outside. The team rushed out to find one of the girls, 16-year-old Beatriz, cowering behind the car of one of our English volunteers, Georgina, while in the middle of the road a group of five girls holding rocks hollered threats and obscenities. Among them, and the one doing most of the shouting, was Layane – the girl known as Little Fire. One of them lobbed a stone which missed Beatriz but dented the roof of Georgina's car. As Orlindo, who was visiting from our office in Belo Horizonte, rushed out to try to protect the terrified girl, another rock scraped his shoulder.

Georgina managed to bundle Beatriz into her car and drive off as Layane — being held back by Orlindo — screamed and swore. It had been a traumatic day in which Layane, a troubled girl with a volatile temper, had stormed out of the Pink House, incandescent that Beatriz, and not her, had been picked as the lead dancer for an outdoor performance. It wasn't the first altercation between the two girls — things were always tense when they were together and staff had noticed a growling animosity between their families too. Nevertheless, with Beatriz safely delivered back home, they hoped the feud would blow over by the morning.

It was around 10pm when Holly, who was preparing to go to bed, heard a loud banging on the metal door at the bottom of the steps that led to her flat. She peered down onto the street to find Beatriz and her mother Soraya, both hysterical and in floods of tears, begging for her to let them in.

"They're coming to kill us," shouted Soraya between gasping breaths. "Layane and a whole gang... they've got knives and metal bars... we only just managed to escape... they're coming after us. Please, you've got to help us."

A startled Holly hurried them inside and locked the door before calling Orlindo, who promised to get over as soon as possible. First, though — worried that the gang, which now included known members of the local drugs gang Layane's family were part of, could be about to storm Holly's flat to attack her — he called the police station. A girl's life was in danger, he explained, they needed to send back up quickly. But no sooner had he described the situation and who was involved that the call handler hung up. Orlindo knew that the military police station was just a block away so he ran over, taking Joseph with him, his camera rolling. He knocked persistently on the door until an officer answered. Orlindo, now increasingly exasperated, again explained that a gang wielding knives could be at that moment attacking a frightened young girl and her mother.

But as soon as Orlindo mentioned Layane's name, the policeman visibly lost interest. "Oh, I see. Those girls," he said nonchalantly, edging back behind the door. "There's nothing we can do, sorry."

Orlindo asked what he meant.

"It's Friday night, this police station isn't allowed to process people caught committing a crime over the weekend. The nearest one is an hour's drive up the motorway. If it were someone else, then OK. But those types of girls, they're not worth us wasting our time over."

As shocked as Orlindo was at the policeman's ready acknowledgement – fully aware that he was being filmed – that girls like Beatriz and Layane weren't deserving of justice and protection, he knew there wasn't time to argue. He and Joseph set off to Holly's flat, but as they raced past the town square they came across one of the members of the guardianship council, relaxing with friends at a a roadside snack bar.

Orlindo explained the situation to him too and while his reaction was similar to that of the police officer, matters involving children in town were his job and he reluctantly agreed to go with them. They found Beatriz sobbing quietly on Holly's sofa next to her mother.

The guardianship councillor, clearly riled that his evening out had been cut short, listened impatiently as Soraya told him all that had happened. He stopped her before she had finished, assuring there was nothing he could do as it was clearly another tawdry clash between two of the town's troublesome girls. It was then that Soraya slumped forward and burst into tears.

"You see, no-one helps us just because we're poor, we're worthless," she sobbed. "We don't have money, so they don't care."

Holly tried to reassure her, handing her a mug of tea. "You're not worthless, please don't think that."

"Of course we are. That's why... when that awful thing happened to my daughter, they didn't do anything either."

The room suddenly fell silent, apart from the sniffles of the mother and daughter. The councillor, clearly aware of what she was referring to, asked to turn off the camera, and when Joseph refused moved out of sight, and eventually made his excuses and left. Soraya, too, seemed startled that she had blurted out what was clearly a closely-guarded family secret, but over the following hours she opened up about the day their lives were destroyed.

Back in the previous June, Beatriz had been walking home from school with her best friend when a taxi driver, someone known to the family, called her over. He knew one of her dreams was to play the guitar, so told her he knew of someone who was selling theirs and offered to take the two girls to see it. The place was in a community down a dirt road outside of town and on the way he stopped to give them a drink, which he had spiked. Soon after, he turned into a deserted clearing, threw the other girl out and raped Beatriz before dumping both on the outskirts of Cândido Sales. Beatriz, still under the effects of the drug, eventually managed to stagger back into town, half naked, her clothes torn, into the arms of her horrified mother.

Soraya immediately brought her daughter to the police station, but officers told her they couldn't arrest the man as the crime was no longer taking place – another of the unfathomable aspects of the Brazilian justice system. And the next day was a holiday, so she would have to wait until the third day to report it. Knowing that by then the chances of catching him would be close to zero, she took Beatriz to the hospital, demanding that they carry out a rape kit test. That evening, apparently knowing she had reported the crime, the man sent his sister-in-law to their house, offering Soraya money or food if she agreed to never again talk about what had happened. "I was disgusted that he would try to buy my silence," she remembered. "I told her to tell him: 'Do what you like, I'll never sell my daughter.'"

At that point Soraya still believed her daughter's rapist would be arrested, even though he himself appeared to know otherwise, arrogantly striding the streets of Cândido Sales without a care. They reported the crime, making a statement at the guardianship council which was sent, along with the rape kit results, to the civil police station. And that was where the case stood still. The police never investigated, in fact the man wasn't even questioned and for the next year and three months, Beatriz and her mother had to watch her rapist walking past her on the street, confident that he wouldn't ever pay for what he did.

The next morning, Orlindo called me and told me everything that had happened and my heart burned with anger. Not long after, the guardianship councillor called Meninadança's office in Belo Horizonte, threatening legal action because of the "discomfort" he'd felt when we'd carried on filming him without his permission. That made me even more furious. How quick he was to use the law to defend his own feelings, while a traumatised young girl had endured months of distress and humiliation precisely because people like him hadn't had the will or inclination to do the same for her. We decided to take up Beatriz's fight and requested a meeting with the town's judge to discuss her case.

After reading her statement and the rape kit results that had been sent to the police, he issued an arrest warrant for the man. I was delighted and surprised that we had managed to get a positive outcome for Beatriz in such a short time. When Joseph called Soraya to tell her the good news she burst into tears, hardly able to believe that her daughter would finally get justice. It wouldn't take longer than a few hours for police to go to the man's house, execute the judge's order and bring him in... or so we thought.

****

Other girls in our Pink Houses were beginning to bravely share with our staff things many had never even uttered out loud. It felt like these houses were finally becoming what I'd always envisioned for them – places where girls would find safety, people they could trust and a way out. But it also meant we needed to meet the expectations they were investing in us and that was the part that concerned me. Despite the recent breakthroughs, the truth was we didn't have the know-how to navigate Brazil's complicated legal system, or the resources yet to take on a lawyer of our own. Yet – like Beatriz and Soraya – the girls were starting to believe that we could take away from them the greatest weight they had to carry: injustice. One day, Cristiane called me from the Pink House in Medina, her voice trembling.

"It's Julia. She's just told us everything. I had no idea. Matt, this is huge. I don't know what to do."

Julia was a 14-year-old girl who had been going to the Pink House for almost a year. Bony and thin with dark brown eyes in sunken sockets. She was skittish and uneasy at first, but over time she had begun to relax more inside the house, although she still clammed up if she was ever asked to say anything in the conversation circles. We didn't know much about Julia, except that she lived in the dusty sticks outside of town with her elderly father in a wattle-and-daub house, the only dwelling at the end of a long dirt track stretching up from the motorway's edge.

That was until today, when Julia finally decided to spill her years of silent pain. She told how her father, a clandestine gemstone miner, would pass her around his colleagues when she was just 11. How she was only able to go to school because those men would give her books and school supplies in exchange for doing what they wanted with her. How she fell headlong into a dark world of prostitution, egged on by her own father, who would nag her to call her contacts whenever things at home, like rice or cooking gas, ran out.

But Julia wasn't just talking about a nightmare from her past. Things were worse now than they'd ever been, she told Cristiane. As tears rolled down her face she told how she was being controlled by a gang of men who were forcing her to do whatever they wanted, whenever they wanted. Cristiane gasped as she told her their names. They were all outwardly upright and respected men in town, community leaders, shop owners, church-goers, family men. And the ringleader, who she said would threaten her with violence, was no other than the town's estate agent, the man we were renting our Pink House from.

"After I started coming to the Pink House I started to see how much I was really worth and I told them I wouldn't do it anymore, but they didn't let me," sobbed Julia. "They keep sending me WhatsApp messages telling me when and where to meet them. I've told them I'm not doing it anymore, but they keep telling me I'll regret it if I don't."

It was difficult to hear what this timid, trembling young girl was telling us, and remain calm and rational. But we knew we needed to snare these men and if we went straight to the police with only the word of a poor girl, already labelled and looked down on, it was likely they would find a way to escape justice. We decided to try to gather as much evidence as possible ourselves before contacting the authorities, so asked Julia to send us every message she received from the men from then on. For the next few weeks, I entered into Julia's terrifying world, every ping on my phone filling me with disgust, indignation and genuine fear for this young girl's life.

The first messages were vulgar and explicit, the men, most past middle age, asking the young girl to send them photos or telling her to go to their homes, describing what they would do with her. One sent a photo of the key to his motel room where he was waiting for her. Then, as she ignored them or told them to stop contacting her, the messages became threatening.

In one exchange, the estate agent demanded, "Julia, sleep with me in my house tonight. If not, I'll go there and get you by force."

She didn't answer, but the messages kept coming, "If you don't come I'll call your dad, and you know that he'll force you to spend the night here."

After several minutes, he continued, "If you don't come here I'll call some of my friends to rape you out there on the path to your house."

"We'll rape you good and proper," he wrote next, along with three devil emojis.

Later, he wrote, "I called your dad and he said that he's going to make you come here in the morning. We're going to eat you, Julia."

A few days later, another message arrived on my phone. They were photos Julia had taken of her face, one side of which was swollen and bruised purple. She explained that two men had ambushed her as she walked home that night and beat her up, leaving her in a heap on the dirt floor. She knew it was a warning and she had a good idea who was behind it. The screenshots she sent next, of her messages to the estate agent, confirmed it.

"Did you send those guys to beat me up," she asked.

"Yes," he replied.

"Why did you do that to me?"

"Because you deserve it, you worthless whore."

That was enough. Julia was in real, imminent danger and the gang, who clearly viewed her as nothing but a piece of meat, were capable of anything. We needed to protect this vulnerable teenager, both from those men but also from her own father, who we now knew was just as involved in her exploitation. We called Alexandre, the town's police chief who had taken the Danish film crew on the operation earlier in the year and, despite my misgivings that time, always seemed happy to help us. After the problems we encountered in Cândido Sales, he arranged for Julia to be interviewed in another nearby town, in case any other officers or staff at Medina's police station found out and tipped off the men. With Cristiane again at her side, she bravely gave her statement before her mobile phone, containing all their messages, was sent away to a specialist federal police lab for forensic examination. Because of what she had said about her own father, a place was found for her at Medina's newly-opened children's shelter while proceedings were ongoing. Her life had been turned upside down, but that night, as we dropped her off at the shelter with a bag of clothes she had managed to take from home, she seemed relieved that her nightmare was over. And, knowing that the police had taken her claims seriously, hopeful that she would see justice come soon.

24

BEFORE THE NIGHT COMES

A year after our first walk along the BR-116, and despite vowing to never put my body through it again, we decided to attempt another walk, this time going south from Medina. The first one, from Medina to Cândido Sales, had been successful in drawing attention to our cause and increasing our base of supporters, but it had also been enlightening, allowing us to better understand what was happening in other communities around the motorway and hear for ourselves the plight of young girls living there.

Although we now knew much about the Jequitinhonha Valley, we had recently heard about another region, the Mucurí Valley, which lay directly south of it and was also an area of extreme deprivation, despite also being rich in precious metals and stones. We decided to set off again from our first Pink House and walk along the motorway all the way to Mucurí, a district of the industrial city of Teófilo Otoni, on the valley's southern edge. This time the walk would last a week and we would cover a distance of 170 kilometres.

Once again, a team of young volunteers were mobilised to go into communities along the route as we walked, doing dance and drama performances and giving talks to children in local schools and public spaces. This time our theme was 'For the end to the culture of sexual violence', a slogan that was printed in the form of a stamp on our T-shirts, leaflets and stickers. We also created a card in the format of a smartphone to give to girls along the way, inviting them to join a WhatsApp group where they could get help and advice and where they would receive positive and empowering messages – a way of reaching vulnerable girls even when there wasn't a Pink House close by. The message on the card was in the form of a WhatsApp conversation, starting: "You know something? You're so special. It's true, you really can realise your dreams. We believe in you."

The reason for our walk became even more urgent when, a few days before we set off, I received some tragic news and a shocking photo. That night, three 15-year-old girls had jumped off a truck as it sped through the first town we were due to walk through, Itaobim, 26 miles south from Medina. One of the girls had died on impact and the other two sustained serious injuries, with one fighting for her life in hospital. The truck driver had just carried on his way without even stopping. The photo, sent by a friend in the town, showed one of the girls lying face down and motionless on the dark road. She was barefoot, wearing a purple crop top and denim shorts. The girl, we later found out, was from the next town down along the motorway, Ponto dos Volantes, and had fallen into a life of prostitution on the motorway after being rejected and mistreated by her own parents – an identical story to so many others we had heard from hurting young girls in Medina and Cândido Sales.

The photo was harrowing, but that night I decided to send it, blurred, to our supporters. It was proof, if it were needed, of just how urgently we needed to reach so many other lost girls along this motorway. "From our experiences in Medina and Cândido Sales, it isn't difficult to persuade girls like these of their value and potential," I wrote. "They just need to hear that they are loved and that there are people who care for them and will not abandon them."

This time, Holly, our volunteer in Cândido Sales, and Lorene from the Belo Horizonte office, joined Warlei and me, setting off early on Monday morning from Medina along a winding road through the hills towards Itaobim. Again, we were stopping at every kilometre sign, tying on pink ribbons as a sign to everyone passing by that girls living along the BR-116 were no longer forgotten or alone. But this time the first day's walking was far more punishing, with steep inclines, dips and climbs and no cloud cover from the blazing sun. Half- way through the 25-mile trek towards Itaobim we were all flagging and wondering if we would manage to make it to Mucurí and the finish line. Holly was struggling the most, at one point peeling off her socks to reveal blisters covering both feet. It was already dark by the time we hobbled across Itaobim's municipal boundary, just a mile from that day's planned destination. It was then that we heard a groan and a thud behind us. Holly had fainted, keeling over onto a pile of builder's sand on the pavement edge. We rushed back and helped her sit upright as we waited for Orlindo, who had been waiting for us to arrive in the centre of town, to come with a car to pick her up.

It was just a few hours into the second day's journey that Holly decided she couldn't go on, although she still bravely insisted she would join us for stretches of the rest of the walk. Then, soon after, as we were trudging up a long hill towards the next town, Ponto dos Volantes, Warlei, who had been lagging some way behind, let out an agonised shout. Lorene and I found him sitting down on the hard shoulder, rubbing his ankle. Convinced he had torn a ligament, he also decided to drop out, and the walking party was now down to just two.

Darkness had fallen by the time we arrived at that day's destination, the town of Padre Paraíso, and a place that was already familiar to me. The last time I had been in this poor remote town, where the motorway sliced through a steep mountain valley, was five years earlier with Dean, during our first fact-finding trip along the BR-116, and from where we'd left weighed down with the grief of desolate mothers who knew they would never see their daughters again. It was also the place from where, two years before, brave journalist Evany had been snatched, before being barbarically tortured and murdered. I shuddered as I opened the metal shutters of my hotel window that night to see the shabby pousada where he had left his open laptop and fan on the night he disappeared, directly opposite on the other side of the motorway.

After I had showered and changed, I met up with Warlei – now hobbling on a walking stick – for a bite to eat on the town square. He was with Sonia, the local woman who had also warmly welcomed Dean and I during that first visit, who over decades had been a mother-figure to the town's destitute children, particularly its young girls. A battle-axe held in awe and affection by many in town, she had helped open the doors for the outreach team in Padre Paraíso, including taking them to meet local government leaders and members of the guardianship council, who had gone with them to areas of the town where they knew girls were most in need.

Warlei, who I had last seen trudging languidly up a steep hill, was now tripping over his words as he told what had happened there. "Matt, girls have been coming up to us begging for help," he said. "They all know a friend who has got into a truck and never come back. Most of them knew the girl who died the other day falling off the truck. But they weren't shocked, some said they knew it would be them next. They just can't see a way out."

On the next day Lorene and I walked to the next town south, Catují. It was an easier stretch, mostly downhill and helped by the fact that, halfway along, we found a stunning waterfall cascading down the rocks to a pool into which we dangled our aching feet. After a long decline, we found another community which clearly revolved around the highway, where the town's entire commerce seemed to face towards it and where trucks constantly rumbled along, their brakes hissing at each speed bump. I remembered this place too, as soon as the stalls dotted along the motorway's edge, selling precious stones and jangling gemstone windchimes, came into view. It was where, the day after Dean and I had met Leilah, we had stopped and bought some green tourmaline stones on our way north towards Medina.

Again, the team who had been visiting schools and gathering crowds on squares and streets while we'd been walking were full of stories about what they had seen and heard. In one secondary school, after they had performed a mime in a morning assembly, urging students to not stay silent about sexual abuse, several girls stayed behind to speak to team members. One 12-year-old sobbed as she confided, for the first time, about how she had been raped by a family member who was suspected HIV positive. That night, after the team led a service in one of the town's churches, also facing the motorway, many of those girls went to find them, imploring them not to leave the next morning. One girl gripped the arm of one of the volunteers, telling her, "You're the only people who have ever given us hope and now you're leaving us... what are we supposed to do now?"

Lorene and I, joined for the last stretch by Warlei and Holly, finally arrived in Mucurí the following afternoon where the team welcomed us with singing and firecrackers and had spray-painted our names in giant letters on a nearby cliffside. As soon as I crossed the finish line, whatever it was that had kept me going until then suddenly evaporated and I crumpled to the ground. As I was carried to a nearby community centre which had laid on food for us, I vowed, once again, to never let myself attempt anything so foolish again.

The pain went away after a few days, but what was left tormented me even more. Over the next weeks, what we had seen and heard on that journey consumed me. Those young girls, barely into their teens but already giving up on life, even wearily resigned to death. How within minutes of meeting us they had shared secrets that for years had buried deep inside because they knew no-one else would care or try to help. The way they held onto us, like someone falling to their death might flail at the last ledge. My instinct was to immediately start a Pink House in both towns, but I knew we didn't have the money to do that in either and I ended up coming to regret doing the walk at all. What were we thinking, taking ourselves to those places, giving those girls that glimmer of hope, when realistically it could be years before we could go back there and try to offer them a way out?

****

It was around six months after our walk along the motorway, as

I was returning from a trip to the coast with Milo and Tainara, that I received a message from Sonia in Padre Paraíso, who had heard we would be passing through the area on our way back home. She asked me to stop by, then sent me the address where I should meet her: 192, Juca de Matos, a road in a part of town I'd never been before. I was even more intrigued when we pulled up outside the place, a small, decrepit brick building with a rotten wooden door and a sagging terracotta roof on a narrow cobbled road a block up from the motorway. Sonia was already waiting outside, sheltering from the midday sun under an umbrella. We hugged and exchanged the usual pleasantries.

"Do you remember that I told you I once opened a soup kitchen because children here were dying of hunger?" she explained. I remembered how, during my first passage through here with Dean, she had talked of the young girls whose lives she had saved, but who later became the 'living dead' after falling into prostitution on the motorway.

"Well, this was the place," she went on. "This road, it used to be the red light district of town. Our creche was right in the middle, most of the children we fed were the sons and daughters of prostitutes. It's been boarded up like this ever since we closed, twenty years ago. Want to see inside?"

Rather perplexed as to why she had brought me here, I followed Sonia as she unlocked the rusted padlock, pushed the door unstuck and spluttered into a shuttered room filled with decades of dust. Stabs of sunlight pierced through cracks in the broken roof tiles. As the dust settled and our eyes adjusted to the darkness, we found ourselves in a long, thin hall, deceptively spacious compared with how it appeared from the road. The room was empty, apart from a scattering of debris. At the far end there was a sink and stone worktop, the remains of the old creche's kitchen. We stood for a few minutes until Sonia's memories of the place had dried up.

"It's fascinating," I said after a long pause. "Thanks for bringing me here, Sonia... I'll need to get going though, the kids are waiting in the car and we've got a long journey ahead."

"Matt," she said, turning to me. "I want to give you this house. I want it to be your next Pink House."

I gasped, lost for words. I had imagined she just wanted to show me the place that had held so much importance to her, where her life of helping others had started.

Sonia carried on. "During your walk, I went around this town with Warlei and your team. I heard everything the girls were telling them. They are desperate. It broke my heart to hear them saying they thought they wouldn't make it to adulthood alive. It made me realise, they are just as much in danger today as they were back then, when we saved their lives in here."

Tears rolled down Sonia's face now. Her love for the girls of this remote, oppressed and forgotten town burned just as fiercely now as it had when she was a young woman, doing whatever she could to prevent another toddler from dying from hunger and disease. She told me that the building was hers, registered in the name of the organisation she had founded, now part of the local Catholic diocese. Then she took both my hands and said something I will never forget.

"Matt, there's no more time. These girls, they know the night is coming for them, always chasing them, always there right behind them. We have to do something now. Please, use this building to save their lives again. We have to get to them first... before the night comes."

25

I CAN'T DO THIS ANYMORE

But we were too late for Laura. That stubborn yet sensitive girl, whose swagger and swear words were just a way of getting people to notice her, of covering up all the hurt and loneliness. Who seemed to take pleasure in shocking others with her talk of her late-night motorway hold-ups, of casually aborting her unwanted babies, or of feeling only hatred and no love. Just like Sonia had warned, the night came for her suddenly, when we least expected it, and just when we thought we had started to see her genuinely reaching out for help.

Among the Lowlands gang girls, Laura had always been the hardest to get through to. And while Bia turned her life around and was now working in the Pink House, Sacha had gone off to do her hairdressing apprenticeship in Belo Horizonte and Patricia had decided to stay out of trouble after her terrifying brush with death on the motorway, Laura had become even more entangled in Medina's dark underworld. Without the company of the other girls, and even more vulnerable, she gradually drifted beyond the reach of the Pink House, rarely turning up as she became involved with some of the town's most violent men. By the time she began to come along again she was 16 and living with one of the local gang leaders.

In recent months Laura had been dropping by the Pink House whenever she could, but especially when she felt afraid or afflicted, or needed someone to talk to. The team would give her all the time she needed, sometimes just listening or offering her a loving embrace. A week earlier she had knocked on the door asking if someone could pray for her because she was scared after a rival gang had issued her boyfriend with a death threat.

It was in the early hours of a muggy January morning when six armed men burst into the house where she was living with the gangster deep inside Lowlands's maze of dirt streets. The boyfriend jumped out of bed and escaped through a window, leaving Laura behind. She tried to run too, but the group chased her through the house, spraying her with bullets before she could even reach the front door. That's where she died, face down in a pool of blood, gunned down just as she was about to pull on the handle and find her way to freedom.

Once again the girls of the Pink House were having to deal with losing one of their own, a girl who, like them, had already suffered so much, whose life had been violently snuffed out before she had found the strength to find her way out. And once again we found ourselves reeling from another senseless tragedy, one that came just as we were feeling the tide turning, that girls like Laura no longer had to feel they had no choice but to run to the first man who offered protection and a roof above their heads. We'd already got used to the rollercoaster of emotions along this journey, where successes and progress were almost inevitably followed by disappointments, setbacks and tragedies. But after the high of being gifted Sonia's house and the prospect of a new purpose in reaching those girls who had begged us for help, this low – losing a girl who was so dear to us and who we felt was so close to choosing the right path – hit us like a hammer blow.

Once the grief had settled, though, losing Laura made us even more determined to reach those girls in Padre Paraíso, who felt helplessly condemned to a similar fate, before it was too late. Georgina, the English volunteer who had been helping in Cândido Sales, had shown herself to be capable of both inspiring the girls and galvanising the staff, a team player who had impressed with her hard work and humility. When I called to ask her what she thought about moving down to a new town and pioneering a new project from scratch with just a derelict old house to start with, she only had one hesitation: her German Shepherd Lua would have to go with her.

It was just a few months later that Georgina was waved off by her friends in Cândido Sales as she embarked on a new adventure, her rusting Chevrolet Celta packed with all her belongings and a bemused Lua strapped into the back seat. With Sonia's help, she rented a small house, close to the blue-washed colonial Catholic church in the town centre. It wasn't long before she got to know her neighbours – opposite her, a house full of friendly, elderly nuns, and behind her a warring couple who would keep her awake at night with their constant screaming and door banging. Things got worse after one of the road's tightly packed dwellings got burgled and residents decided that each should have a whistle they would blow whenever they heard something suspicious. That led to even more disturbed nights, especially when one family started sending their children out onto the street armed with machetes whenever the makeshift alarm system went off.

Georgina didn't waste time getting to know her new home, again thanks to Sonia, who spent long days with her trekking up and down the red dirt roads cut into the steep valley sides to visit the homes of girls she knew, or the places where she knew they hung out. Every outing would take much longer than expected as Sonia, who seemed to be on first name terms with everyone in town, would stop every five minutes for a natter with those she met along the way. Georgina didn't mind, though – those long walks helped her to get to know the town and its people, their concerns and needs, the nuances of the local culture and, most importantly, the girls.

Among the first girls she got to know was 11-year-old Joana, an affectionate, chatty girl with tight curls and a bright smile who she and Sonia would often meet on their walks around town and who Georgina had already become fond of. Joana would always yelp with glee when she saw them and run over for tight hugs, but the encounters, especially those after dark, would always leave Sonia visibly troubled.

"Joana's mum Marcia is a good woman, but she's had the most awful bad luck," she explained one day. "Last year her partner died of alcoholism. Then her teenage son started mixing with the wrong crowd. He was hiding the gang's guns in her home, then started stealing from her... one day she went away and he'd stripped the whole house, the stereo, washing machine, everything she'd worked hard to buy. It was too much, she became depressed, she couldn't even face leaving the house. That's when Joana started spending her time on the streets and she started to be exploited, too."

Recently, Sonia had discovered that Joana had been seen walking the streets at night with a 19-year-old who she knew was deeply involved in prostitution. Rumours swirled that she had been touting the girl around older men in the town and, of course, taking her cut from whatever they paid. But what was even more agonising for Sonia was that she knew the older girl – she was one of the girls she called the 'living dead' who, years ago, she had saved from starvation as a toddler, only to see her fall into the death trap of child prostitution when she grew up. In her attempts to keep Joana safe, Sonia had even helped her mother by giving her a job cleaning her house and then, after she was recruited by the drugs gangs, paid the girl's bail when she was arrested for drug possession. None of that had worked and now she was watching helplessly as another young girl's life spiralled out of control.

The next afternoon Georgina and Sonia climbed a steep, cobbled road to Joana's home high up on the hilltop, where they found a mother in pieces, knowing her youngest child was in danger but wallowing in such deep desolation that she couldn't find any strength to protect her. Since her partner's death, Márcia had been working as a street cleaner to pay the bills, getting up at 4am then spending the rest of the day and night asleep in a gloomy, permanently-shuttered house. It was no wonder Joana wanted to spend as little time here as possible, thought Georgina as she scanned the gloomy interior, where clothes were strewn over the dirty floor and unwashed plates stacked up in the sink. Sonia asked her if Joana was at home and she shook her head sadly.

"I don't know where she is. Most days she only comes home in the early hours. One night she didn't come home at all, then arrived in the morning, stinking of cachaça. I shouted at her, but she just ran off again. What can I do? I can barely get myself up in the morning."

Each day brought more distressing stories, more lost, hurting girls who desperately needed to feel loved by someone. They kept Georgina awake at night, especially as we hadn't even started renovating Sonia's old crèche building to turn it into a place where the girls she was getting to know could find help. One day the nuns living opposite her told Georgina about two sisters, aged 13 and 15, whose mother, a hospital cleaner, would get them out of their beds when she got home from her shift in the middle of the night and take them to the motorway to offer to truck drivers. In fact, she and Sonia had already met the girls, who lived in the sprawl of low-income housing on the top of the hill, next to the town's huge rubbish dump. The girls had been withdrawn and quiet, but their mother was friendly and talkative, convincing them that she was exasperated by her daughters' bad behaviour – without mentioning of course that she was the one who had robbed them of their innocence. Without a place where they could speak to the girls in private, there had never been a moment when the girls felt safe enough to open up and tell them the truth.

Later, they also visited the home of a 16-year-old who they had heard was being pimped by her own stepdad, with her mum's knowledge. They managed some moments with her in private, when the girl whispered how she hated living there, although didn't say why. But before they could get closer to her they found out she'd gone off with a man from the rural zone, a vast dusty wilderness which stretched for hundreds of miles outside of town. They never saw her again.

One day, Georgina called me. She was her usual polite and softly-spoken self, but this time there was exasperation in her voice. "Matt, I just wondered how long it's going to take until we can open the new Pink House. It's just that these girls... they really need us. It's so hard telling them we're going to help but not being able to say when."

The truth was, while we had enough new monthly support from the last 'adopt a kilometre' campaign during our last walk, we hadn't factored in the considerable extra cost of renovating Sonia's dilapidated building to make it safe and suitable for the girls. One local builder had a long look around and concluded that the only solution was to demolish the whole house and build another one from scratch, at an eye-watering cost. Another was more reasonable, but told us he would need to replace the entire roof and replaster the walls, besides the other necessary work such as building a new bathroom and a new interior wall to create a kitchen space. It would still require a large financial outlay, something we'd imagined we'd have at least a year to raise before Georgina and Sonia were ready to start. Now, with Georgina's impassioned plea, we knew we had to find the money as quickly as possible. The blessing came out of the blue in the end, when Phil, an English volunteer who was doing admin work in our Belo Horizonte office, said he wanted to donate a portion of the sale of his late mother's house to Meninadança. It was probably the first substantial lump sum we'd ever received and we knew exactly where we were supposed to spend it.

The work was still predicted to take six months to complete. In the meantime, Georgina found a temporary place to start working with the girls – the local rural workers' syndicate headquarters allowed her to use the disused second floor of their old building close to her house by the Catholic Church. She and Sonia started inviting the girls they had been meeting to go there and take part in activities like dance, arts and craft, beauty salon and cookery classes. Just like with the other Pink Houses, the girls arrived timid and wide-eyed at first, hardly able to believe that someone would set up a space, however sparse and simple, just for them. And just like the other projects in Medina and Cândido Sales, it didn't take long before they were beginning to believe life could be different.

Within a few weeks there were around 24 girls coming along to the temporary Pink House every day, including Joana and many of the others they had got to know over the past few months. As word began to spread, they would bring their friends, or sometimes Georgina would go downstairs to find new girls sitting timidly on the pavement outside the door, asking if they were also allowed to take part. Just a month in, Georgina and Sonia decided to put on a special dinner at the centre to mark Mother's Day, the second Sunday in March in Brazil, to which girls could invite their mums to a meal cooked by Sonia's sister Mara. They didn't expect many to show up, but by the time the event began the place was packed with 60 girls and their mothers. Some of the women, their faces ravaged by hardship and struggle, struggled to contain tears as their daughters each performed a solo dance just for them, then together sang a song about the love between mothers and daughters, holding candles of hope.

Two months later was the national May 18th day against abuse and sexual exploitation of children, a date marked every year by local authorities in Brazil, although, as we had observed in the other towns, it was often little more than an annual nod to children's rights before life carried on as normal. As always, Padre Paraíso was putting on an event in the town square and organisers had offered Georgina a spot during the main show for the girls to dance. At first she and Sonia were unsure about putting them to perform in public so soon, especially in front of hundreds of people in their own town square. But their minds were changed by the girls themselves who – just like our first ever public performance six years earlier in Medina – insisted they were ready and wanted to show their town how they had changed.

One in particular, 11-year-old Aline, threw herself into the preparations with a notable zeal. She didn't miss a single rehearsal and on the day of the event was at the front of the girls as they walked to the town square and the first to her place on the steps in front of the sky blue Catholic church. "Hey, you, stand still and watch!" she hollered at some passers by before the music began, riled that people were going about their business instead of stopping to hear what they had to say.

A few days later, a local school teacher knocked on Georgina's door. During a recent class activity she had asked pupils to write a 'message to God', she explained. One particular letter – by Aline's 13-year-old sister Amanda – took her aback. The content was so disturbing that she even wondered if she was making it up. The message revealed how as a child living in another town she had been abused by her mother's ex-partner and how, when locals found out, she saw him brutally beaten to death in front of her by an angry lynch mob.

Sonia made enquiries and confirmed all that Amanda had described and the team rallied round her, making a special effort to make her feel safe and cherished. But the more Georgina got to know the young teenager, the more troubled she was by Amanda's emotional turmoil.

It was clear she was still carrying an unbearable burden, both from the years of abuse and from witnessing a violent murder, along with other feelings that had been forced upon her of guilt and blame, which was affecting her mental health and preventing her from fulfilling her potential and being truly free. The closer Georgina became to her, the more she realised that Amanda was going to need more than just the love, affirmation and positive messages she was receiving in the Pink House. Yes, the dance, the safe environment, the loving acceptance and honest conversations were hugely important in helping her find hope and inspiration, but to recover from this kind of profound emotional trauma she needed another kind of intervention – a professional who knew how to reach down to the deepest of wounds.

Not long afterwards, Georgina received a phone call from Amanda late at night. She was sobbing quietly.

"I've just taken a whole packet of Mrs Branca's pills," she whimpered. "I can't do this anymore. I just called so I could say goodbye." The line cut out before Georgina had a chance to respond. Mrs Branca was an infirm old woman who would pay Amanda to clean her house.

Georgina immediately dialled for the ambulance, explaining that a girl's life was in grave danger. It was only when the call handler asked for Amanda's address that Georgina realised she had no idea. She knew how to get there on foot – a journey that took at least half an hour – but had never noted the street name or number. "It's the white house with the blue door… it's that long street halfway up the hill, with a bar on the corner," she blurted, panic in her voice. But it was no use, the crew wouldn't be able to find the girl if she couldn't be more specific. She called others who knew her, but they also didn't know the street name and house number. Exasperated, Georgina hung up and ran out onto the street, at a complete loss as to what she should do, her heart twisted as she imagined Amanda on her own, in pain and thinking that no-one was coming to save her.

Thankfully, the episode didn't end with yet another girl gone before we could rescue her. One of the volunteers in the Pink House, Andreia, spoke to her husband, a biochemist, who assured her that while the blood pressure tablets Amanda had taken could make her very ill, they weren't strong enough to kill her. When Georgina finally reached Amanda's house, she found her not slumped on the floor, but cooking food on the stove and insisting she wasn't going to let her take her to hospital to have her stomach pumped. She'd had another fight with her mother, she explained, who had hurt her with cruel words. It was just a desperate cry for help.

Even so, it was a turning point for Georgina, the moment she realised there was no more time to lose, that she needed to find a way of getting through to damaged young girls before they decided they'd rather be dead than have to live with their painful memories. It was the beginning of a journey of knowledge and discovery that would transform our work with the girls of the BR-116.

Georgina began to spend long hours and late nights hunched over her laptop, researching, reading, posting messages on online groups and sending off emails. The girls deserved the very best, she reasoned, so she thought nothing of knocking

on the doors of some of the world's most respected profession-
als and professors, telling them about the girls and asking for
answers. Her search even took her back to the UK, where she
attended seminars, met up with child trauma specialists and,
on one occasion when I was also in the country, took me with
her to spend a day at a specialist centre which offered advice
and support to those working with young victims of abuse. One
expert, who was especially sympathetic, was author and psy-
chotherapist Betsy de Thierry, renowned for developing the
'trauma continuum' to discover the degree and intensity of
trauma in children and how best to care for them. Offering her
time free of charge, Betsy spent hours imparting her knowledge
and experience and even led an online training seminar on
child trauma for all our Pink House staff.

Georgina called me and came straight to the point. "Matt,
there's no other way, we need psychologists working with
the girls. Those like Amanda who have been so profoundly
damaged... I don't think we can heal them without help from a
professional." And before I had finished explaining that we just
didn't have the resources yet to pay a psychologist's salary, she
said she knew that – it was why, while searching for expertise
and advice, she had also approached potential funders and now
had the money to pay for a psychologist's salary for each of our
three Pink Houses, one day a week, for the next two years.

26

HOUSE ON THE HIGHWAY

The building works on the new Pink House in Padre Paraíso were several months away from completion when something incredible happened.

For the last year I'd accompanied the new team in Padre Paraíso with a sense of satisfaction that we were finally reaching out to girls in that town, where eight years earlier Dean and I had been shocked by stories of young girls taking trucks and never coming home and where, more recently, during our walk along the motorway girls had begged us for help. What I'd pushed to the back of my mind was that there were in fact two towns where we had felt an urgency to open our next projects. In Catují, the next town south and also sliced in half by the BR-116, we'd left with even heavier hearts after young girls had implored the team not to leave, gripping their arms and asking with tear-filled eyes what they were supposed to do without them.

Then one day there was a knock on the glass door of our offices in Belo Horizonte. Warlei, Orlindo and Lorene were on the mezzanine first floor and when they went downstairs found three men, dressed in jeans and short-sleeved shirts, peering through the clear shop window. One of the men, the youngest and first to reach out his hand, introduced himself as Fúvio, the mayor "of a town called Catují".

"Yes... I know the place," said Warlei as he ushered the men inside, showing them upstairs to our meeting room table. Orlindo went to brew coffee, but the mayor was impatient to get started. He introduced his two companions – his chief of staff, and the town's culture secretary.

"I've heard about the work you do, rescuing the girls from prostitution," he explained. "We have this problem too. There are so many girls in my town who need help. I came here to ask if you would like to open a project in Catují too...?"

The team were astonished. In every town where we'd opened a Pink House the local government had proven to be one of the biggest obstacles. Sometimes they were even part of the problem, or at least needed convincing that a problem existed. Yet here was a mayor who had come hundreds of miles to the state capital to ask for our help.

Warlei, though, seemed less upbeat. "We'd very much like to, Sir, in fact it's one of our dreams," he began. "But at the moment we just don't have the resources to consider opening a new Pink House, at least for the next few years."

Fúvio was undeterred. "Then tell me what you need," he insisted. "We can give you a building, we can pay all the bills, water, electricity, telephone and internet. We can make the municipal buses available for you and put our social workers at your disposal. I need to do something for these girls, and I can't wait that long."

The mayor seemed sincere, but it still took several other

meetings with him and other members of his staff for us to be confident Fúvio and his administration were serious – and allay the instinctive distrust of politicians, which in Brazil is almost a byword for corruption and self-enrichment. That last time Warlei and I had given an ear to someone from the political sphere was a few years earlier, when an aide to a state government minister had asked to meet us, explaining that they had access to a social work fund and wanted to give us a million reals – about two hundred thousands pounds at the time. There was just one caveat: we would have to employ him and a number of other people on hugely inflated salaries; or rather, they wanted to use us to fill their own pockets with public money. As we politely declined and stood up to leave, he quipped, "If you don't do deals like this you'll always be a poor charity."

The more we got to know Fúvio, though, the more we felt that he was different. We also began to understand why he was in so much haste to firm up an agreement. The heir to a local yoghurt manufacturer, he only had a few months to go until the end of his four-year term as mayor and wanted to do something while he could to give hope to the girls whose plight had distressed him for so long. He was also astute to the fact his successor would probably reverse any agreements he'd made, so made sure the founding of a Pink House in Catují was voted through by the council chamber so it would be enshrined in municipal law and would require another majority vote to undo. That process took several months but several years later we would realise how crucial the mayor's forethought had been.

Once the law was passed, Fúvio asked us to take a look at a building he thought would be perfect for the new project. He was right. It was a large one-storey house right on the side of the BR-116 as it cut through town, its concrete steps descending directly onto the dirty ribbon of earth and rubble between the motorway and the edge of town. It was where girls would stand, beckoning for truck drivers and not far from where, on the last night in the town during our walk, girls had held on to team members, begging them to stay longer. Inside, there were several spacious rooms – one which could be a cosy living room, another we knew would be ideal for a dance studio. I imagined the faces of those girls we'd met, dancing in that place, just metres away from where trucks were rumbling by yet safe from harm and no longer alone.

Georgina began to oversee preparations for opening our new Pink House, splitting her time between Padre Paraíso and Catují, a half an hour drive south. Over the next few months she also helped sound out and interview the local staff we would need, a coordinator for each house, educators, workshop teachers and now psychologists too. We planned to inaugurate both new Pink Houses on one big celebratory weekend, but then we got some bad news. The builder in Padre Paraíso reported that the ground had sunk substantially, almost a metre below street level, and he would need to raise and reinforce the floor and walls before he could even start fitting a new roof... or rather, he would have to practically demolish the house and start again, possibly setting us back by as much as six months.. The girls in Padre Paraíso would have to continue meeting in temporary premises – now a local Baptist church after cracks began to appear in the walls at the syndicate headquarters and staff admitted they'd been warned the building could collapse at any moment. It didn't matter. If the last few months had taught us anything it was that everything happens at the right time and the most important thing was that girls in both towns that had weighed most heavily on our hearts just a few years ago were no longer alone.

It was a breezy but cloudless October day when, just six months after Fúvio had appeared out of the blue at our office in Belo Horizonte, we held an opening ceremony at the new Pink House in Catují. Now painted our preferred shocking pink with the Meninadança name and logo on a sign outside, it was our first house on the highway, visible – unmissable, even – to anyone travelling up or down the BR-116. Inside, the house had been transformed into a space which exuded safety and positivity and instantly lifted the spirits with bright walls, comfy seats and bean bags in a cosy living room, loudspeakers ready to burst to life in the dance room. I especially liked one detail: a big truck tyre swing hanging from the ceiling of the veranda, where girls were already playing, giggling and squealing. It seemed to reflect the essence of the place, where girls whose innocence had been stolen by the motorway got the chance to be children again.

Fúvio and others from the council were there too, as well as Sonia, who was just as thrilled to see a new Pink House come to life, as impatient as she was for the one in her own town to finally open its doors. As we declared the project open, Warlei, Fúvio and Sonia gave speeches to the assembled girls and guests. Sonia took the microphone with tears in her eyes. "This has been my dream for my whole life," she said. "A place where girls can finally be safe and now, Meninadança is doing it. I can't wait until I see a Pink House in my town, too."

****

My drives up the BR-116 now included four stops and a lot of time in between to reflect with gratitude and some incredulity on how far we'd come. But while things were moving forward perhaps faster than any period since we'd begun this journey, there was one area where the lack of any kind of progress was causing me increasing frustration. Two cases we had been certain we would swiftly see girls find justice seemed to have ground to a complete halt, if they had ever started moving at all.

It had been almost a year since Beatriz's mum had cried with relief that finally her daughter's rapist would soon be hauled before a judge, but despite the arrest warrant he was still a free man.

The police in Cândido Sales hadn't lifted a finger, it seemed, except perhaps to warn him that the warrant had been issued, allowing him to leave town and go off the radar. Although he was officially a fugitive of justice, we'd heard numerous reports that the man would return regularly to Cândido Sales, where his wife and children continued to live, and even that local police were allowing him to come and go unperturbed. Several people told us that a member of his family worked at the town's civil police station – the same person who had let the original rape investigation be mothballed was also ensuring him free passage in and out of town whenever he wanted.

Beatriz's case weighed increasingly heavily on my mind. It just seemed preposterous that a young girl had been brutally raped, with forensic evidence, two witnesses and even an arrest warrant, yet police were behaving as if it was nothing that deserved their time or attention. They were even helping the poor man come back to see his family, as if it were he who had been most inconvenienced by the whole affair. Meanwhile, for

Beatriz and her mother Soraya, the trauma of both the rape and the months of stagnation and impunity became too much to bear and they were left with no choice but to leave Cândido Sales, moving to live with relatives 800 miles away in São Paulo.

In Medina, meanwhile, another girl was losing hope in our promises that she would see justice. It had been nearly a year since Julia had bravely given her statement about how a group of well-heeled men in town had been passing her around for abuse, coercing her with threats of violence, and actual violence. Police chief Alexandre had gone through the due process, transcribing her testimony and sending her mobile phone to be forensically examined, but a few months had passed without any news and when we tried to find out what the hold up was he never got back. We eventually discovered one of the reasons for the impasse.

As was normal for children who reported sexual abuse, the guardianship council had visited Julia at the children's home and written a report on how she was coping which would be annexed to the case files. But the report was withering, describing Julia as untrustworthy, prone to lying, with a history of wrongly accusing others of crimes and who was known in the town for being a willing participant in prostitution. Far from being an innocent victim, the guardianship council – which was supposed to stand up for children – had painted a picture of Julia as cruel, calculated and deceitful, a document that would inflict huge damage on her claims if it were ever seen by a judge and jury. It was no wonder the police had suddenly gone cold on pursuing her case through the courts.

It didn't take long before we discovered the reason. The report was signed by the president of the guardianship council – who was also the sister of the man named by Julia as the ringleader, the town's estate agent who had ordered her beating when she had refused to obey their orders. Once again, a family member within the system had managed to smother the investigation and convince others that the case of a poor victim of violence and sexual exploitation wasn't worth pursuing.

During my long trip up the BR-116 with Dean 10 years earlier I had heard many stories of young victims of abuse and exploitation who had been denied justice, their cases filed away or swept under carpets simply for being poorer and less powerful than their aggressors. Now I was seeing it with my own eyes, to girls I knew and cared for personally. It made my blood boil. But I didn't feel I had any answers either.

The Brazilian justice system was perplexing even for Brazilians, deliberately abstruse and bewilderingly complex, probably so no-one except the very well-educated could benefit or profit from it. Even Warlei, who'd studied at postgraduate level in Brazil, found it hard to understand what legal avenues we could use to force the authorities to act, or where to even begin. Then there was another obstacle we'd identified as we had knocked on doors looking for answers. Inside that legal world there wasn't much space for anyone without a law degree and registration in the Brazilian Bar Association. Once judges, prosecutors and lawyers knew we were unqualified lay people their interest visibly waned and conversations quickly dried up.

We knew that what we really needed was to employ a lawyer, but also knew not to seriously entertain such an idea. We were already stretching every centavo that was coming in just to keep the work going in what would soon be four different towns. We couldn't see any time in the near future that we could afford anything like an attorney's level of salary. It was beginning to feel like justice would remain something within reach of only the rich and powerful.

As I thought about how else we could persuade the police in Beatriz's case to arrest her rapist, I remembered how successful our letter-writing campaign had been in catching the fugitive mayor of Taiobeiras. Without a qualified lawyer to get the ear of the judge and make the correct legal representations, it seemed like the only card we had. Once again I convened our supporters around the world, asking them to put pen to paper and write a letter to the town's police chief. After the last time, though, I was certain he would receive a deluge of letters and I was quietly hopefuly that, given the hundreds of people around the world who were aware of Beatriz's case, he would be compelled to act

****

In Padre Paraíso, with the work on the new Pink House now nearly complete, the countdown had begun to their own opening day. The whole team was over the moon that after nearly two years in borrowed premises they could finally offer the girls their own permanent space. None more so than Sonia, who would spend long evenings excitedly discussing with Georgina all her plans. I'd dreamed of a safe place for girls in Padre Paraíso since I first visited the town nearly nine years earlier, but it had been in Sonia's heart for decades, even more so as she saw the girls fall into a downward spiral of exploitation. Now she had the building, the resources, the team, to finally bring all those dreams to life and she couldn't wait to get started. First, though, she wanted to begin with a bang as she set about organising an opening day that no-one would forget.

A few weeks away from the inauguration, her plans were interrupted when Sonia fell ill with a bad case of bronchitis, enough to keep the battle-axe in bed for a week then send her grudgingly to hospital for drip antibiotics. When Georgina went to see her after she was discharged back home, she was already getting back to her old jolly self, chastising herself that her ill health had put back the opening day preparations and eager to get started again.

Georgina was woken up at half past midnight by her phone ringing the following night. It was Mara, Sonia's sister, so upset she could hardly get the words out. "It's Sonia," she sobbed. "She's dead."

Without stopping to digest the news, Georgina grabbed her coat and sprinted through a bleak and drizzly night over to Sonia's house where she found her adopted teenage son sobbing uncontrollably as he clung onto her body, which was still lying on her cold tiled bedroom floor where she had crumpled and died. Sonia had taken a turn for the worse earlier that night then, as Mara did what she could to make her more comfortable in her bed, she suffered a heart attack, dying in her arms. As news got around town, others began to arrive until the house was packed with people whose lives Sonia had touched, who she had cared for, helped, nurtured and loved. Many were teary and distraught, hardly able to believe they had lost her, but determined to talk about her and what she meant to them. Most stayed for the entire night, even after the funeral car had taken her body away. For a woman who had never had children of her own, she had been a mother to so many.

Sonia would have insisted we go ahead with her opening day ceremony so, two months after she died, that's what we did. We knew she would have hated for it to be a sombre or melancholy day, so we turned it into a celebration of life, especially hers, with music, dance, light, colour and hope.

Of course it was a tough day for those closest to her, and implausibly tragic that she never got to see her dream come true, but Sonia was there in so many ways, in the displays around the walls telling the girls they were loved and precious, in the thoughtfully confected decorations, in the potted plants each guest received with a message of hope. She was memori-alised in the speeches and conversations among those present and, of course, in the bricks and mortar too. As we unveiled the sign on the front of the building and declared the new project open, there was a gasp of satisfaction – we had named it the Sonia Viera Pink House.

I had many cherished memories of Sonia too – how she had welcomed Dean and I into her home when we first knocked on her door, immediately treating us like sons, making cheeky jokes and roaring with laughter; how whenever I dropped by she would open her fridge, lay out a banquet of food on her big wooden table and insist that we ate everything; the time she took us to her family's homestead in the parched countryside, where we spent a lazy afternoon playing table tennis, drinking beer and where she killed and cooked one of her favourite chickens.

It was her passion for the poor and powerless, though, that had made the greatest impression on me, her determination to do whatever it took to bring hope to the hurting people she saw around her, most of all the girls she so dearly loved. Even today, I strive to make Meninadança a reflection of how passionately, selflessly and intensely Sonia lived her life.

27

WHAT ARE YOU,
LARA?

An icy wind was swirling around Trafalgar Square. I tightened my coat around my neck and quickened my pace as I crossed diagonally, the winter morning sun casting long shadows across my path. Waiting for me on the other side was Charlotte, our UK coordinator, with Joseph, the young filmmaker who had spent time in Cândido Sales and Sérgio Utsch, the Brazilian TV reporter whose despatches from the Jequitinhonha Valley had made such an impression on me when I first started researching the region while working for the *Mirror*. Since then Sérgio had become the SBT channel's Europe correspondent based in London, a good friend and also now one of our charity ambassadors.

It was Sérgio who had set up today's meeting with the Brazilian ambassador to London in the grandiose embassy building just a short walk away along Pall Mall. I imagined it would have been uncourteous for him to have turned down the request from a TV journalist like him who was watched by millions every night on one of the country's main nightly news broadcasts. I also wondered if he might take exception when he found out he had actually been taken away from his important diplomatic duties to hear about one poor girl from an obscure back country town.

It was a thought I quickly shrugged off though, as I remembered Beatriz and her long wait for justice. It had been six months since we'd asked supporters to write to the police chief in Cândido Sales and although I knew he had received over a thousand letters from all over the world, her rapist was still a free man while the one person with the duty to arrest him had still not lifted a finger. After we'd conceded that requesting action from the police was pointless, we then asked supporters to send more letters, this time to the town's public prosecutor, but those appeared to have also fallen on deaf ears. Whether through complicity, corruption or lack of interest, we clearly weren't going to get anywhere with the authorities in Cândido Sales, so I decided we needed to petition a higher power. If we could get the Brazilian ambassador in London to bring up Beatriz's case, then surely we'd see progress.

The meeting began with the expected niceties and polite exchanges as Sergio, clearly held in esteem by the ambassador, introduced each of us. We sat down on upright upholstered chairs as an assistant brought in a tray with water and fresh coffee. I pulled out a photo of Beatriz from my bag.

"This is one of the girls from our Pink Houses," I began. "A man drugged and raped her in broad daylight. Her mum took her to do a rape kit the next day and there are statements from her and a witness. But that was nearly three years ago and absolutely nothing has been done to bring the man to justice."

I explained how this was about more than just one girl, how Beatriz represented thousands of others who, because they were poor, powerless and girls, were last in anyone's priorities –

from the police to the protection network right up to the upper echelons of the justice system. We wanted him to intervene, not just to take away the weight of injustice from Beatriz and her mother, but to give home to thousands of others.

The ambassador listened kindly, nodding and quietly murmuring agreement. Once I had finished I handed over the photo, along with a petition including over 400 signatures I'd collected during a recent speaking tour, which he thumbed through as we all watched in silent expectation. I imagined him figuring out a diplomatic way to let me down, to explain that this – one case of injustice out of many millions in Brazil – just wasn't something that was normally brought to the table of one of the country's top international envoys.

"Well first of all, I want to congratulate you on the work you are doing," he began. "We've been receiving the letters your supporters have been sending. I want you to be assured that I will send them, along with all these signatures, to the Ministry of Foreign Affairs in Brazil, who will send them on to our office in the state of Bahia. They will make sure the public security department, which is responsible for the police, is aware of the case."

As we stood up for a round of warm hand shaking I was quietly buoyant. I didn't quite know what to expect from the meeting, but this seemed like the best possible outcome. Surely, now, with the ambassador intervening on Beatriz's behalf, no-one would be able to ignore her case or sweep it under the carpet any more. We walked out into the city hubbub with a sense that, just maybe, we had managed to break the stalemate that had put a girl's life on hold for so long.

****

Back in Brazil, we held out for news as our attention turned back to the day-to-day needs and challenges of the Pink Houses. The new projects in Catují and Padre Paraíso were already in full swing with girls arriving in ever greater numbers, trusting our newly-recruited staff with their innermost hurts and heart-aches. I'd always insisted that our Pink Houses should be led by local women and we had found two gems.

In Catují, our coordinator was Ellen, a bubbly, impassioned young woman who would think nothing of trekking for hours around the poorest districts or deep into the outlying rural zone just to find a girl who needed help, or just a hug. And in Padre Paraíso, Andréia, an older mum-of-three who was equally devoted to the girls and radiated a reassuring air of calm and control.

As in the other towns, those women began by offering a loving embrace to the girls, awakening them to their true worth and potential. And just as in the other towns, it wasn't long before they needed to protect and defend them as well, as it became clear their rights were being ignored or flagrantly denied. In their small, close-knit communities, where most people were connected by one or two degrees of separation, fighting for girls regarded as good-for-nothings, or even dangerous seductresses, required an extra dose of courage and resilience.

This was especially problematic in Catují, where the town council was our official partner, lending us the Pink House premises and paying many of our bills. A new administration was now in place after Fúvio had stepped down at the last council elections, but as Ellen and her team became more involved in the girls' lives they became increasingly alarmed at how little those in the local institutions and government departments that were supposed to be a safety net for vulnerable children were actually willing to do for them.

The girl who worried them most was a petite 14-year-old called Lara, a girl whose heartbreaking story was well known to the town's natives. Ellen herself remembered finding out about her when, aged 16 and working at a hairdressing salon, she would hear a girl's constant terrified screams coming from a house on the other side of the street. It was Lara, then aged seven, and her mother who would lock inside on her own all day while she went out to work.

Now aged 10 and able to roam the streets while her mother was out, Lara was abused by a man who lived nearby. Locals remembered how the little girl went around telling anybody who would listen, but her cry for help only made her nightmare worse as other men began to take advantage of her, rewarding her with some food or a few reals. By the time she arrived at the Pink House for the first time, Lara's journey of abuse had gone the same way as so many other girls we had got to know – she was the local 'little whore', despised by women and seen as 'used goods' by men, now selling her body to truck drivers on the motorway. She was still only 14.

Ellen and the other women at the Pink House knew she was none of those things. Although Lara was often spending whole nights away from home, she was one of the most regular girls and often one of the first to burst excitedly through the doors on the motorway's edge, her bright smile and happy chatting lighting up the whole house. She would eagerly take part in the activities, loved to help in the kitchen and would often melt into the arms of one of the staff, staying for as long as she could and telling them she loved them. What Lara liked most of all, though, was dolls. The team would find her in a quiet corner of the house dressing them up, styling their hair and lost in her imagination as she played out stories. Whenever the fancy dress cupboard was opened she would dress up as a doll and when the girls had TV time she pleaded for a Disney princess film.

For Ellen, getting to know the real Lara – the affection-ate, communicative, childish Lara – made hearing how she had been seen climbing into a truck late at night all the more agonising. Likewise the rumours that she was running drugs up and down the motorway for the local cartel. Yet while everyone in the town knew of the mixed-up girl's unbearable existence, no-one ever tried to help her, not the local people who had seen her grow up around their streets and much less those in town whose job it was to protect and support girls like her.

Ellen decided to take them to task, following the procedures set out in Brazilian children's law to inform local government departments of Lara's situation and requesting the interven-tions they were legally required to make.

Over several weeks she sent referral letters to 10 different council departments and requested meetings with three of them to discuss the case. She also enlisted the help of a local policeman and family friend who would go and find Lara every time news reached her that she had been seen offering herself to truckers on the motorway. He would take her back home, inform social services and log an incident report, which would also alert the relevant authorities and was supposed to trigger a response.

But all those letters and reports were met with silence – the same disinterest and inertia we'd seen many times before. Lara, it seemed, just wasn't seen as the kind of child they thought their services were duty-bound to help. She was a motorway girl who everyone saw getting up to no good as they drove back to their homes at night, not an innocent child, not deserving of the time and resources that would be required. "I've tried everything, Matt," an exasperated Ellen once told me. "No-one wants to do anything to help her. It's like Lara just doesn't exist here."

Up until then the team in Catují were still managing to gently coax Lara, and other vulnerable girls, away from the path of self-destruction. But then two unexpected things happened which combined to cast her and many others way beyond their reach.

It was Ellen who first suspected something wasn't quite right after noticing that some of the girls were turning up at the Pink House dolled up in going-out dresses, heels and heavy make-up. She had an inkling what might be going on. Recently a construction company had set up in Catují to fulfil a two-year government contract to erect mobile phone masts in the region and a workforce of over 1,200 men had descended on the town. The workers had boosted the local economy as they filled up local guest houses and spent money in local commerce, but they had also become known for drunken antics and rowdy parties and Ellen had worried if their presence might affect the town's vulnerable girls.

In that day's conversation circle Ellen decided to approach the theme of sexual exploitation, using stories and pictures to help the girls understand its different forms. Afterwards one girl, 13-year-old Shirley, asked to talk with her in private.

The girl fidgeted with embarrassment at first as they sat down in the Pink House office. "It's just… it's because I have a boyfriend. I just wanted you to know," she said.

Ellen feigned matter-of-factness "Oh, thanks for telling me, Shirley. Does your mum know?"

"Oh yes, she's very supportive. He's really generous, you see, he does the supermarket shop and buys lots of things for the house."

"Oh really?"

"Yeah. He makes sure we never go without. I'm very happy."

It turned out that Shirley's 'boyfriend' was in fact one of the managers of the phone mast firm, a stubbled, pot-bellied man in his late fifties often at the centre of the rowdy late-night disturbances. The mixed-up youngster had believed the relationship was normal, especially given her mother's encouragement, but something in Ellen's talk that afternoon had clearly sowed a seed of doubt in her mind. She wasn't the only one. Over the coming days other girls came to Ellen for private chats, telling how they were involved with other men from the company who were also giving them things that they would never have been able to afford – clothes, mobile phones and Nike sneakers they'd always wanted, taking them on weekends away or giving money to their families. The effect on the fledging but so far successful work of the Pink House in Catují was devastating, with many of the most vulnerable girls coming less often and some dropping off the radar altogether. One of those was Lara, who one of the construction workers had persuaded to move out of her mother's house and into his lodgings. The young teen abruptly stopped coming to the Pink House. Soon, Ellen heard the man was a drug addict and that he and Lara were using together – it was the last thing that vulnerable, love-starved girl needed.

One morning Ellen was sat chatting with a 10-year-old as she swung on the truck tyre swing on the outside of the Pink House when she noticed a man, wearing the firm's dark blue scruffs and hi-vis vest, looking over and making a hand signal to the young girl as he walked past outside. Aghast, she called him over and demanded to know what he was doing. "Oh no, miss," the man, who appeared to be in his sixties, protested. "It wasn't meant for her, I was waving to my friend walking by over there, behind the house."

But that night a friend of Ellen's, who worked at the budget inn on the side of the motorway where many of the workers were staying, told her she'd found the same 10-year-old girl inside the hotel. It was the last straw.

The next day Ellen marched over to the company headquarters, demanding a meeting with those in charge, then went to the town council offices too, then the police station, until she'd managed to get everyone to agree to sit in the same room together and discuss what was going on. Later that week two representatives from the firm arrived at the council's Social Assistance Centre, where Ellen opened the meeting by describing how their male workers were grooming and abusing the poorest children in town and that even 10-year-olds were not safe.

The company reps had clearly been sent with instructions to limit any damage to their reputation in town and keep locals on side. Appearing meek and sincere, they listened intently to the discussions, then made assurances that measures would be put in place to keep their men under control, including not letting them use company cars at night and promising to educate their staff about the kind of behaviour that wasn't acceptable. Once all had been said, everyone present – except Ellen – seemed satisfied that the meeting had produced an acceptable solution, shook hands and went on their way.

When Ellen reported back what had happened, I was just as

incensed. Those men had committed crimes, ones which even under Brazilian law are classed as 'heinous', punishable with up to 20 years in jail. Yet there was not a word about bringing charges, or even dismissing those men who had abused children in the town, just that they would take away their car keys and give them a good talking to. And, of course, nothing changed. The men continued to prey on the town's girls, grooming them with money, possessions or drugs, or paying for their mothers' approval and those who should have been protecting them continued to turn a blind eye, knowing how important the firm was to the town's economy. Within months dozens of girls who at the Pink House had been starting to awaken to their dignity and self-worth were drifting further astray than when we'd first found them, some seemingly beyond reach.

Then the second catastrophic event hit – COVID.

The pandemic swept through Brazil with frightening speed, overwhelming hospitals, morgues and cemeteries with terrifying scenes in some cities as health services collapsed and patients suffocated in their beds as supplies of oxygen ran out. Before long, everybody knew somebody who had died. Among them was Meninadança's accountant at our office in Belo Horizonte, Vitor, aged just 26, who called Warlei in tears just before he was put on a ventilator and lost his fight for life two months later. The virus tore through the rural areas of Brazil with as much speed and ferocity as the big, overpopulated cities with the difference that there was often just one doctor in the town and no ICU for hundreds of miles. With mixed messages from central government, local lockdowns were ordered in the towns where we worked and, for six months, all our Pink Houses had to close their doors. Suddenly, the girls were denied the safe space which had become such an important part of their lives. And in many cases, they were forced to stay with their abusers inside their own homes.

While the buildings had to stay shut, our teams kept working, stepping up to the challenges of the pandemic with their usual determination and creativity. Despite being forced apart, they still found ways to look the girls in the eye, so they would still feel cared for and could whisper if they needed help or advice. That often involved delivering them lovingly-wrapped pieces of cake, brigadeiro sweets or a handmade card with a special message, or even sending them a film via WhatsApp and then turning up on their doorsteps with popcorn, hotdogs and a can of Coke to enjoy while they watched it. The dance teachers would give online classes while conversation circles would still take place via WhatsApp with most of the girls still relishing the daily chats about their lives which had helped them stay strong and positive when the houses were open. The teams would even deliver packs of art materials so the girls could take part in the online workshops. In Cândido Sales our new coordinator Keyla organised dance contests where each of the girls would record their own attempt at dancing to a piece of music on their phones and send it to the group. The girls who came third, second and first won a prize – again delivered to their homes by the whole team, determined that the bonds of trust and friendship they had worked so hard to form wouldn't be broken.

In Catují, though, even that work was exacerbated by the ongoing problems caused by the construction workers, who remained in town even though their work was on hold. With the hotels and lodgings now bound by law to not allow anyone but guests inside, the men started renting houses in the countryside surrounding the town where they would put on clandestine parties to drink, use drugs, and transport the girls to abuse. Ellen and the team there would often arrive at a girl's home to deliver a cake or gift and find she wasn't there, with her family unable to say where she was or when she might be back.

One evening, Ellen's mobile phone rang. It was Melissa, a 13-year-old girl who even before the Pink House was a cause of worry for her and her team. Soon after she had started taking part a year earlier her mother had died from alcoholism. The confused, inconsolable girl had gone to live with her 16-year-old sister, who had recently brought her boyfriend – one of the construction workers – to live with her. She had been sleeping on the kitchen floor of the tiny two-roomed home, inside which she had been shuttered since Catují had ordered a lockdown weeks earlier.

Melissa was sobbing and gasping. "What's the matter?" asked Ellen.

"It's my brother-in-law. He... just abused me," she whispered.

Ellen's instinct was to run right over to Melissa's home and bring her back, but she knew that was impossible – the authorities were strictly enforcing the lockdown. This was exactly what our teams had been most worried about, knowing girls would have to stay inside the very places where many were most at risk. "Melissa, you need to be strong," she told her. "Where is he?"

"He went out, he was drinking," she whimpered.

"If you tell the police they have to act, it's your right," Ellen told her. "Do you think you'd be able to go down to the police station?"

"Only if you stay on the line."

Melissa put the phone on mute, then in her pocket, and ran

out into the road. Ellen kept her ear to her phone, listening first to the patter of her flip-flops on the cobble-stoned hill, followed by her knocking on the door of the police station and bravely asking for help. As she went with an officer to give her statement Melissa told Ellen she could hang up. The next she heard was a police siren echoing around the town's deserted streets and Ellen knew the police were on their way to pick him up.

There was no satisfactory conclusion, however. Several days later, Melissa's older sister persuaded her to retract her police statement – her boyfriend was financially providing for them, she had told her, and without him both would be homeless and destitute. It meant Melissa had to spend the next four months living in a tiny, two-roomed house with the man who had abused her. Thankfully, being arrested had been a sufficient enough shock that he didn't try anything again, but for Melissa, already reeling from the death of her mother, that traumatic period would take a devastating emotional toll.

It was also during these dark months of the pandemic that Lara's situation went from bad to worse. After the man who had convinced her to live with him tired of her and kicked her out his house. Her mother didn't want her back either and the teenager inevitably fell off the radar, probably sleeping in brothels and drug dens, until Ellen heard she had fallen into the claws of the feared local drugs trafficker, who was using her as a mule ferrying cocaine between Catují and Padre Paraíso. He would provide her with lunch, according to those who knew, but in return she was expected to buy food for dinner, and the drugs they were both using, by selling her body on the motorway. The news floored Ellen – her worst fears for Lara were coming true. She desperately wanted to go after her and persuade her to come home, but knew, with both the pandemic restrictions and how deeply she had become enmeshed in the criminal underworld, that even to attempt that would be incredibly reckless. The gang she was involved with was almost certainly the same one that had so brutally tortured and decapitated journalist Evany. In fact it was after his murder that I first heard of Catují – it was where he had been investigating a child prostitution ring in the months leading up to his death.

Ellen could only wait, pray and hope. But when she did get news, it was always worse than the last. One day a friend who worked in the forecourt of one of the motorway gas stations forwarded her a video that had been sent around a WhatsApp group of Lara in a skimpy pair of jeans shorts and black bra top, her cheeks red with blusher, thumbing down trucks on the motorway at the entrance to the town. Around her were a group of crossdressers, who Ellen later found out were using the girl to travel to the lockdown-busting parties outside of town, making her sell her body in exchange for their lifts to and from the clandestine events. "What are you, Lara?" asked one filming the video as the camera zoomed in on her face. "A prostitute," she replied, smiling yet with a look of deep sadness in her eyes.

Several months later Ellen heard that Lara had moved out of town and was now living with another, even more dangerous man, the leader of the drugs gang in Padre Paraíso. But she was still transporting drugs between the two towns and still being exploited by pimps and prostitution gangs on the motorway. One day, the man found out that she had 'cheated' on him by doing a 'programme' on the motorway and viciously beat her up, leaving her black and blue. He broke all of her front teeth before kicking her out onto the streets again.

What Are You, Lara?

Ellen knew Lara couldn't survive much longer and that the next story she heard about her could be the worst news of all. She started searching for her around town, going out at the dead of night to walk around the deserted streets in the hope that she'd find her, but always arrived home empty-handed and even more worried. One day, when Ellen was at the Pink House, sweeping the dust from the rooms that hadn't seen girls for months, she looked up and saw Lara standing sheepishly in the door frame.

"Lara!" Ellen cried, dropping her broom and running towards her. They both wept as they held each other in a tight embrace – neither cared about COVID restrictions at that moment. Lara was in a state: emaciated and dirty, her face still bruised and disfigured and her once-captivating smile a mess of broken teeth. But she was alive. Ellen whispered into her ear how much she had missed her and how loved, precious and beautiful she still was.

"I was so worried. I was always looking for you, but never found you," she told her, stroking her hair.

"You would have found me here," whimpered Lara.

"What do you mean?"

"I would come here, after midnight, and sit on the stairs outside and cry," said Lara. "I was here every night. I'd cry so much, but all to myself, no-one saw me and no-one heard me."

"But Lara, why would you come here to the Pink House to cry, in the middle of the night?" Ellen asked her.

"Because I knew that I used to be safe here. It was the only place I'd ever felt safe in my life."

28

JUSTICE

When COVID restrictions were finally lifted it was like the waters receding after a devastating flood. In its wake the pandemic had left lives shattered, families pummelled by hunger and malnutrition and many so destitute they were having to beg or scavenge just to make it through each day. As always it was the most vulnerable who suffered the most. Our staff were shocked at how different the girls seemed as they tentatively started coming back through our doors. Many were quieter and more withdrawn, their eyes betraying whatever they had been made to endure behind closed doors or out on the streets without the safety net of the Pink Houses. Several girls had also fallen pregnant, the youngest aged just 12. Some, like Lara, had gone through hell.

It was clear the girls were going to need more support than ever, but as the Pink Houses started referring girls to local services, or reporting cases of abuse or domestic violence to the authorities, they encountered even greater levels of indifference than before. The budgets of council departments, we found, no longer stretched to helping the motorway girls, who even before the COVID tsunami hit were seen as wayward, delinquent and less deserving of public resources.

Justice

One of those was Melissa, the 13-year-old who had been abused by her sister's boyfriend during lockdown, then forced to live with him in the same house for four months after. She was one of the girls who returned to the Pink House on the first day, albeit subdued and less communicative than before. Despite her unbearable situation, Ellen's meetings with council departments asking to find a place in a children's home for Melissa had proved futile – they were inundated with many other requests for help from local destitute families, she was told.

Then, just a few weeks later, the sister's boyfriend was killed at work in a freak accident when a metal pole fell on his head. While his death, however tragic and untimely, meant Melissa was finally safe in her home, it also plunged the two sisters into a different dark chasm. Without the only breadwinner, they now had no-one to sustain them and she would often arrive at the Pink House hungry, sometimes saying she had only eaten a spoonful of rice the whole day. Ellen managed to get the council to deliver some food parcels, but later heard that Melissa's older sister, now aged 17, had been visiting the lodgings of the telecommunications firm workers as desperation pushed her towards prostitution. The team rallied around Melissa, caring and nurturing her and providing for her as much as they could, but Ellen had to watch helplessly as the two girls' situation went from bad to worse.

Then there were the girls who had been waiting for justice even before COVID. In Medina, Julia had been staying at the town's children's shelter after testifying against the local businessmen who had enslaved and exploited her. But nearly two years on, there was still no news, while the town's police chief Alexandre – the same who had only acted on a report of child prostitution that had gathered dust for two years after a film crew showed up – was still being deliberately evasive. My heart sank when I learned that, during the pandemic, Julia had withdrawn her statement against her father and gone back to live with him in his dirt-brick house at the end of a pitch-black track on the motorway. It was better to go back to her abusive home and try to carry on with her life, she had decided, than for her life to remain on hold, waiting for something she now knew would never happen.

And of course there was Beatriz, the girl from Cândido Sales whose rapist was still on the run, aided and abetted by the police. Again, a year after we'd handed over the hundreds of signatures to the Brazilian ambassador in London, we had heard nothing, and the man was no closer to being caught and brought before the courts. Both Beatriz and her mother, now living in São Paulo, stopped answering our calls. They were trying to rebuild their lives a long way from the town, forget about what had happened and move on, we heard. Why keep replaying such painful memories when it wasn't going to change anything?

The girls seemed more on their own than ever before. And although the Pink Houses were open again and giving them love and support, some needed more than we could provide – government interventions, specialist medical care, a place in a children's home, a police force and judiciary that would take them seriously. They were all rights that are guaranteed to every child under Brazilian law, but to which these girls apparently weren't allowed to access and we seemed powerless to do anything about it. I was becoming increasingly dissatisfied with where we were as an organisation. Yes, we had opened four

Pink Houses in 10 years, we were gradually gaining space and recognition... but what good were we really doing if we were failing to secure those things that would really change the girls' lives?

I met up with Warlei and we both knew what we needed to do. To truly fight for these girls, we needed lawyers who could take on their cases, force authorities to fulfil their legal duty of care to them and pursue their aggressors and abusers through the courts. The problem was, lawyers in Brazil were prohibitively expensive – exactly the reason why justice was an almost exclusive privilege of the wealthy. We would need a lot more money and we would need to find someone to work for us who wasn't only qualified and licensed by the Brazilian Order of Attorneys, but who also shared a passion for the cause and would do most of their work on a pro-bono basis. Based on my experience with Brazilian lawyers, and knowing how stretched our finances were already, especially after months unable to do any speaking engagements and raise more monthly donors, that seemed like an almost impossible task. We were back to square one.

The answer came only a few months later. Before the pandemic a friend in the UK with experience in writing funding proposals had helped us by sending off some letters to foundations and charitable trusts. When the world locked down a few months later he stopped, knowing that it was very unlikely that trustees would even be meeting to discuss grant requests, let alone agree to support an organisation in Brazil when everyone was facing unprecedented struggles at home. It was several weeks after Warlei and I had spoken when we received a reply from one of the trusts, informing us that they had agreed to help us with a modest one-off donation to help with monthly costs. It was enough to pay a minimum salary to two people for a couple of years and we knew exactly where we were going to spend it.

Warlei had a suggestion for who could lead the justice team – Pryscilla, a young Brazilian woman who was herself working with poor families in the nearby town of Jequitinhonha, but who also had a law degree and was passionate about getting justice for the poor and powerless. As Pryscilla had become more involved in our work I had been impressed with her activism, her refusal to accept the status quo and her knowledge of how the legal system could benefit – but most likely fail – girls like ours. She called herself a 'hopeful pessimist' and was under no illusion at how hard justice was to get, but she was determined to never give up trying… just the type of person we needed.

With Pryscilla on board, we set about trying to find a lawyer. Pryscilla introduced us to her childhood friend, Luisa, who had grown up in the region and was now a practising attorney, specialising in issues relating to children and families. Where most ambitious young lawyers dreamed of making their names and fortunes with a big city firm, she had chosen to stay in the region and had spent years battling the flawed and under-resourced police and protection networks that would let down so many underprivileged children. Warlei and I set up a Zoom meeting with Luisa, who surprised us by accepting our invitation to work with us before we'd even finished our introductory pitch. Just as unexpected was finding out she had an elder brother who was also a lawyer, Antonio, a specialist in criminal law, another area we knew we needed expert knowledge. He, too, took up our offer without hesitation and suddenly we had a team of three, each with something different to offer, all with a shared passion – justice for the girls of the BR-116. The feeling that we had found just the right people became clearer when it was time to ask for their bank details so we could set up their monthly payments. It was only a meagre minimum wage, but both Luisa and Antonio couldn't understand at first, as they'd actually thought they'd be working on a voluntary basis.

It wasn't until the justice team got to work that I realised what a game changer this was going to be.

They started by visiting the Pink Houses to get to know the girls, who at first couldn't quite fathom that they had their own lawyers who would use the laws and constitution to defend them... that was something only rich and important people had. When Luisa and Antonio would do group sessions with the girls to help them understand their rights they would sit as close as they could around them, hanging on each and every word. I sat in on a few and teared up on occasion as I saw how the girls' demeanour completely changed, sometimes breaking into a broad smile or breathing a long sigh of relief as they listened, finally understanding they were no longer alone.

Perhaps, most consequential, was the way the lawyers were received by everyone else in town. Pryscilla had talked of how in the small towns you could only get things done by 'having coffee' – that is, sitting down with someone, looking each other in the eyes and creating a personal connection. That was hardly ever possible before as prosecutors and judges generally kept their distance from the general population, perhaps to maintain their aura of authority. Getting local council staff to even turn up to a meeting to discuss a girl's case, let alone agree to a course of action, was equally problematic. But that all changed when our lawyers arrived. With members of the judiciary there were no more formalities. They naturally treated them as equals, who knew the law as well as they did and who were fellow fluent speakers of that deliberately confusing legalese. Having smartly-dressed attorneys turn up to meetings with members of local children's services, their leather briefcases full of case notes, made all the difference too. Perhaps the reaction would have been different in the big cities, but in these remote towns where lawyers were still regarded with a certain awe, people took notice, listened to what they had to say and tried harder to please – while all the time clearly perplexed about the reason they were there. The motorway girls were, in most people's minds, the ones least worth defending.

****

Over the next months Pryscilla, Luisa and Antonio travelled up and down the motorway between Catují and Cândido Sales, making their presence felt, reassuring the girls, training the Pink House staff, holding community meetings and taking on girls' cases. The girls grew in confidence, believing they really could find hope, and began to reveal the crimes that had been, or were being, done to them. Even those cases which had been causing us so much frustration, which had been forgotten or deliberately left to stagnate in the system, slowly began moving again. It felt as if we had finally found the missing piece of the puzzle. And yet it was so obvious. How can you offer hope to young victims of abuse and sexual exploitation without also giving them the one thing that would truly set them free – justice?

One of the early breakthroughs came in Medina where, with Julia's stalled case in mind, the justice team had worked hard to build bridges with the community and get to know the main players in the police and judiciary. They decided to hold an evening event at the Pink House and invited key townsfolk, including local businesspeople, council workers and law enforcement, including the town's police chief, Alexandre. Guests were treated to the typical Pink House charm offensive – a personalised welcome gift, beautifully decorated, candle-lit tables, drinks and canapés, before the evening began with a special presentation of dance and drama which the girls had spent the week practising. After the dance, Pryscilla stood up to give her talk, welcoming everyone just as cordially and deliberately directing her words to the members of the police and judiciary in the room. The town's police force had made headlines recently for several operations in which they had arrested gang leaders and disrupted the drugs and arms trade in the area.

Officers smiled bashfully back as she gushed, "I would like to congratulate you on your excellent work. You have honoured your people and your badge by protecting the town from criminals and the dangers of drugs and guns."

She went on, "I also want to remind you of something in our constitution called the 'principle of absolute priority'. It's a requirement to always put the investigation of crimes against children and teenagers first. It's very clear that if that doesn't happen, if those who abuse children are not being brought before a court, then we are failing in our duty."

Pryscilla delivered the message with so much kindness that no-one in the room appeared to feel offended until police chief Alexandre, sitting with other officers towards the back of the room, put his hand up, asking if he could say something. Pryscilla held out the mic and heads turned as he stood up and made his way to the front.

Alexandre tapped on the mic, hesitated for a moment, then cleared his throat. "I just wanted to say, thank you, thank you, Meninadança," he began, looking around the room. "You see…" He paused, perhaps momentarily wondering if he should go on, or to fight back tears. "I didn't used to believe that a man who paid a teenage girl for sex had committed a crime. But now I know differently. There's no such thing as consensual sex with a child, it's statutory rape, no excuses. I want to assure you that I will never make that mistake again."

It was an astonishing confession – almost unbelievable coming from a long-standing police chief. It also helped explain our troubling trip out with his patrol a few years earlier, when he had only followed up a report of child prostitution that had been filed away for two years to impress a Danish film crew. But it was also a turning point. Within days he had dug out Julia's case, reopened the investigation, urgently requested the evidence from her mobile phone and brought the men she had accused in for questioning. It was too late to see one of the three men face justice though. The case had taken so long that he had died while we had been waiting. Soon, though, the other two men had been charged and a date set for the trial.

Everything happened so quickly I didn't have much time to stop and reflect, but when I did I began to worry. It wasn't the first time we had been involved in a court case in Medina – the first was Emilly's murderer and then the trial of Samara's father, both of which had generally had the approval of local people. But this time it was different. The people we were hauling before the judge were well-known and respectable businessmen – the town's estate agent and the owner of a local hair salon. The girl we were defending had been a helpless victim of predatory men for most of her life, but in the eyes of most townsfolk she was just a cheap local prostitute, who many remembered seeing standing by at the side of the motorway or waiting in street corner shadows with no right to accuse anyone. Thankfully, right at the beginning, before the arrest, we had insisted that Julia be interviewed in another town to distance the Pink House and its staff from the case. In the time that had passed since then, during which the Pink House wasn't even open because of COVID, very few were making the connection with Meninadança. Even so, on the day of the trial our lawyers would need to go to the town to be at Julia's side, questioning the accused and petitioning the judge and we had no way of knowing how safe that would be.

It was only a few days before the trial when we heard it would be held remotely by video call – COVID restrictions for court hearings had not yet been lifted, so only those testifying were required to attend in court. While the team had felt they should be there to support Julia, we were relieved they didn't need to attend in person. Luisa joined the Zoom call as prosecutor's assistant, while Julia went along accompanied by our social worker, Leticia, with assurances she wouldn't come face to face with the two men in the dock. Over the last months, however, Julia had formed a strong bond of trust with Pryscilla and the other lawyers and within a few minutes the fact they were not there to support her began to show. After a lifetime of abuse and years waiting to tell what these men had done to her, when the moment finally arrived, she clammed up. She became upset and disappeared from the screen.

Several streets away, Cristiane was in her office in the Pink House, waiting anxiously for news, when her phone rang. "I can't do it, I just can't do it," Julia sobbed from the courthouse corridor.

Cristiane helped her to calm down and control her breathing. "It's perfectly normal to feel that," she reassured. "But this is the final hurdle, don't let them stop you now. The judge needs to hear from you. You can do it, you're strong enough."

Several minutes later, she appeared again on the screen, her face wiped of tears, composed, determined. "I was just fourteen years old," she began. "They would send me a message, tell me the place I should go and when I was there they told me what I should do. When they finished they would give me 10 reals, fifteen at the most, and tell me to leave."

Julia spoke quietly and carefully, giving places, dates, times, names, details of the abuses she had endured and the brutality of those who had inflicted them. Perhaps for the first time in that courtroom, one of the motorway girls had given a full, unabridged account of her suffering. I remembered what Evany had told me back on the first night I met him — how child prostitution was "this town's dirty secret. No-one ever talks about it, no-one wants to hear about it." Well, now they were hearing about it, in excruciating detail, evidence that would be recorded and kept on file about how a helpless young girl had been robbed of her innocence, violently raped and degraded, passed round and sold on, trafficked, threatened, beaten up. How one time when two men tried to drag her into their car she escaped into a thick scrub, then heard one of them calling the estate agent to tell him the 'kidnap' hadn't gone to plan. How she had been beaten black and blue when she tried to make a new start and had ignored their orders. How she felt trapped, helpless, worthless and sometimes just wanted to end it all so she would no longer feel any pain. She was describing her own life, but it could have been any young life among the thousands being destroyed by men on this motorway.

Next, it was the two men's turn to be questioned. First, the hairdresser was asked about the messages which had been found on his phone, telling Julia to go straight to his house, how much he would pay her and what he would do to her.

"Well, it wasn't me who wrote them... it was her, that girl," he said confidently.

The judge looked puzzled. "How could she have written them if they were sent from your phone to hers?" he asked.

"Well, you see, Your Honour, she got hold of my mobile phone, without me knowing and wrote the messages pretending to be me."

"How on earth could she have managed that?" the prosecutor interjected, pointing out that his phone was password protected and by his own admission he never left his house without it.

He threw up his arms. "This girl... you don't know who she is, she's a bad, bad person... capable of anything. All I know is that I never did anything to her. She took my phone when I wasn't looking and sent those messages, just to incriminate me, I swear."

The next defendant, the town's estate agent, was equally arrogant, although he hadn't even concocted a cover story, however bizarre. He just kept insisting that Julia was lying and that he had never had sexual relations her, despite the vulgar messages from his own phone, the vile threats to gang rape her and his written admission that he had ordered two men to beat her up because she "deserved it".

By the time the hearing was over few in the room were in

doubt that the judge didn't believe their story – even 'optimis-tic pessimist' Pryscilla, who was both astonished and thrilled at their pathetic attempt to explain their way out of a guilty verdict. However, I was also guilty of assuming he would deliver his ruling and send the men down that same day. The judge's deliberations, we were told, would take months, maybe even a year – another absurdity of the Brazilian legal system which was supposed to treat children as the absolute priority. In the meantime, and despite our confidence in a guilty verdict, the two men were free to go back to their normal lives while Julia's life remained on hold.

TAKE A WHOLE TOWN TO COURT?

The justice team had also been building bridges in Cândido Sales where Beatriz's rapist still hadn't been captured, despite an arrest warrant and incriminating evidence. They especially focused on building relationships with members of the town's judiciary, meeting with them to chat and 'have coffee', inviting them to visit the Pink House and get to know the girls. They were hindered, however, by the revolving door of new prosecutors in the town, with some staying for just a few months before moving on, meaning that work had to be started all over again with each new incumbent. Slowly, though, they managed to make progress.

One prosecutor agreed to change the conditions of the man's case so that the time he spent on the run wouldn't be subtracted from his eventual sentence. The next ordered that he be included in the national 'wanted' list so he would be flagged up to police if he was stopped for any reason – someone had prevented his details being automatically added to the database. The next to take up the post was a young prosecutor who seemed most eager to help, especially after spending an afternoon at the Pink

House where the girls even managed to get him to join them in a dance class. Examining Beatriz's case, he noticed that an order had never been made to lift the accused's confidentiality – a legal prerequisite to the police being able to access his private information such as his mobile phone and bank records. It was proof that the police had never made any effort to track him down. He promptly got the order signed off by the judge.

They were all necessary steps, but the truth was we were no closer to catching him than we had been three years earlier and now even less confident that the town's police officers would do their job. We decided to ask for another meeting with the prosecutor to discuss what more could be done. In another chat over coffee, Luisa, who was joined by Warlei, told him everything they had discovered through their own investigations – the rumours he was regularly returning to see his wife and children, how records showed he was picking up his pension, had registered for a COVID jab and returned to vote at the last election, and how most believed he was being protected by the police whenever he was in town. The prosecutor listened carefully, then mulled over his words before leaning forward and lowering his voice.

"I'm here because of an investigation into something much bigger," he began. "Into the criminal gangs that have set up their operations here. What you've told me has helped confirm some of the information we've also received, about how they have infiltrated the police and civil service. You've given us another piece of the jigsaw. This man isn't the only one being protected by those in power."

What the prosecutor was telling us helped explain why, despite all our efforts, hundreds of letters from abroad, and even representations from the Brazilian embassy, nothing had been done to catch him. But it was also incredibly disheartening. What he was confiding to us meant it was even more unlikely we'd see progress on Beatriz's case. Why would they risk blowing a dangerous investigation into organised crime – the reason, apparently, for the prosecutor having been placed in the town – to pick up one of them just because he had once also raped a girl?

Now knowing that even the good guys had reason not to touch Beatriz's case, we decided to try one last thing: hire a private investigator to find him ourselves. Once again, we appealed to supporters around the world, this time for the money to pay him, and once again they stepped up. By now, many were feeling as passionate about getting justice for Beatriz as we were. It was some weeks later that Antonio and I met up with a man calling himself Sidney, a serving police officer currently on leave but who could still make arrests himself, who assured us that he could fade into the shadows in Cândido Sales, gather intelligence, and catch the suspect if he appeared. We agreed the terms and set him on. We had no idea if it would work, but it seemed infinitely better than the other alternative – admitting defeat.

Some weeks later, Sidney was still undercover, but we did get some unexpected good news from Cândido Sales. It came in the form of a photo sent to Georgina's phone, who was now back in the UK, of a girl in a white dress being baptised in a river. I had to do a double take when I saw it. It was Layane, the girl nicknamed Little Fire because of her riotous reputation in town. I'd met her on my first visit to the town, for a newspaper story on child prostitution at the World Cup, when, then just 13, she had told me how she had decided to go off with a trafficking gang to Salvador. But the photo showed a very different young woman, smiling and looking to heaven as she emerged from the waters of a river and a group around her clapped.

In the message she explained how, despite her bravado and bad behaviour, all that she had received from the Pink House had been changing her, little by little. She had left behind her late-night antics, turned her back on the gangs and prostitution, found a young man who loved her and got engaged, then joined a local church, found faith and had just been baptised. Her message was full of affection and gratitude, for always believing in her when no-one else did and when she had not given anyone any reason to either.

We were thrilled for Layane, who for many in town was a hopeless lost cause just like Bia in Medina, but like her had managed to find her happy ending. It was the reassurance we needed that, even when it felt we had tried everything without success, we should never think of giving up.

**

In Catují, our team were still trying to convince the local authorities to meet their legal duty of care to Lara, now 15 and still living hand-to-mouth on the streets in brothels or drugs dens, still being exploited by pimps and gangs. Once again, it was the justice team that eventually forced change. Once Ellen had filled in Luisa and Antonio on her situation, they too called meetings with representatives of local government departments, but found them even more resistant, now ignoring their calls, emails and hand-delivered letters. We knew the reason – protecting Lara in the way defined by Brazilian law would mean paying for her to stay in a children's home, and they didn't want to spend precious municipal resources on that.

It was during a Zoom meeting as we were thrashing through what we should do when Luisa had an idea.

"The authorities in Catují are refusing to do their legal duty to Lara. So, why don't we use the law to force them to comply?"

I asked what she meant. "We can file a civil lawsuit," Luisa explained. "Against the whole town. The law states that they are the ones who should be protecting her. So we can make them responsible for the human rights violations she is suffering."

I gasped. "Take a whole town to court? But how would that help rescue Lara?"

"We could ask the judge to fine the council for every day she is still on the streets. It's a big decision, I know, but we've tried everything, it's the last resort we have."

We imagined that such an extreme tactic had never been used before to oblige a town to protect one of its children, especially a despised motorway girl like Lara. But there was another factor to consider. We were in an official partnership with the council in Catují – if we took them to court we risked losing that support, even being evicted from the building they were providing for us. Fúvio was no longer mayor and we now saw just how foresighted he had been in making sure the partnership had been voted into law before he left his post. It could still be undone, though, if the new mayor was determined enough. As we discussed the case, we were all in agreement. Lara was in real danger, not just of violence and exploitation but of losing her life. That was far more important than any other concern. If the council took away their support we would just have to find a way of covering the extra costs.

We filed the petition with the nearest district court and within weeks the judge had returned his decision – in our favour. He not only ordered that the council pay a fine for every day Lara hadn't been placed in a children's home, he also held the mayor personally responsible, ruling that if they didn't pay the money should be deducted from her own bank account. It was the beginning of a legal tug of war with the council over the life of a vulnerable girl.

Firstly, the council appealed the decision, with their lawyer claiming that because Lara's absent father lived in a different town, she wasn't their responsibility. Luisa was furious. They knew full well that Lara's mother had lived in the town all her life, while everyone in town knew the girl spent all her time on the streets of Catují.

She found one of the council's own reports which showed that Lara was in fact enrolled in one of the town's social programmes, only open to residents, and despatched it to the court in her counterclaim. It blew their argument apart. The judge promptly rejected their appeal, setting the daily fine running that same day. It was then that Warlei got a heated phone call from the mayor's assistant, demanding that we withdraw the lawsuit immediately. "The mayor can't stop crying, this is so stressful for her," he told him, before alluding to taking away the council's support. "She can't understand how a so-called partner would do this to us?" he said.

Warlei explained that we were just fighting to save one of the town's own girls who was in grave danger. And besides, we wouldn't be able to withdraw the lawsuit even if we wanted to, which we didn't. The assistant ended the call abruptly. In a conference call later that day, Luisa was worried. "I'm afraid about what might happen to Lara now," she said. "I've heard of local authorities taking children like her and dumping them hundreds of miles away just so they don't have to spend money on them. We need to be vigilant."

Three days went by, then the council informed the court that Lara had been taken to a children's home some distance away and was safe. We were overjoyed, until a few days later when it turned out to be untrue, a fabrication just to stop the daily build-up of fines. We only found out when Lara was picked up on the streets of Padre Paraíso by policemen who, when they put her name in the system and found out about the court order, took her straight to the municipal children's home. For Catují's town council, the game was up. They could no longer pretend she wasn't their responsibility, nor keep up the lies that she was being cared for somewhere else. After trying every trick to avoid giving a homeless, exploited girl the protection that was hers by right, they finally agreed to foot the bill.

Two weeks later, Ellen's phone rang, and she squealed with delight when she recognised Lara's voice. The same affectionate, chatty tones she had missed so much at the Pink House without her. Lara seemed thrilled to have a roof above her head, meals she didn't have to pay for with her body, people around her who didn't want to abuse and exploit her. All the things most girls her age would simply take for granted. She even enthused about the house rules, the washing up rota and the strict times for waking up and going to bed.

"I'm being taken care of. I feel really happy. Thank you for never giving up on me," she told her.

"It's because you deserve it, Lara," said Ellen, her voice breaking with emotion. "You're so, so precious."

There was a pause before Lara ventured, "Ellen, can I ask you for something?"

"Yes, of course. What do you need?"

"A *Frozen* princess dress. I really want to play at dressing up, but I need a princess dress. Do you think you could send me one?"

****

We were thrilled that we had been able to use the law to save Lara, but the fact we had to employ a team of lawyers just to force an authority to protect its children from harm felt more depressing rather than something we should celebrate. It remains the most infuriating part of the landscape where we work, where still a large proportion of the cases we take on are kicked so far down the road that they seem to be in perpetual limbo.

Just months after our successful court battle over Lara, our bubble was burst again when we lost the next case over Beatriz. Nearly five years since the judge had ordered her rapist's arrest and he − forewarned by the police − had gone into hiding, his lawyer had applied for the warrant to be rescinded, on the outrageous premise that it was such a long time since the crime that there was no danger he would try to sway the witnesses' testimonies. I laughed when Luisa first filled me in on the impending hearing. Surely it would be preposterous for any judge to reward a fugitive for managing to successfully avoid arrest long enough? But that was exactly what happened. Despite Luisa's objections as Beatriz's representative in the hearing, the judge − newly appointed and the fifth in town since we first took on the case − agreed with the accused that it was he, not his victim, who was being unduly inconvenienced, and ordered that the arrest warrant be annulled. The ruling, and the fact the friendly prosecutor we'd spoken to just months earlier had been suddenly removed and replaced, made me wonder if Cândido Sales' criminal gangs' tentacles had now reached the town's judiciary too. The next day the man was already back, confidently strolling the streets and welcomed by friends and family as a returning hero.

The criminal case against him wasn't over and would continue to run its course, albeit at Brazil's achingly slow pace, but it was easy to see why young victims, particularly poor girls, never dare to imagine being on the winning side of justice.

"We are incredulous with this decision," I wrote to support-ers, many of whom had invested time and money to support Beatriz's case. "It shows that those who abuse or exploit girls are able to get away with their crimes, with even arrest warrants withdrawn if they hide for enough time. But we will continue to fight for her."

UNSTOPPABLE

It was no longer the pink ribbons tied to kilometre signs along the motorway that were the only things getting us noticed. Our struggle for the girls of the BR-116 was now reverberating all over the region and beyond. News of our audacious court cases, and with it word of the bright pink houses standing up for girls' rights, started to reach the big cities too. Brazil's second-largest television network, Rede Record, asked to come and see what we were doing, leading to an hour-long documentary on their flagship Sunday night news programme entitled *The Exploitation Highway* in which they showcased the work of the Pink Houses and interviewed some of the girls, including Bia and Julia. It was the first time a major TV network had devoted so much time to an issue that had for so long been hidden from view, about which even Brazilians living in the same state had little knowledge. Scenes such as that of Bia, walking around the now abandoned brothel on the side of the BR-116 where she had been forced to work, telling the reporter how her mother would send her to the motorway aged 10, beating her if she didn't come back with money, were met with shock and outrage by many.

Some months later we made headlines again when an influential think tank, the Jose Luiz Egydio Setubal Foundation in São Paulo, placed us among the 10 most innovative social projects in Brazil. ""Meninadança shows how urgent is the work of empowering girls," their report said, "inviting them to see themselves as whole subjects, potent and artistic, capable of elaborating their own stories and weaving narratives for themselves through art and conversation circles."

It turns out that we had also caught the eye of public prosecutors in state capital Belo Horizonte, who had been looking for an organisation to help girls affected by another tragedy. Three years earlier, in January 2019, the dam of the Brumadinho iron ore mine, in a countryside community just outside the city, had suddenly burst, unleashing a devastating river of sludge that had engulfed everything in its path, killing 270 people and poisoning rivers for hundreds of miles around. The disaster cost the lives of a third of all men in the area, leaving hundreds of grieving mothers and children. But as reconstruction efforts brought thousands of male workers to the region, they began to see another sinister consequence – the same we had found in Catují with the mobile phone company: many already bereaved and traumatised young girls falling victim to sexual exploitation.

The prosecutors were in charge of the fund, paid for by a fine levied on the mining company, which was supposed to go towards social projects in the region affected by the disaster, as well as other parts of the state where rivers had been polluted. Knowing about what we were doing on the BR-116, they asked if we could bring the same activities to girls in Brumadinho and two other towns which had been devastated, in exchange for more funding for our Pink Houses, for a period of two years.

The deal was done and we put together a team which began working in schools and community centres in some of the neediest neighbourhoods, reaching hundreds of the girls most at risk of exploitation. It was an unexpected new direction, but one which meant we could finally give the very best to the girls of the BR-116. For all these years we had done what we could with the bare minimum.

We still only had one social worker, in Medina, and our psychologists, paid for with what Georgina had managed to raise, worked only one day a week in each house. Now, with the prosecutors' funding, everything changed. We took on more staff, including more workshop teachers, educators and, crucially, a full-time social worker and psychologist for every Pink House. And that meant we could do more, open our doors to more girls and provide the highest quality of care. It was a dream come true.

****

In the coming weeks, fresh support came to us from a source I'd never expected. When Dean and I had found Leilah on the side of the road that night, dust and exhaust fumes swirling round us on that lonely patch of red earth, a good proportion of the trucks thundering by next to us probably belonged to a company called SADA. It was one of Brazil's largest haulage firms, with over 7,000 vehicles on the roads every day with most taking their cargos on the most direct route south to north, or north to south, along the vast BR-116. On that night, and every night since when I'd stood by the side of that road, often trying to persuade a girl to go back home or choose a different life, those trucks often felt like our nemesis. It was one of the reasons why I had mixed feelings, and more than a little suspicion and scepticism, when representatives from the company called us, requesting a meeting.

In fact it turned out the leadership of SADA had also been following our work for many months, and had been particularly moved by the Record TV documentary. They knew what we were talking about, they told us, they recognised the places, the stories and the numbers, that on the BR-116 every 10 miles, on average, there was a place where underage girls were being sold for sex. They had always felt they should be doing something to bring it to an end, but never knew how.

The way Elisa, the head of the company's social responsibility sector, spoke took me by surprise. She was passionate, her voice sometimes cracking with emotion. It was clearly something in which she, and the Medioli family which owned SADA, felt personally and deeply invested. Even so, I still expected the online meeting to be a preliminary chat, just a get-to-know-you before we started talking about what we could do together, which is why what Elisa said next was an even bigger shock.

"We've seen what you do with these girls, taking them in, transforming them, giving them hope," she said. "We want to be part of that too."

First of all, they wanted to fully fund a new Pink House on the BR-116, she explained. Warlei and I immediately knew where it would be – Ponto dos Volantes, 25 miles north of Padre Paraíso. It was where the three 15-year-old girls were from who, just before our second walk along the motorway, had fallen out of a truck onto the motorway, one of whom was killed instantly. Warlei and I had stopped off at the town on one of our recent trips up to the projects and heard heart-wrenching stories from members of the guardianship council of girls being abused and exploited in impunity. The town owed its existence to the motorway – its name translates as 'Steering Wheels Place' – and was famed far and wide as a stop off for prostitution. Now we could begin to bring hope to girls there too and it was a truck company that was making it happen.

But that was not all. Elisa went on, "We are very aware that our trucks are on all of Brazil's highways, every hour of the day," she said. "That's why we don't just want to join this fight as a company – we want our drivers to as well. We don't want them to be the problem, we want them to be part of the solution." Their idea, Elisa explained, was to train up their drivers to become 'agents of protection' on the motorways, who would know how to report and intervene when they saw children being trafficked or exploited. They would have badges and bumper stickers warning others that it was a crime and know how to talk about it to other truckers they met on their journeys. Elisa pointed out that their company was a leading member of Brazil's truckers' association. They would start with their own 7,000-strong workforce, but their intention was to roll this out to many thousands of other truck drivers over the coming years.

When the call was over, I switched off my camera and slumped back on my seat and tried to process everything that had been said. For years we had fought what often felt like a lonely battle against what seemed like an indomitable evil. It didn't feel like that anymore. Suddenly, it felt like anything was possible. Maybe even a world where girls were no longer robbed of their childhoods on the BR-116.

Once again my mind darted back to Leilah. Back then, even

with that first glimpse into this tragedy, making any kind of meaningful difference seemed as remote as the dark, lonely place where we found her. Even in the following years, while seeing individual girls finding hope, the problem itself always felt as unstoppable as the constant barrage of trucks pounding every kilometre. I'd always hoped that we might help some girls find a way out, but if someone back then had told me we would one day be making waves all over this country, bringing abusers, exploiters – even whole towns – before the courts, convincing truck companies to play their part and turning thousands of drivers into the girls' guards and protectors… I'd have struggled to believe it.

But there was even more to come. Soon after, we received an invitation to speak about the plight of girls on the BR-116 in the British Parliament. It was the kind of opportunity we'd only ever dreamed about – to finally bring this hidden scandal out of the shadows and possibly even mobilise the very people with the power and influence to bring about lasting change. As we considered the invitation, though, we decided we didn't just want to talk about the girls, we wanted the girls themselves to do the talking. How much more powerful, more compelling, would that message be if it were they who were delivering it?

So it was that, later that year, with our fifth Pink House already up and running, new projects in the towns deluged by the dam disaster, thousands of truck drivers already acting as 'agents of protection' on the motorways and our teams now working with over 500 teenage girls a day, I watched Rany, Moany and Maluiza move a roomful of politicians and dignitaries to tears. The three girls were from Cândido Sales, a place where we had faced so much hostility and opposition, where the police and prosecution service had once tried to silence us, where criminal gangs had smothered our attempts at getting justice for girls, where we had often wondered if we would manage to save even one young life... and yet here they were, undaunted and empowered, determined to tell the world about what they had come through and how they had found their way out. When the music stopped the cheers and applause were so loud other parliamentarians meeting in committee rooms nearby came to find out what was going on. Many stayed as the girls returned for a final encore, their nervousness now gone as they beamed wide, excited smiles.

And as we left that place, past the ancient wood-panelled corridors, through the cavernous Westminster Hall, and out onto the street again, it felt less like a successful conclusion and more like another beginning. If we'd come this far in 13 years, what might the next bring? What else could we achieve that we couldn't even dream or imagine today? How much further could we go, how many more could we bring along with us, how many more lives could we change? I couldn't wait to get started.

Things were changing. The tide was finally turning.

A new chapter was beginning.

ACKNOWLEDGEMENTS

Thanks to my agent Oli Munson for believing in this book before anyone else. Paul Dove for being the second to believe, and my editor Christine Costello for making it a reality.

I wouldn't have a story to write if it weren't for many, many people who have believed in the cause, and some who have dedicated their lives to it. The incredible, brave women of our Pink Houses, the team in our Belo Horizonte office, our lawyers, and specifically, Warlei Torezani. Our UK office team and volunteers, our trustees past and present, and all the people who down the years have trusted us with your support, many before we had anything to show for it.

The girls, too many to mention, whose strength, bravery and determination to be different – and be the difference in their communities – have made every day of this journey worthwhile.

ⓞ meninadança

Meninadança continues to change the lives of some of the world's most vulnerable girls. Every day the teams in our five Pink Houses work on the frontline of Brazil's child sexual exploitation epidemic on the BR-116, helping them discover their worth and potential and take control of their lives.

Scan the QR Code below to find out what happened to some of the girls described in this book, and hear them describe in their own words the difference Meninadança made in their lives

Yet we know there are untold numbers of girls who we haven't yet reached, who are still on their own and don't yet know there is a way out. You can help us find and rescue them, and be part of the rest of this story.

To donate, adopt a km of the BR-116, or get involved, join our movement for girls at www.meninadanca.org.